Georgian Harlots
and Whores

Georgian Harlots and Whores

Fame, Fashion & Fortune in the late Eighteenth Century

Mike Rendell

PEN & SWORD
HISTORY

First published in Great Britain in 2022 by
Pen & Sword History
An imprint of
Pen & Sword Books Ltd
Yorkshire – Philadelphia

ISBN 978 1 52679 102 3

Typeset by Mac Style
Printed and bound in the UK by CPI Group (UK) Ltd,
Croydon, CR0 4YY.

Pen & Sword Books Limited incorporates the imprints of Atlas,
Archaeology, Aviation, Discovery, Family History, Fiction, History,
Maritime, Military, Military Classics, Politics, Select, Transport,
True Crime, Air World, Frontline Publishing, Leo Cooper, Remember
When, Seaforth Publishing, The Praetorian Press, Wharncliffe
Local History, Wharncliffe Transport, Wharncliffe True Crime
and White Owl.

For a complete list of Pen & Sword titles please contact

PEN & SWORD BOOKS LIMITED
47 Church Street, Barnsley, South Yorkshire, S70 2AS, England
E-mail: enquiries@pen-and-sword.co.uk
Website: www.pen-and-sword.co.uk

Or

PEN AND SWORD BOOKS
1950 Lawrence Rd, Havertown, PA 19083, USA
E-mail: Uspen-and-sword@casematepublishers.com
Website: www.penandswordbooks.com

Dedicated to all women, everywhere, who live with prejudice.

Contents

Preface

A Peep into Brest with a Navel Review.

I t is a curious confession to start with, but necessary to explain where I came from in my decision to write this book: I confess that I was inspired to write it because I was thinking of Kim Kardashian at the time. Or rather, the whole Kardashian Clan – the entire family and its entourage, a collection of people famous for being famous, stars of a parallel universe based upon reality TV.

Let me explain. I am not for one moment doubting the morals of the Kardashian family, or implying that they are successors to that other parallel universe of three centuries ago, namely the demi-monde inhabited by the leading prostitutes and courtesans of the day. But there are similarities. The Kardashians are fashion icons, their products and beauty ranges are loved, and bought, by millions. They are influencers on a grand scale, with millions of Followers on Twitter and on Instagram. And yet when it comes to dressing, they do not choose, by and large, to bedazzle us with their good taste and grand style, rather they elect to display acres of flesh on an almost gynaecological scale. Even Khloé remarked on one occasion that her elder sister Kim was dressed like a street walker. And that is where there is such a contrast with the eighteenth century. Nowadays our celebrities do not dress to impress, they dress to shock. The eighteenth century had its own version of celebrity, although the word was not used to describe an individual (as opposed to a status) for another one hundred years. Those celebrities, the stars of the Georgian universe, were the sex workers at the pinnacle of their profession: and they wanted the world to know it. Not for them a dress style which emulated the common whore. For them, success meant dressing like a duchess, showing their finery for all the world to admire.

Look at the mezzotints and prints from the second half of the eighteenth century and it is hard to tell the difference between the bejewelled harlot and the haughty duchess. Both had their images painted by the leading artists of the day, and both had their portraits exhibited alongside each other at the Summer Exhibition of the Royal Academy. Then, as now, the celebrity status of the most successful strumpet owed nothing to the amount of good these people did for their fellow human beings. They were catapulted into stardom because of their prowess in the bedroom, because of their promiscuity, because of the company they kept. Nowadays we award fame and adulation to WAGS – the wives and girlfriends of famous sportspersons. Then, it was the whores, harlots and mistresses who reaped the rewards that fame brought. They were termed demi-mondaines, or given the collective name of 'the Cyprian Corps', or 'the Thaiis' or called 'the gold-touching sisterhood'. Sometimes they were termed 'the Paphian priestesses', the 'impure sisterhood' or the 'votaries of Venus.' Otherwise known as 'the Cytherians' or 'the amorous phalanx', their leaders were revered as being the 'Toast of the Town'. The press, especially the precursors of the modern red tops, reported their every appearance in public, invented rivalries and indiscretions and ensured that their antics were never out of the news. Sound familiar, Ms Kardashian?

Nowadays, celebrities monetise their fame by bringing out their own fashion lines, appearing to believe that fame alone gives them the skill to act as a designer. It reached the stage where the great designer Oscar de la Renta, speaking at the 2012 Fashion Institute of Technology's Couture Council Award for Artistry annual lunch, commented: 'Today, if you play tennis, you can be a really good designer or, if you're an actress, you can be a designer. I've been at it for forty-five years and I'm still learning my craft on a daily basis.'

He had a point: multi-Grand Slam winner Serena Williams has her own fashion line; her sister, Venus, promoted her footwear brand known as *EleVen*; Kim Kardashian has her *Skims* line of shape-wear; Sarah Jessica Parker launched her own fashion line, *Bitten*, in 2007 and still promotes a line in shoes under the name *SJP*. However, there is nothing new about this trend, which dates back 300 years to when Mary Robinson gave the world hats, caps, muffs, dresses – even gold stockings. The difference is that she inspired others to make and sell copies of what she herself was wearing, rather than selling the items herself. The important similarity, then as now, is that the general public are influenced by what the celebrities say and wear – and what a fashion icon wears in public one day will often be on sale in shops before the month is out in every High Street in the land. In the latter years of the twentieth century women would be familiar with 'the Rachel' (Jennifer Anniston's trademark hairstyle from her role in *Friends*). It helped define the mid-nineties look, just as the Farrah Fawcett 'flip' or 'Farrah-do' had defined the seventies, lasting well into the eighties. Two-and-a-half centuries earlier, the Fanny Murray hat and the Robinson chemise captured the zeitgeist of the period in exactly the same way.

In the eighteenth century nothing succeeded like success. If a girl became pre-eminent in her profession as a sex worker, then not only did other working girls aspire to be like her, but the male customers jockeyed for position to be seen in her company. It is a bit like a modern-day Premier League footballer parking a Bentley outside his property in leafy Alderley Edge, even though he doesn't hold a driving licence. So, 200 years ago, young blades would go to the opera just to be part of the glittering circle which surrounded the doyens of society, the hookers who shared their favours with the princes, dukes and earls.

I use the words 'whores', 'harlots' and 'courtesans' to differentiate between the different groups of sex worker. The whore was basically a purveyor of sexual favours for money – and that could be a term bestowed on everyone from a woman happy to provide what was colloquially known as 'a threepenny stand-up' in a shop doorway, to a high-class prostitute in one of the seraglios in London's St James's. But it is fair to point out that to the lexicographer Dr Samuel Johnson 'whore' could have two meanings, only one of which involved money. He included two definitions in his *Dictionary*:

Whore
1. A woman who converses unlawfully with men; a fornicatress; an adultress; a strumpet.
2. A prostitute; a woman who receives men for money.

Indeed, Johnson used courtesan, harlot, doxy, drab, strumpet and hackney more or less interchangeably, whereas over the intervening centuries some of those words have evolved, while others have fallen into disuse.

Harlots were not necessarily being paid – they just enjoyed having sex. They shared their favours with whomever they chose. And then there were mistresses, kept women who may sometimes have received an annuity from several men at the same time. 'High keeping' was the name given where their male admirer provided them with a house and picked up the bills for the running costs. The term 'courtesan' may have started off as describing a royal paramour living in court, but by the eighteenth century it was applied to mean any prostitute with wealthy or upper-class clients, regardless of where she lived or practised her craft.

The important difference between the courtesan and the whore was that the courtesan was not just selling sex, she was selling her company. In modern parlance she was offering an RGFE – a real girlfriend experience – one where men were paying her to accompany them to the opera, to masquerades and to balls. She was expected to be able to converse fluently, to be able to hold her liquor, to add refinement to the company. She might be able to play a musical instrument, she might simply be a trophy girlfriend dripping with jewels on the arm of her keeper, but she was expected to be able to act a role, and also to know her place. She could be picked up; she could be put down. She had no rights, but she could certainly expect financial benefits way beyond those enjoyed by the rest of the sisterhood.

And as this book shows, there were no rigid boundary lines between whores, harlots and courtesans – many of the women who are featured in this book moved from one category to another. In the case of Elizabeth Armistead, she encompassed all three categories before ending up as a happily married woman. In others, such as Mary Robinson, she never resorted to selling her body to hoi-polloi on the open market – but she still sold herself in the sense of becoming a mistress, first of the Prince of Wales, and later of several other men of rank and fortune, before falling head over heels in love with a man who deserted her after sixteen years. She was looking for love – and she never really found it.

More than anything else I wanted to show that these were women who dared to play men at their own game – and win. They may have been sex workers, but then, as now, they should not be judged merely because of what they chose to do for a living. First and foremost, they were women trying to survive, finding a way through the maze of a totally male-dominated world. In general, women were denied an equal education, were offered appallingly limited job opportunities and were treated to male hypocrisy on a grand scale. If they dared to resort to supplying sexual favours for money they were never taken seriously. They were judged as unfit to enter the homes of their noble clients, dismissed out of hand if they sought to express views in print, and were ridiculed for their literary aspirations. Some of them took enormous risks with their health and personal safety. Then as now, they were simply trying to succeed and make the most of what they had to offer – themselves.

They were the true female entrepreneurs of the eighteenth century. Then as now, they do not deserve to be disregarded or pushed into a separate cubby-hole marked 'sex worker', as if they were in some way different or inferior to the rest of us. They strove to run a business, and often to support a family. They put up with defamatory press speculation, were the object of endless gossip and lies in the press, were lampooned by the likes of James Gillray, and yet still came up smiling. They had to put up with legal inequalities, and a police force that treated them as second-class citizens. They faced the risk of rape, and without any possible redress in law because no one would ever believe that a sex worker would say 'no'. They were, and still are, the object of extraordinary hypocrisy and criticism. So let's not judge the whores, the harlots and mistresses of the eighteenth century. Let us instead salute them for their perseverance and doggedness, and for daring to succeed in a man's world.

I should perhaps just mention my rationale in selecting, and omitting, the stories of individual courtesans. In general, I wanted to select women who did more than simply work as prostitutes. I decided not to include Sally Salisbury (born Sally Pridden) even though she was one of the first celebrity whores, because she never really made anything of her life. She made money, she lost money, she stabbed her lover, she was sentenced to a spell in prison, and died of syphilis while serving her sentence. She may have been typical in the sense that many of her fellow sex workers led brief, sordid, unhappy lives, but she never aspired to anything other than being a whore. So I missed her out. I also missed off Harriet Wilson, the foremost courtesan of the Regency period. She was a brazen whore, and proud of it. She slept her way to the top of her profession and then retired from harlotry, married, and published her memoirs. In doing so she turned the tables on the men who had so casually used her. She, like all the women highlighted in this book, worked the system to her own advantage, but she is missed off the list of celebrities because she came along 'after the show was over', in the sense that she was never painted by the leading artists of the day, never influenced fashion, and peaked in popularity after the gossip columns and scandal sheets had passed their prime.

I decided to include one of the stars of the show – Kitty Fisher – even though her life story did not differ substantially from that of her exact contemporary Fanny Murray. Both started off in the gutter, rose to pre-eminence in their profession, married, and died young. Kitty was a glittering star, and although she achieved nothing different from Nancy, I felt that anyone who could beguile Joshua Reynolds so that he painted her multiple times and counted her as his friend deserves to be included for the part she played in developing celebrity status. And it wasn't just Reynolds who was fascinated by her: she also had her portrait painted by Nicholas Hone, Philip Mercier, James Northcote and Richard Purcell.

I looked at Pat Woffington, a highly influential actress. She was always rumoured to have had a number of lovers, reportedly including David Garrick, but at the end of the day she was not selling her services and was an actress of considerable ability and fame. To dismiss her as a whore would be wholly unfair. On the other hand, I felt that Frances Abington deserved a place because she technically satisfied the criteria of being willing to sell her body, at least when she started her career, but then used her abilities to raise herself to become not just a competent actress but a woman of immense influence. Her taste in fashion inspired followers across the country, and this was enhanced by the number of times she had her portrait painted by Sir Joshua Reynolds, as well as by Richard Cosway. Hers was an allure that has travelled well through time – you can look at her portraits and immediately understand why she was so famous, which is more than you can say for some of her contemporaries.

I missed off Martha Ray, daughter of a corset-maker, teenage mistress of John Montagu, 4th Earl of Sandwich, and a fine singer. Her life was tragically cut short, murdered by a deranged former soldier on the steps of the Royal Opera House in Covent Garden when she was aged thirty-two. Frankly, she hadn't done enough outside the bedroom to merit inclusion.

Sophia Baddeley was dead by the age of forty-one and had lived her life to the full as a beautiful courtesan and actress, but she died in 1786 and never really achieved superstar status. Also, I wanted to focus on women who went further than they had any right to expect. I thought long and hard about including Grace Elliott – an extraordinary woman who was a top courtesan by any standards, with a list of lovers that included the Prince of Wales and a significant portion of the nobility both in Britain and France. However, she was, unlike the women profiled in this book, born into a world of privilege and class. She befriended Madame du Barry, mistress of King Louis XV, got caught up in the aftermath of the French Revolution, helped spirit away a number of aristocrats from under the noses of revolutionaries, spent years in various French prisons and died in France in 1823 just shy of her seventieth birthday. Extraordinary, yes, but not sufficiently part of the London scene – too much involved in French politics to earn herself a place as a superstar in Britain. Besides, her story has been excellently told in the recent book *An Infamous Mistress* by Joanne Major and Sarah Murden.

I gave some consideration to including Nelly O'Brien, a prostitute whose fame was enhanced by being a friend of Joshua Reynolds. He painted her twice, and the mezzotints based on his portraits sold in their thousands. She was the lover of Lord Bolingbroke, and later of the Earl of Thanet, but at the end of the day she was a victim; she never controlled her own destiny and died in 1768, leaving three young sons, but little else. She never attained the heights of being acclaimed as the Toast of the Town, and if it were not for Reynolds she would have died unknown.

There was never any doubt that Nancy Parsons and Gertrude Mahon would be included, because they both had that extra 'something' that made them special. Likewise, Elizabeth Armistead and Mary Robinson towered above their contemporaries, and both lived lives that were so much more than that of 'just a whore', and which must have been an inspiration to many.

By and large, the women who gained a place in the book are those who used the one thing they had – their sexual allure – to try and make something of their lives. They were the 'It' girls of the second half of the eighteenth century, enjoying a status, fame and influence that would horrify the Victorians. As such, they provide an interesting counterpoint to our own obsession with celebrity.

Part I

Components of Celebrity – Then and Now

Liberality and Desire, by Thomas Rowlandson.

So, what makes celebrity? Is it just fame – or is it rather more than that? Can you be a celebrity if you are poor? Or not beautiful? Can you ever be a celebrity if you follow a 'serious' profession such as being a doctor or an accountant?

In most definitions, celebrity status is generally awarded to people who are *not* renowned for their importance to society. They may well donate large sums of money to charity, but that is not why they became celebrities. And it is hard to think of a poor celebrity. Some may achieve star status, for instance, by winning a talent competition – Susan Boyle, winner in 2009 of *Britain's got Talent*, would be an example. But she is not a 'typical celebrity'. Celebrities are the 'Beautiful People', people who live aspirational lives, who are followed by the paparazzi and are featured on television programmes. A celebrity has to be 'open to view', not shut away as a wealthy recluse. And nowadays you get celebrity status because of a fortuitous coming together of the power of television – especially reality TV programmes – and social media. The reach of celebrities is astonishing – it encompasses the whole world.

Three centuries ago celebrity was a much more parochial affair, and in reality was confined to London. Fashion and manners were highly esteemed and as the idea of 'ton' developed more and more people aspired to join those arbiters of taste and style. The 'haut ton' – literally, 'high tone'– was perhaps represented by as few as 400 families. It covered the absolute crème de la crème of people of high fashion and manners. The 'haut ton' had, since 1769, referred to the prevailing mode or style and to fashionable ways. Later, the term 'haut ton' might be extended to those whom the Lady Patronesses deemed eligible for inclusion as members at Almacks, and for that you needed to have impeccable manners, good breeding and, preferably, a title. But that can be distinguished from the other phrase used at the time – the 'bon ton'. In 1823 a Dictionary of Slang was published by John Broadcock and it defined 'bon ton' as follows:

The Bon-ton: Highflier Cyprians, and those who run after them; from "Bon" – good, easy – and "ton", or tone, the degree of tact and tension to be employed by modish people; frequently called 'the ton' only. Persons taking up good portions of their hours in seeking pleasure, are of the Bon-ton, as stage-actors and frequenters of play-houses, visitors at watering-places, officers, &c &c. In Paris they are both called "le bon genre". The appellation is much oftener applied than assumed. High life, particularly of whoredom: he who does not keep a girl, or part of one, cannot be of the Bon-ton; when he ceases, let him cut. Bon ton – is included in haut-ton, and is French for that part of society who live at their ease, as to income and pursuits, whose manners are tonish.

For some, the idea of the ton was interchangeable with the phrase 'the beau monde'. It meant the fashionable world, or high society, and clearly the pursuit of pleasure was not in any way limited to people with titles. It had nothing to do with education or refinement. It had everything to do with an ostentatious display of wealth, of time spent at the gaming tables, of drinking and fine dining – and, of course, whoring. The ton involved being bang up to date with fashion. It was shallow and uncaring – think 'airheads' – but it was also incredibly aspirational. Those at the pinnacle of tonishness were the courtesans themselves – the girls who could afford to be seen dripping with diamonds, dressed up to the nines, occupying the best boxes at the theatre, cavorting with the rest of the beau monde. Those who did not possess 'ton' wanted it badly, were dazzled by it, were fascinated by those who possessed it – and were delighted to read every minute detail about what these hedonists got up to. The ton comprised relatively few people and although some were famous, only a few were celebrities in the modern sense of the word. These exotic few did not of course have television to make their faces famous – but they had the next best thing: they had their portraits painted by the leading artists.

They were helped by an explosion in the market for prints – especially mezzotints – enabling their image to be purchased by all and sundry. And they had newspapers, in particular scandal sheets with gossip columns, giving the public details of their everyday life. It was this coming together of newspapers, prints and portraits which provided the breeding ground for celebrity status, in much the same way as reality TV programmes and social media create celebrities today. There was an insatiable desire for information about 'how the rich live'. You needed public arenas where celebrities could be seen – the theatre and places such as Ranelagh, the Pantheon and Vauxhall Gardens – but you also needed exclusivity and privacy, leading to a sort of 'what are they getting up to behind closed doors' mentality. You needed extreme wealth – or at least the ostentatious display of wealth – and you needed style and an awareness of fashion, because more than ever before, the Georgian era was one where fashion was king. Celebrity status, then and now, was earned by those who flaunted their success, who revelled in their place in the spotlight and who made little or no attempt to hide from the press. Shy introverts cannot be celebrities, but they can be stars. It takes an extrovert, someone who says 'look at me, I'm famous for being famous' to fuel the fires of celebrity. And in the eighteenth century that sort of attitude was most likely to be exhibited by the trollops who filled the gossip columns, sat for the leading artists, packed out the print shop windows, and entertained the onlookers at the opera.

Dealing with those various elements – portraits, prints, newspapers, wealth, public places and fashion – leads inevitably to the world of the demi-monde, to the sex workers who strutted their stuff across the London scene. Because they ticked all the boxes: after all, they were rich, they were beautiful, they were highly visible, and they were fashion icons to a remarkable extent. And they not only occupied acres of type in the newspapers of the day but actively manipulated the press by releasing stories about themselves, or by going out of their way to flaunt their success and to be seen in all the right places, where the hacks were bound to observe and comment on their activities.

Chapter 1

The Press: Newspapers, Magazines and Gossip Columns

Eighteenth century newspapers gave the public information about the great and the good – here, the Evening Post of 26 September 1761 listing the precise order of attendance at the coronation of George III. But what would fill those column inches when there was nothing going on?

Newspapers were not born in the eighteenth century, but in many ways that was when they came of age. Tracing their origins back to partisan broadsheets in the Civil War (known as corantos, or notebooks) they developed into organs for disseminating government notices and information (e.g., the *Oxford Gazette* from 1666, which eventually emerged as the *London Gazette*, still in use today). By 1702 the first daily newspaper had been launched in London (the *Daily Courant*) but the first 'modern' journalist (in the sense we know today, of a person who gathers information and opinions and tries to present them as an accurate picture of events) was probably Daniel Defoe. His story of the Great Storm of 1703 was based on eye-witness accounts from across the country. But newspapers tended to concentrate on bare facts. Some specialised in shipping movements, for instance Edward Lloyd's thrice-weekly *Lloyd's News* which was first published in 1703 and then grew to become *Lloyds List*. The papers themselves were expensive – roughly half of the cost equated to taxation – and therefore information in the papers was shared around, in coffee houses and in lending libraries. In time, weekly periodicals appeared such as *The Tatler* (1709) and *The Spectator* two years later.

More and more titles were launched with an anti-government bias. *The Weekly Journal, or, Saturday's Post* was launched in 1716 . It later became known as *Mist's Weekly Journal* and developed a tradition of including a front-page essay giving opinions about the news, a tradition followed by the *Craftsman* in 1727. All newspapers were subject to the payment of a stamp tax linked to the number of pages in the publication. The *Universal Spectator* came out in 1728 followed by the *Grub Street Journal* two years later, both consisting of four pages of which the front page was an essay (often highly critical and vitriolic). Two pages of news were then followed by a back page containing advertisements.

Up until then the papers tended to concentrate on events at court, at home and abroad, and on major news stories. They were not, at that stage, heavily reliant on gossip or tittle-tattle about the rich and famous. The list of titles became an avalanche as the public appetite for news grew exponentially, as shown by the amount of revenue generated by the Stamp Acts. A combined circulation figure of perhaps just under two-and-a-half million copies a year in 1713 grew to over seven million in 1750, eleven million by 1773 and a whopping sixteen million copies by the start of the next century. By the time *The Morning Post* was launched in 1772 it was one of fifty-three titles produced in London alone, with many provincial cities having their own titles.

The pressure was on to fill those column inches, and gossip was to emerge as one of the principle topics. *The Morning Post* was in effect a scandal sheet, produced by John Bell, who went on to launch a number of newspapers and magazines, particularly with an emphasis on fashion and prevailing style. Two of its early editors were vicars, given the respective nicknames of 'Reverend Bruiser' and 'Dr Viper', which gives some idea of their determination and zeal used when attacking their chosen targets.

The full title of *The Morning Post* underwent numerous changes while it developed a reputation for gossip-mongering. It mattered little to the editor whether the stories were true or false, as long as the revenue from sales exceeded the fines and bribes paid to the parties being defamed. It was not the first or only scandal sheet. The *Town & Country Magazine* first appeared in 1769 (so called because the paper had offices in urban Clerkenwell as well as in rural Highgate). Whereas its founder, Alexander Hamilton, may have originally intended to concentrate on politics, it quickly built up a following on account of its Tête-à-Tête series, featuring aristocratic rakes and their adulterous liaisons. The têtes-à-têtes always started off with a facing pair of oval portraits of the lovers, their names thinly disguised either by omitting letters from their true names or by giving hints as to their identity by referring to their occupation or to historical characters. There then followed a brief history of the exploits of the parties, not necessarily entirely true, but often based on shrewd guesswork and a vivid imagination. The public lapped it up, and indeed they worried that the paper would run out of scurrilous rumours, only to be reassured by the publisher that they had enough stories in the bag to last at least for the following two years. In practice the *Town & Country* ran until 1796.

At much the same time, caricaturists started to hint at sexual impropriety between those suspected of adultery – for example by showing a couple sharing a meal at the breakfast table together, perhaps with the lady's husband in the background, identified as a cuckold by the addition of a pair of horns. In such a way the inference of adultery could be expressed without the likelihood of prosecution for libel. In those days, before the Libel Act of 1843, the truth of the allegation was not in itself a defence to a charge of libel, but a successful prosecution would necessarily involve a huge amount of 'dirty linen being washed in public'. The party claiming to be libelled was much more likely to keep quiet and hope to avoid publicity.

This undoubtedly gave rise to some scurrilous newspapers writing deliberately false stories of alleged indiscretions. A messenger could then be sent to the home of the victim of the false allegation, explaining that the story would appear in the paper later that week, unless a payment was made to hush the whole thing up. Even *The Times* newspaper, founded in 1785 under its original title of *The Daily Universal Register*, was not averse to printing scandals and fake news. Its founding publisher, John Walter, went too far when he libelled the Prince of Wales and two of his brothers by suggesting that they were consorting with enemies of their father, the king, and were seeking to promote the republican cause. For that, Walter was sentenced to a spell in the pillory (never carried out) fined heavily and forced to spend sixteen months in prison. In those days, incarceration did not prevent Walter from continuing to publish his scandal sheet, which makes it all the more remarkable that *The Times* survived to be given the nickname of '*The Thunderer*', one of the most respected newspapers in the whole world. Back in the 1780s it was no different to any of the other scandal sheets, meaning that for nearly a hundred years journalists were generally regarded as the lowest of the low, echoing Ned Ward's comments in 1693:

> The condition of an Author, is much like that of a *Strumpet*, both exposing our *Reputations* to supply our *Necessities*. The only difference between us is, in this particular, where the *jilt* has the Advantage, we do our business first, and stand to the Courtesie of our Benefactors to Reward us after; whilst the other, for her Security, makes her *Rider* pay for his Journey, before he mounts the *Saddle* ... and if the Reason be requir'd, Why we betake our selves to so Scandalous a Profession as Whoring or Pamphleteering, the same ... Answer will serve us both, viz. That the unhappy circumstances of a Narrow Fortune, hath forc'd us to do that for our Subsistence, which we are much asham'd of.

That link, between the literary hack and the brazen whore, was to work to the mutual advantage of both parties. The whore thrived on the publicity and the journalist could profitably spend his time rootling around in the gutter looking for more tales of intrigue, corruption, sexual incontinence and venal behaviour.

The 1770s saw an explosion of what were known as 'crim. con.' cases. Criminal conversation, to give it its full name, was in effect a precursor to divorce and was based on the idea that a man could be sued for damages if he led a married woman astray. The ball had really started rolling in 1769 when the Duke of Cumberland, brother to the king, was sued by Lord Grosvenor after the Duke was found *in flagrante* with Lady Grosvenor. It wasn't the size of the damages (£10,000, equivalent nowadays to over a million pounds) which shocked and intrigued the public – it was the minutiae which the trial revealed in terms of the royal lifestyle. Details as to when he rose for breakfast, when he went to his club, what he ate and drank, and so on, helped feed a frenzy for more and more intimate details about how royalty and the aristocracy lived. The fact that they were 'no better than the rest of us' was an added bonus. Reports of the trial were avidly read, and books were written containing transcripts of the love letters which passed between the amorous pair, along with witness reports from servants about what they had observed through the bedroom keyhole. Accounts as to whether or not the bolster had been rumpled merely added to the frisson of excitement for the reader: everyone could be a voyeur at this act of illicit fornication.

Magazines were published devoted almost entirely to the more low-brow elements of the beau monde. So, you had *The Rambler's Magazine: Or, The Annals of Gallantry, Glee, Pleasure and the Bon Ton*, which was published between 1784 and 1791. Not to be confused with Samuel Johnson's *The Rambler*, the magazine boasted that it was 'calculated for the entertainment of the polite world, and to furnish the man of pleasure with a most delicious banquet of amorous, bacchanalian, whimsical, humorous, theatrical and polite entertainment.' Each issue came out monthly, and consisted of around forty pages, brim-full of bawdy anecdotes, letters, poems, songs, and general gossip. There were engravings to lighten the text, usually tongue-in-cheek depictions of such things as 'Abelard studying the use of Eloise's globes.' It was the precursor to the sort of gossip magazines that supermarket bosses place nowadays by the check-outs, designed to catch the eye with lurid tales and screaming headlines. The public, then as now, happily paid their pennies and got their fix. As stated in the June 1787 issue of the newspaper *World and Fashionable Advertiser:* 'Scandal, if related in an entertaining manner, will always be acceptable.'

It was a century when literacy levels had almost doubled to around 60% of the male adult population. We can just imagine a footman, seeking to entertain his fellow servants around the kitchen table, choosing not to regale his audience with accounts of what the Portuguese ambassador said or did when he was introduced to the king, but instead concentrating on stories about Lady M... being caught having rumpy-pumpy behind the gorse bushes in the local park. Or lurid tales of Lady S... being seen getting into the coach with Lord T...., the blinds being pulled down, and the carriage standing stationary for twenty minutes while the springs were observed to be going up and down in a rhythmic motion. Even better if the story related to one of the Toasts of the Town: for example, the coach of a leading courtesan seen outside the house of the Duke of C... for the whole night. You can just imagine the cat-calls in the servants' hall of 'you go for it, girl'. It was, after all, 'one of us' making a success of an unfair world, and therefore there was much to be celebrated.

The regular reports of crim. con. cases led on to other, more pornographic tales. The Georgians were a prurient lot and loved nothing more than to read about their social superiors bonking like rabbits. If there were stories about servants observing bedroom antics through the keyhole so much the better. And if those stories gave intimate details of the lady undressing, and who-did-what-to-whom in titillating detail, then that was what would sell the papers.

There was nothing new about pornography, although the word only came into general use in Britain during the following century. Pornography, from the Greek words *porneía* meaning 'prostitute' and *gráphein* meaning 'to write about', was therefore originally intended to describe biographies about whores. On that basis, there was an explosion of pornography in the mid-eighteenth century, from stories about semi-fictional characters like Fanny Hill in Cleland's *Memoirs of a Woman of Pleasure* through to allegedly autobiographical accounts written by or on behalf of leading sex workers, such as those ostensibly written by Fanny Murray and by Mary Robinson. It also provided the climate in which *Harris's List of Covent Garden Ladies* could flourish, acting as a directory of whores plying their trade in and around the City, with details of their sexual proclivities, physical appearances, and cost.

In this way the printed word created the platform of fame upon which the leading whores could operate. Famous men with deep pockets would happily pay to be seen with a woman who was portrayed as being at the top of her profession – if she was the best, then every man wanted to be seen in her company. And, of course, the more important the male admirer, the more the press would report – and the more the papers were sold and read. Superstar status was within reach of any girl who was in the right place at the right time, and who was prepared to play the system.

It is worth remembering that it was almost impossible for women to find pictures of fashions, at least in the first half of the eighteenth century. Nowadays we are used to a plethora of magazines on the news-stands, each catering to women of different ages, ethnicity or lifestyle. But up until the launch in 1770 of *The Lady's Magazine; or Entertaining Companion for the Fair Sex* there was nothing aimed at the British female market. Here was an early monthly periodical for women and it dominated the market for many years. Its first edition featured as its frontispiece a plate titled 'A Lady in Full Dress in August 1770'. It was the first magazine either in Britain or France to issue regular plates featuring contemporary fashions. Twenty years later the magazine introduced hand-coloured engravings, making the publication more expensive but also very much more popular with its female readers.

In 1798 *The Lady's Monthly Museum or Polite Repository of Amusement and Instruction* hit the streets of London on a monthly basis. It was considered to be of a useful pocket-size, at seven inches by five inches, and it included a *'Cabinet of Fashion'* with coloured engravings. This section was renamed and expanded in 1812 as *'The Mirror of Fashion'*.

Meanwhile, *La Belle Assemblée or Bell's Court and Fashionable Magazine* was to become one of the most important women's magazines of its time. It was founded by John Bell who was also founder or part-proprietor of several other periodicals including *The Morning Post*, *The World of Fashion* and *Bell's Weekly Messenger*. He launched *La Belle Assemblée* in February 1806, aiming at fashionable society, and although its first fashion plates were originally in black and white, by the end of that year the magazine was being issued in two forms, uncoloured at 2s 6d or hand-coloured at 3s 6d. At last women in Britain could see the latest styles and fashions in a way that had previously been the preserve of the French. Above all, these magazines showed that fashion sells, and it meant that the reign of George III really was the age when style and fashion became major obsessions.

Chapter 2

Portraits and Prints

Kitty Fisher after Sir Joshua Reynolds.

I t is hard to think of a celebrity without bringing to mind their facial characteristics. The point is: celebrity status involves people knowing what you look like. Someone famous may choose to lead the life of a recluse, but there is always someone who is able to take a grainy photograph of the 'target' relaxing on a sun lounger with a telephoto lens. There may be interviews on television with a school friend, who just happens to have a photograph. In general, we are surrounded by images of the famous – on our TVs, in newspapers and magazines, on billboards. Paparazzi ensure that literally dozens and dozens of pictures are taken of the selected 'star' performing everyday operations – like getting out of the car, or carrying their designer shopping bag, or walking their pampered pooch. Frame after frame is there for all to see, with or without the consent of the person concerned.

This image familiarity was not always present. Go back three or four hundred years and people often had no idea what the rich and famous looked like – which certainly reduced their chances of achieving celebrity status. People would know what the monarch looked like – because his or her image appeared on the coins that the public handled every day. But for the vast majority of leaders and high achievers, they could pass unnoticed. When they died, people could see their tomb in Westminster Abbey. The public might pass by their statue or look at an engraving in the frontispiece of a book. If they were invited as a guest to a stately home they could see portraits of the owner and his family, past and present, hanging in majestic splendour – but for the general public this was effectively out of bounds. By and large, people were not recognised outside of their immediate circle of contacts.

All that changed in the eighteenth century. Portrait painting moved into the public domain, printing techniques changed so that lifelike representations were mass-produced, a mania for buying caricatures and prints developed, and slowly but surely by the 1750s celebrity status started to emerge. By the 1780s the desire to know everything and anything about these new heroes and heroines had reached crazy levels. And the more we knew about these 'Beautiful People' the more we wanted to copy what they looked like and to mimic their style. The growth in consumer demand meant that shops could expect to bring out copies of the latest fashions within days of their first appearing.

Art moved out of palaces and fine houses and into public galleries. Thanks to mezzotints, the images then migrated into the homes of the general public. It had all started with the very first academy in England, founded by Sir Godfrey Kneller, a leading painter in the reign of Queen Anne. He appointed himself governor of the modestly named 'Kneller Academy', based in Great Queen Street, London, until he was ousted by his great rival James Thornhill, who took over in 1716. Thornhill didn't fare much better than Kneller in keeping his artists together – in 1720 they all fell out and Thornhill upped sticks and started a new school in Covent Garden, while his son-in-law William Hogarth took the remaining members off to a new site in St Martins Lane. Thornhill's school originally met at Slaughters Coffee House. He had one attempt at formalising the gatherings – but the man nominated as treasurer embezzled all the funds.

Hogarth founded his Academy in 1735. It was this academy, in St Martin's Lane, that thrived under him, and he formulated the plan for a British academy for all the arts. He helped introduce the rococo style to England and was closely associated with the Foundling Hospital, founded by Thomas Coram. In 1742 the Foundling Hospital became the first art gallery open to the public. Pictures were selected by the Dilettante Society, a group of art lovers who had all been on the Grand Tour, and who believed that if it came from Italy or was Italian in style in must be good, and if it didn't, it wasn't! In other words, it was heavily influenced by classical art. Hogarth helped organise the display of paintings in the supper boxes at Vauxhall Gardens. For the first time the public could wander round and see paintings without having to go into someone's private house, and viewing the pictures on display became a fashionable pastime.

Into this happy scene stepped William Shipley. He was not an easy man to get along with and he decided to form an arts society which became known as the 'Royal Society for the encouragement of Arts, Manufactures & Commerce', or 'the Royal Society' for short. But the full title gives a hint of why it was unpopular with painters, who did not particularly wish to be lumped together with manufacturing and commercial interests. The artists wanted more control over how their works were exhibited, how they should be framed, where the pictures should hang. They couldn't get what they wanted with Shipley, so in 1760 a loose association of artists was started under the name 'The Society of Artists of Great Britain'.

The Society of Artists of Great Britain split down the middle after an unseemly leadership dispute between two leading architects, Sir William Chambers and James Paine. Paine won, but Chambers used his strong connections with George III to create a new body and the Royal Academy was formally launched on 10 December 1768. There were two founding objectives of the Academy – firstly, raising the status of the artist through training; and secondly, arranging exhibitions of recent works. It was this two-fold approach that led to a distinctive 'British' school of art, different from its French and other Continental counterparts.

There were originally thirty-four founder members of the Royal Academy, with an additional two 'nominated members' added later by George III (William Hoare and Johann Zoffany). They were a decidedly mixed bag: one Frenchman, a Swiss, a German, an American, an Irishman and four Italians. There were two sets of brothers, a father and daughter, and they included not just painters – there were also a number of architects, cartographers, designers and so on.

Many of the founders have been largely forgotten, but they included such fine portraitists as William Hone, Thomas Gainsborough, and Sir Joshua Reynolds, the Academy's first President. Born in 1723, he painted as many as 3,000 portraits during a career of over fifty years. More than anyone else, Reynolds brought portraiture into the public domain, and helped launch the whole idea of celebrity. He was happy to be associated with the idea of 'beauty', so quite apart from painting portraits which had been commissioned by others, he kept back pictures of well-known beauties – especially the leading courtesans – and displayed them in his studios. Potential sitters could visit his studios and select similar poses, or choose to be painted in similar costumes. In this way the courtesan provided the template for her social superiors, blurring still further the distinction between the two. Reynolds certainly knew how to churn out his pictures with amazing speed, even considering the fact that he may only have painted in the face and hands of the sitter, leaving his minions to finish off the boring bits such as the folds in silk fabric of the dress, or adding in the obligatory spaniel.

The first exhibition of the Royal Academy was in 1769, held in cramped quarters in Pall Mall where some 136 works were on display. This then became the Summer Exhibition the following year, a tradition which has remained unbroken ever since. By 1780 the exhibition had moved into the Strand end of the new Somerset House, and the following year the Summer Exhibition included some 547 paintings. Twenty years later there were almost double that number, with over 1,000 paintings on display.

By a curious irony, the Hanging Committee responsible for deciding which-painting-was-hung-where often placed the portrait of the courtesan immediately alongside the likeness of the aristocratic lady. Both were symbols of beauty, both displayed the same glamour and both were regarded as being equal. Because the pictures were hung without differentiation as to the rank of sitter, and without any indication as to her identity (save in the catalogue), viewers therefore saw the portraits without any preconceptions – they saw them as *fashionistas* in all their finery, setting trends especially in their choice of clothes, the way they styled their hair, and the accessories and jewellery they wore to complete their ensemble. Not everyone approved of this classless display and as early as 1785 a writer to the *Morning Herald* had complained at the Reynold's portrait of Letitia Smith, notorious mistress, and later, notorious wife of Lord John Lade, being seen in juxtaposition with other more respectable personages.

Reynolds may have ensured that the spotlight rested on him and his chosen beauties, but other artists such as Joseph Wright, John Hoppner and George Romney were great portraitists, along with Thomas Gainsborough. The latter did rather get button-holed into painting famous faces, lamenting: 'I'm sick of portraits and wish very much to ... walk off to some sweet village, where I can paint Landskips.' He never really got the chance. Portrait painting become popular with a burgeoning middle class, and therefore irresistibly profitable for an artist of talent.

In its Somerset House years the Royal Academy became inextricably linked with some really great artists who went through the system, including Thomas Lawrence, JMW Turner, John Constable and William Blake. Lawrence, in particular, became the Regency era portrait painter of choice, but, unlike Reynolds, steered away from painting prostitutes over and over again, and instead concentrated on the wives and daughters of the seriously wealthy. It marked the end of the celebrity whore as fashion icon, and soon Victorian morality saw to it that 'women of loose morals' were no longer venerated and publicly admired.

The fact that Reynolds was so prolific at painting portraits did not in itself make the sitters famous. After all, most of those portraits would end up in the dining rooms of the sitter and their family, unseen by outsiders. What Reynolds wanted was to be famous for himself – and that meant spreading the word. He did that by working closely with the makers of mezzotints. Within weeks of an original painting going on display the engravers would produce an image which could be mass produced and then pinned up in houses the length and breadth of the country.

There was nothing new about mezzotints – 'mezzo' from the Italian for 'half' and 'tint' from 'tinto', meaning 'tone'. In 1684 the publisher Alexander Browne had been granted a Royal Licence, lasting fourteen years, to produce mezzotints and he worked closely with the artist Peter Lely. Meanwhile, this type of print had become popular in Europe in the second half of the seventeenth century, with Amsterdam emerging as the centre of the print trade. The movement of artists and skilled workers from Holland into England following the accession to the throne of the Dutch-born King William III in 1689 meant that the market in producing mezzotints was soon dominated by London, and the prints themselves were widely known as being in '*la manière anglais*'. By 1753 William Hogarth was writing: 'The copper-plate it [the mezzotint] is done upon, when the artist first takes it into hand, is wrought all over with an edg'd tool, so as to make the print one even black, like night: and his whole work after this, is merely introducing the lights into it; which he does by scraping off the rough grain according to his design, artfully smoothing it most where light is most required.'

The process involved the engraver using a tool called a rocker (similar to a chisel, with a serrated semi-circular blade) to roughen the copperplate to produce an even texture known as the burr. This was then smoothed away in selected places, using a scraper and a burnisher, thereby controlling how much ink was caught in the burr. The resulting half-tones were ideal in facial representations, because they were particularly good at showing shades of light and dark. The textured look went on to be favoured by artists like Reynolds, who worked closely with the engravers so that sometimes the original painting was exhibited alongside the print: you like the picture? You buy the print.

One particular engraver who worked with Reynolds was the brilliant John Raphael Smith, who produced prints of over forty of his works. One of Smith's pupils was Samuel William Reynolds, a man who claimed a family connection with the artist. In the 1820s he issued reproductions of over 350 of Sir Joshua's works, running to four volumes. Another engraver was the Dublin-born Richard Purcell, who, for reasons of financial impecuniosity, used pseudonyms such as Fowler and Corbutt and who produced a number of Reynolds portraits before his death in 1766. Another was James Macardell, of whom Reynolds prophetically said, 'by this man I shall be immortalised'.

There was a symbiotic relationship between artist and engraver – neither could succeed without the other. And the one thing you can say about Reynolds was that he adored success and loved being in the spotlight. He was jealous of the success of others, to the point of being petty and unpleasant, but where he could see his fame spreading throughout the country, thanks to the mezzotint printers, he was more than happy to share that pedestal of fame with the sitters he most frequently portrayed: in other words, the prostitutes given multiple sittings. Rumours abounded that he had affairs with more than one of his favourites. All we can be sure of is that he was happy to provide exposure to girls like Kitty Fisher and Nelly O'Brien, with no evidence to show that their portraits were ever intended to make money for the artist. He clearly enjoyed their company and the celebrity status which he brought to them was echoed in equal measure by the celebrity status which he brought to himself.

There is one final element contributing to celebrity status; the growth in popularity of the print shop. There were dozens of them in the area near the Strand and they catered to a growing demand from the public wanting to know what the great and the good looked like. Rather like when colour television first started, and queues would develop outside the windows of electrical shops, all gathering to see a football match for the first time in colour, so large crowds would gather outside the windows of the print shop, eager to see who was in the news. For the first time the public could make comparisons between different beauties on display – they could see what fashions they were wearing, and make assessments about their beauty.

Prior to 1740 most of the prints sold in the print shops were of French origin but the printer John Boydell hit upon the idea of boosting the English engravers by commissioning prints of London street scenes and famous buildings. He tapped a market for those of the 'middling class' who were prepared to pay for artwork to be taken home and hung on the wall. As the mezzotint came into vogue in the 1760s, only to be upstaged by aquatints in the 1770s and by stipple engravings in the 1780s, the market for better-drawn images developed. The boom years were between 1790 and 1815 and the public proved more than willing to be parted from sixpence for a black and white image, or a shilling for a coloured version of their favourite scene or person.

Printer/publishers such as Carington Bowles grew wealthy by predicting trends. Some produced what were known as 'drolls' – gently satirical looks at society. Other publishers such as Matthew and Mary Darly (husband and wife) specialised in 'macaroni prints'. These poked fun at the mock-Italian fashions, especially those worn by men, with their absurd tight jackets with big buttons, with their wigs tied back in long tails known as queues, and with a foppish air which preceded the regency dandy by half a century. Fashion was suddenly a favourite subject for artists.

Added to the mix were caricaturists, who broke through into the mainstream. William Hogarth may have previously wagged a disapproving finger at the bedroom antics of the aristocracy, usually on an anonymous basis, but then along came the likes of James Gillray, Richard Newton, Thomas Rowlandson and Robert Dighton in the last couple of decades of the century, combining to produce a Golden Age of Satire. Not only could the general public see and recognise the rich and famous – and laugh at what they got up to – they could also see what they were wearing, and discover who was doing what to whom.

The print had become a sort of news item in its own right, and if people wanted the news, they bought the print.

Chapter 3

Meeting Places – Theatres, Gardens and Watering Holes

A Thomas Rowlandson watercolour showing an audience watching a play at Drury Lane Theatre.

To be the Toast of the Town – to be at the very pinnacle of whoredom – you needed to do more than lure a considerable number of well-connected and wealthy men into bed; you needed to be visible, to be seen at all the right places with all the right people. And that meant standing out from the crowds in various places: Vauxhall and Ranelagh Gardens, at the Pantheon, at the opera and at the theatre. In between times it helped to be able to drive a stylish open carriage through Hyde Park, to be seen drinking chocolate at fashionable hostelries and to be invited to balls and masquerades at the private houses of the great and the good. But if you wanted publicity the starting point was to be seen at the public gardens which became increasingly fashionable during the Georgian era, commencing with Vauxhall.

Originally known as New Spring Gardens, Vauxhall had started off after the Restoration as being a rather pleasant garden on the south side of the River Thames. The diarist John Evelyn had talked about a visit to 'a pretty contrived plantation' while Balthasar de Montconys described a visit in 1663 to see roses, beans and asparagus being grown in rectangular beds bordered by gooseberry bushes. But even back then the horticultural aspect of the place was being upstaged, with Adison writing in 1712 that people would be happier visiting 'if there were more nightingales and fewer strumpets'.

Jonathan Tyers had taken a lease of the premises in 1728, determined to upgrade the facilities so that the pleasure grounds could be used to entertain people on summer evenings. It reopened officially in 1736. He enlisted the help of artists such as Hogarth, Hayman and Roubillac to decorate a series of supper boxes housed in pavilions on the site. In the 1740s he added a frivolous rococo structure called the Turkish Tent and then a splendid rotunda, where people could meet, eat, and listen to music. The public loved it and huge crowds thronged to see the attractions. Tyers had originally charged visitors a shilling-a-head entrance fee, and this was doubled in the 1790s. In 1749 a rehearsal of Handel's Water Music had attracted 12,000 spectators and as late as 1786 Tyers had been able to celebrate the golden jubilee of his brainchild by attracting a crowd of over 60,000 people in fancy dress to a gala evening.

If you liked people-watching, you loved Vauxhall. However, it never shook off its reputation for attracting sex workers, no doubt dressed to impress. The gardens were the haunt of prostitutes only too willing to service their clients in the shady corners and dark alleyways, or to lure them off for a night of debauchery.

By the time the Cyprian Corps mentioned in this book were in their prime, Vauxhall had developed a somewhat tawdry, worn-out image and the stage was set for its successor – Ranelagh Gardens. Ranelagh, in Chelsea, was launched as a trendier, more upmarket rival to Vauxhall in 1742. At that stage its entrance fee of half a crown was more than double the amount people paid to visit Vauxhall. Its centrepiece was a giant rotunda, built of wood, some 150 feet wide and housing fifty supper boxes along with viewing galleries around a central stage where musical entertainment was provided. Even the young Mozart played there when he visited London in 1764 at the age of eight. Some idea of the grandeur of the edifice is shown by the words of B. Lambert, writing in 1806 in his *History of London and its environs* when he stated:

The entrances are by four Doric porticoes opposite each other, and the first storey is rustic. Round the whole on the outside is a gallery, the stairs to which are at the porticoes; and overhead is a slated covering which projects from the body of the Rotunda. Over the gallery are the windows, sixty in number, and over these the slated roof. The interior is elegantly decorated, and, when well illuminated and full of company, presents a most brilliant spectacle. Indeed, it may be said of Ranelagh that, as a public place of amusement, it is not to be equalled in Europe for beauty, elegance, and grandeur.

When it had opened in 1742 the *Gentleman's Magazine* contained a report by a French visitor to Ranelagh:

Into this enchanted palace we entered, with more haste than ceremony; and at the first glance I, for my part, found myself dumb with surprise and astonishment, in the middle of a vast amphitheatre; for structure, Roman; for decorations of paint and gilding, gay as the Asiatic; four grand portals, in the manner of the ancient triumphal arches, and four times twelve boxes, in a double row, with suitable pilasters between, form the whole interior of this wonderful fabric, save that in the middle a magnificent orchestra rises to the roof, from which descend several large branches, which contain a great number of candles enclosed in crystal glasses, at once to light and adorn this spacious Rotunda. Groups of well-dressed persons were dispersed in the boxes; numbers covered the area; all manner of refreshments were within call; and music of all kinds echoed, though not intelligibly, from every one of those elegant retreats, where Pleasure seemed to beckon her wanton followers.

When it had first opened with a breakfast celebration in April 1742 the gardens attracted the gossip Horace Walpole. Initially he disliked it, preferring the gardens at Vauxhall. He wrote:

Two nights ago Ranelagh Gardens were opened at Chelsea; the prince, princess, duke, much nobility, and much mob besides were there. There is a vast amphitheatre, finely gilt, painted, and illuminated; into which everybody that loves eating, drinking, staring, or crowding is admitted for twelve pence. The building and disposition of the gardens cost sixteen thousand pounds. Twice a week there are to be ridottos at guinea tickets, for which you are to have a supper and music. I was there last night, but did not feel the joy of it. Vauxhall is a little better, for the garden is pleasanter, and one goes by water.

But two years later he was converted, writing: 'Every night constantly I go to Ranelagh, which has totally beat Vauxhall. Nobody goes anywhere else, everybody goes there ... You can't set your foot without treading on a Prince, or the Duke of Cumberland.'

Some four years later he wrote that Ranelagh had become so crowded that his coach was delayed by over half an hour in trying to disembark. An indication of how important it was to see and be seen at Ranelagh was shown by the remarks of Dr Samuel Johnson. When somebody cynically said that there 'was not half a guinea's worth of pleasure in seeing Ranelagh,' he replied, 'No; but there is half a guinea's worth of inferiority to other people in not having seen it.'

People of fashion flocked to Ranelagh. It became a notorious place for amorous rendezvous, with the historian Edward Gibbon describing it as 'the most convenient place for courtships of every kind – the best market we have in England.' Above all, it became famous for its masquerades. In earlier decades these had been the preserve of the aristocracy, meeting in private houses, but the sumptuous masquerades at Ranelagh were open to all-comers. It offered an opportunity for guests to indulge in role-play and to flirt outrageously. Above all, it gave the whores of London the chance to don their finery and have a splendid and profitable night out. There, a temptress might dress as a shepherdess and flatter a duke or seduce an earl – it was a place where everyone got what they wanted.

Ranelagh could only ever aspire to be a place of summer entertainment. What London needed was a winter setting, indoors, where the fun could continue. The answer seemed to come in the form of the Pantheon. Designed by James Wyatt and opening in 1772 on the south side of Oxford Street, it quickly became famous for its concerts and masquerades. Initially, admission was limited to those people who were recommended by a member of the peerage – a device intended to deter prostitutes and pickpockets. The deterrent failed, and quickly the place became popular with the Cyprian Corps.

When the Pantheon opened on Monday, 27 January it was a grand affair, with one commentator remarking: 'There were present upwards of seventeen hundred of the first people of this Kingdom; among whom were all the Foreign Ambassadors, the Lord Chancellor, Lord North, Lord Mansfield, Lord and Lady Clive and eight dukes and duchesses.'

Dr Charles Burney, the famous musicologist, at one stage invested in the project and went on to lose a significant amount of money when fire destroyed the premises in 1792. He wrote that the Pantheon 'was regarded both by natives and foreigners, as the most elegant structure in Europe, if not on the globe ... No person of taste in architecture or music, who remembers the Pantheon, its exhibitions, its numerous, splendid, and elegant assemblies, can hear it mentioned without a sigh!'

The fashionable season at the Pantheon generally ran from December through until April or May, with the proceedings starting at 7pm. For the annual fee of six guineas subscribers could attend twelve concerts throughout the season, culminating in dancing until the early hours. In addition, at least two masquerades were held each season and on occasions these were sponsored by one or other of the men's clubs: Boodle's in 1774, Goostree's the following year and White's in 1789. On such occasions supper would be served at around midnight in the basement.

The Pantheon, with its central dome based loosely on its more celebrated namesake in Rome, enjoyed a brief but chequered history. It was converted briefly into an opera house. After it was destroyed by fire it was rebuilt to a different design with the intention of housing masquerades, but by then people were beginning to tire of the entertainment on offer. The fad remained in the form of fancy dress parties, but gone were the days of elaborate masked balls, a feature of the social calendar. The building itself underwent various transformations before being pulled down, with its place now taken by the Oxford Street branch of Marks and Spencer.

Its temporary use as an opera house reflected the popularity of attending operas throughout the Georgian period. Opera was never just the preserve of the wealthy – music lovers of all social classes would attend. Not that much attention was paid to the music for much of the performance: going to the opera was an opportunity to socialise, to play cards, enjoy a snack, have a few drinks – and perhaps to pick up a prostitute with whom to spend the rest of the evening. Only when a favourite aria was started would the noise and commotion stop: the audience would listen attentively, applaud vigorously, and then go back to whatever they were doing before.

Much the same was true of the theatre. We tend to think of the theatre as a place where the audience is expected to keep quiet: not just no mobile phones, but no heckling, no interrupting the actors, no active participation. The Georgians would have been amazed at such passivity. For much of the century wags would be permitted to sit on the side of the stage, frequently commenting loudly on what was going on, exchanging repartee with the actors.

The theatres themselves were often opulent affairs, sometimes with two separate royal boxes, one for the monarch and a rival one on the other side for the Prince of Wales. Ever since the Licensing Act of 1737 only two theatres were licensed to put on plays, that is to say, where the spoken word was paramount. Other play-houses and theatres such as Sadler's Wells had to get round the ban by showing burlesques, or combining the spoken word with music, dance and novelty acts. It meant that the two licensed premises, at the Theatre Royal in Drury Lane and in Covent Garden, enjoyed a duopoly over the performance of plays. They became immensely popular, with thousands of people clamouring for tickets. The theatres regularly caught fire (small wonder with naked lights being used on stage and in the auditorium) and on each occasion the theatres were rebuilt on an ever-increasing scale. Often, the public were given a mixed bill, with a play in two acts followed by a third act which was more like a pantomime, often with such delights as slack-rope dancing, music and general tomfoolery. It was the custom to allow the mob into the pit to see this third act for half price. Riots often ensued when the management sought to withdraw this privilege.

As with other popular places of entertainment, the theatres also became venues for people making assignations, either with the actresses on stage or with the prostitutes who thronged the foyer. The leading courtesans even took the best boxes for the entire season so that they could flaunt their success and attract an even greater number of ardent and well-heeled followers. Of course, not all the actresses were available for hire at the end of the performance, but a great many were and some used the stage as a stepping stone to marriage. The actress Elizabeth

Farren was a case in point, marrying the besotted Edward Smith-Stanley, and thereby becoming the Countess of Derby.

For many others, the stage offered a chance to escape from the drudgery of being a sex worker out on the streets of the City: it provided regular employment, a chance to impress a better class of clientele and a spell in the spotlight of fame. Many of the women mentioned later in this book appeared on stage at some time or other during their careers. It was almost a rite of passage for anyone destined for the top. On stage they could learn grace and style, hone their coquettish skills, learn how to mirror behaviour, and even iron out harsh country accents. As long as they had a reasonable singing voice, had a good pair of legs and a vivacious personality, they could go far.

Sadler's Wells had started in 1683 when Richard Sadler opened tea rooms at his premises out towards Islington. When a spring was discovered in the garden he changed the name to Sadler's Wells and introduced singing, dancing and burlesque shows to entertain the paying public. But respectability eluded poor Sadler and the premises were soon renowned as a nursery of debauchery. When the premises were rebuilt in 1765 they developed as an opera house, often offering spectacular re-enactments of historical events and famous battles. These lured Londoners out to see the shows, which also attracted low-life only too willing to part the theatre-goers from their valuables, whether by picking their pockets or by holding up their coaches on the public highway. Prostitutes found easy pickings, whether by day while punters were 'taking the waters' or by night when the 'after-theatre' entertainment took on a whole new meaning.

There were many other springs in and around London where both street-walkers and high-class courtesans vied for custom. Bagnigge Wells was perhaps the most crowded, but not necessarily by people of good repute. In 1765 the chalybeate waters (in other words, rich in iron) were being promoted by Mr Davis, owner of the site, with the words:

> the proprietor, takes this method to inform the publick, that both the chalybeate and purging waters are in the greatest perfection ever known, and may be drank at 3d. each person, or delivered at the pump-room at 8d. per gallon. They are recommended by the most eminent physicians for various disorders, as specified in the handbills. Likewise in a treatise written on those waters by the late

Dr. Bevis, dedicated to the Royal Society, and may be had at the bar, price 1s., where ladies and gentlemen may depend upon having the best tea, coffee, hot loaves, &c

It was soon apparent that the clientele were after rather more than hot loaves! Bagnigge may never have scaled the heights of popularity with the bon ton but it would have been used by a number of 'loose women' in the early stages of their careers, before they became famous. After all, a girl has to start somewhere.

Chapter 4

The Importance of Fashion

'The Bum Bailiff Outwitted, or, The Convenience of Fashion' (1786).

The women featured in this book all hit their stride at some time in the second half of the eighteenth century. It was an era of great change, great flamboyance, and great style. Spending money on clothes took up a far higher proportion of a person's budget than nowadays – think more in terms of what we might spend on our mortgages to see what the fashionable wannabees would spend on their clothes.

In the early 1750s the dresses expected to be worn at court were hideously uncomfortable with an emphasis on the female torso being shown as an inverted cone, created by having boned stays and very full skirts. Hips were emphasised by hoop skirts – even side panniers. These made sitting down impracticable.

Fashions were much less formal beyond the court and the general emphasis was on wearing low-necked gowns called robes, worn with a skirt which opened in front to reveal the petticoat underneath. Where the bodice of the gown was open in the front a stomacher might be pinned to the front so as to ensure a modicum of modesty – or a *fichu* (a type of neckerchief, usually made of lace) would have the same effect. Clearly, there were many 'ladies of ill-repute' (and quite a few others) who were happy to dispense with any such modesty panels and in general males got to see rather more cleavages than they ever saw of female legs. This was because the robes reached down to the floor.

There were two main types of robes – the *robe a la francaise* and the *robe à la anglaise*. The first was also known as a sack-back gown, with the back pleats hanging loosely from the neckline. An example is shown in plate 13 and it contrasts with the English variant which was a close-bodiced gown with back pleats sewn in place so that the skirt then fell from the waist (see plate 12). Another variant was the polonaise (shown in plate 14). This came into fashion in the 1770s and the fabric at the rear was split into three separate puffed sections to reveal the petticoat underneath.

Over the years there were many changes in style for all these types of robe, especially in the mid-seventies when the female figure was padded out in most extreme ways, particularly with cork rumps, sometimes known as 'Chloe's cushions'. The December 1779 edition of the *Town & Country Magazine* reported: 'Bum-shops are opened in many parts of Westminster for the sale of cork bums ... Tall ladies, and short ladies – fat ladies and lean ladies, must have bums.'

Each fashion extreme led to a swing of the pendulum: next up were false stomachs – imitating pregnancy – with pads made of tin. The smaller ones were called 'paddies' and were given the name of 'tin pinafores'. There was even a brief vogue for false calves – stockings enhanced with fleece to give a more muscular calf-muscle – a trend apparently followed both by men and women.

And then there was the actual hairstyle. Whereas men tended to favour the full wig (necessitating a whole-of-head shave every day to prevent itching – and lice!) women tended to choose hair pads or part-wigs, often coated with powder and then ornamented. The powder was often white but could also give a pink, blue, lilac or even violet hue to the hair. The pads, used to give height, were made of cut hair, wire, hemp, wool or tow. The ornamentation might involve pearls, decorative pins, flowers or short ribbons and the wearer's natural hair could be curled, waved, frizzed or left natural. Then came the daftest era for hairstyles – the towering edifices of the 1770s, built upon cork or linen toques (usually heart-shaped) around which a cushion of natural hair would be piled to give a hairstyle perhaps one and a half times as high as the head. In 1774 the Duchess of Devonshire topped that lot off with a display of ostrich feathers and caused a sensation immediately copied by anyone wishing to be 'a la mode'.

By 1780 there was a move back towards more 'natural' styles. Out went the absurd headdresses featuring national emblems, warships and hot-air balloons. Instead, hair was cut shorter on the crown but with a length of hair left to hang down the back of the neck, either braided or left straight, or curled into ringlets. Then came the French Revolution and with it all ostentation disappeared out the window. The tax on powder for wigs, introduced in 1795 to help pay for the war with France, spelled the death knell for wigs. Hair styles became softer, more feminine; in came simple ribbons and restrained ornamentation.

Within this fashion framework there was a huge scope for personalisation: women could add layers of ruffles to the sleeves of their dresses; they could wear belts or sashes; they could add bangles and beads; they could wear brooches and pendant ear-rings; they could set off their outfits with hats worn at a jaunty angle, or caps ringed with curls. And in a world where the court, with its stifling effect on fashion, meant that novelty and innovation were frowned upon, the leaders of change were the nouveau riche – the courtesans. The Fanny Murrays, the Kitty Fishers and the Mary Robinsons were the trendsetters. Unfettered by convention, unjudged by the court, they were free agents and they could indulge every fancy.

In France there were differences, not least because heavy and embroidered silks predominated. Britain, with its close links to the Indian sub-continent, experimented with lighter, more flowing fabrics such as chintzes made of Indian cotton. And it was into this background that Marie Antoinette decided to kick over the traces and embrace a completely new fashion – for plain cottons and muslins, gathered at the waist and around the arms with simple ribbons. The French aristocracy were horrified. Accustomed to the stifling, uncomfortable fashions insisted upon by the court, they regarded the queen's taste as being more appropriate to the bedroom – hence the name *chemise a la reine*.

Otherwise called the *robe de gaulle*, the cotton dress may have been fine for the queen while she was playing the part of a country shepherdess at her retreat at the *hameau* of the Petit Trianon, but it was anathema in polite French circles. It was unpatriotic, it spelt the death knell of the French silk industry, and even worse, it boosted British trade interests. In Britain there were no such prejudices and the simpler style swept the country, largely thanks to the trend being endorsed by the Duchess of Devonshire and the courtesan Mary Robinson. It was a trend which led to a demand for cotton goods that could never be satisfied from India and resulted directly in the development of the cotton growing industry in America, heavily reliant on slave labour.

As the end of the century approached waistlines got higher and higher until costumes were tied tightly under the bust, leading to the Empire line which was a world away from the styles of fifty years earlier. Once again it was the harlotry that was quick to embrace the new, softer, more feminine styles, based upon figure-clinging fabrics. Where they led, others soon followed.

Above all, it was an era when fashion accessories came into their own and this was where trends could be set. Think tippits (similar to a shawl, often made of fur); think lappets (decorative lace hanging parts of a cap or hat); think muffs (typically of fur or feathers); think capes, parasols, ruffs, cuffs and wristbands. Think shoes and sandals, hats and headdresses – all of them coming in and out of vogue at different times in the final quarter of the eighteenth century. The Thomas Rowlandson image of Beauties, dated 1 December 1792 and shown in plate 1 gives some idea of how these accessories could be brought together to create fashion. The figure on the left, with blonde hair, holds a fan and wears a full-skirted dress and overshirt decorated with ruffles at the neck. Her sleeves come down to just below the elbow. She sports bracelets on both wrists and wears a large straw hat decorated with bows. Her companion on the right has dark hair and has opted, not for a revealing decolletage, but for a loose gown with deep decorative cuffs and with a floppy collar or capelet.

Plates 7 and 8 give more examples of some of the other accessories available for the fashion-conscious young lady to consider wearing.

Chapter 5

The Cyprian Corps

Two high-class prostitutes plying their trade at London's Bagnigge Wells, a popular watering hole at Clerkenwell.

It has been suggested that up to one in five women in eighteenth-century London resorted to one sort of sex work or other during their lifetime. With a population of around a million living in the city, if we take the gender split as being equal that gives a potential 100,000 potential sex workers. But that figure does not mean that a hundred thousand prostitutes were lining the streets or living in brothels – it included the servant girl willing to offer her favours for a few shillings to the randy son of her employer. It included the kitchen maid, sacked from her employment, who sold her charms to men in the room above the local tavern while she looked for a new job. Daniel Defoe, writing in 1725, was certainly of the view that young servant girls made up the majority of London prostitutes, and that they took to prostitution when they were unemployed, as a way of supporting themselves. 'This is the reason why our streets are swarming with strumpets. Thus many of them rove from place to place, from bawdy-house to service, and from service to bawdy-house again.'

Many moved on to other areas of work once they reached their mid-twenties, if of course they lived that long. *The Times* of 31 October 1785 famously quoted a figure of 5,000 prostitutes dying every year in London. Of those who survived, a few (a very few) lived the dream, with money, fame and glamour, but for the majority it was a seedy life of depravity, degradation, poverty and debilitating illness. Not that that ever put off the wave of newcomers entering the City every year, eagerly snapped up by the bawds and procurers who scoured the coaching stations and inns on the main arterial routes coming in from the country. Some of them were victims from the outset – raped or seduced and then abandoned, unable to return to their family homes because of the shame they had brought upon the family.

At the other end of the scale the rather loose definition of sex workers included the unhappily married woman who had left her husband and cohabited with a man who was willing to pay her bills and give her a dress allowance. It certainly included the street-walkers who thronged to watering holes like Bagnigge Wells, or infested the dark corners in Ranelagh Gardens where they pestered male company for a quickie behind the bushes. It also included the raddled old whores, their bodies ravaged by venereal disease and malnutrition, living by the docks and offering their services to passing sailors willing to pay them sufficient pennies to enable them to drink themselves into oblivion.

It included the girls living in garrets in the St Giles district, offering their services for a few shillings, dreaming of securing a regular benefactor, just as it included the women working for a madam – not necessarily living in at a brothel, but occupying rooms nearby where they could be called to a 'selection parade' whenever a gentleman turned up. And then, right at the top of the profession, were the superstars – the ones who had worked their way up through the ranks, who had perhaps snared a wealthy gentleman willing to pay them an annuity of a few hundred pounds a year, who had bought their own house, had managed to get invited to masked balls where the nobility held private parties, and who had thereby come to the attention of randy dukes, libidinous earls and the morally incontinent scions of distinguished families. These were the Toasts of the Town –

famous for being handed around among a seemingly closed group of aristocratic friends, all of them willing to be seen in public sporting such a glamorous commodity on their arm.

Make no mistake, women were a commodity. Men could behave as licentious rakes and get away with it. They were simply 'gallants', entitled to sow their wild oats. Women, on the other hand, who had multiple sexual partners were seen as sluts, shunned by the haut ton. They were never invited into the dining rooms of the homes owned by the class of men they associated with. And yet, such was the wealth pouring into the capital and cascading down through the ranks, that these same women were able to afford to dress like the aristocracy, move in the same circles, drive the same carriages, sport the same jewels, play the same part in the bon ton. Theirs was the demi-monde, a parallel universe where the pursuit of pleasure was seen as justifying everything.

In 1758 a book was published by G. Burnet (author unknown) with the long-winded title of *A Congratulatory Epistle from a Reformed Rake to John F...g Esq upon the new scheme of reforming prostitutes*. The book urged readers to accept that the higher-class sex workers were just as likely to corrupt the morals of the nation as the lowly street-walker:

If low, mean, Whores are a Bane to Society, by debauching the Morals, as well as Bodies, of Apprentices, and Lads scarce come to the Age of Puberty; if they frequently infect them with venereal Complaints, which almost as often terminate in as fatal Consequences; if they sometimes urge these youths to unwarrantable Practices for supporting their Extravagance in Gin; do not those in a more dazzling Situation produce still worse Consequences, by as much as they are above the others? Are not youths of good Family and Fortune seduced by these shining Harlots, who more frequently than their Inferiors in Rank, propagate the Species of an inveterate Clap, or a Sound-pox?

The same book puts the blame fairly and squarely on women for corrupting men, rather than the other way round:

There is a Lust in Woman that operates more strongly than all her libidinous Passions; to gratify which she sticks at nothing. Fame,

Health, Content, are easily sacrificed to it. Fanny M...y and Lucy C....r have made more Whores than all the Rakes in England. A kept mistress that rides in her Chariot, debauches every vain Girl she meets – such is the Presumption of the Spectator, she imagines the same Means will procure her the same Grandeur. A miserable street walker who perhaps has not Rags enough to cover her Nakedness, more enforces Chastity – I had almost said Virtue – than all the moral Discourses, and even Sermons that ever were wrote or preached.

Put simply, the writer felt that society had less to worry about with the sad, destitute, girl who sold her body for a few pennies than with the high-class prostitute in her finery, charging a hundred guineas for a single night of passion. The first, by her failure, would act as an object lesson; the second was an aspirational figure. 'Look at me; you too can have all of this.'

It was an era when life expectancy, at birth, was around forty years. However, so many people succumbed to fatal illnesses shortly after birth, or in their teens, that if they survived and reached the age of twenty, they could expect to live to the age of sixty. By coincidence, the average lifespan of the seven women featured in Part Two of this book was precisely sixty, an average which was made up of the longevity of Elizabeth Armistead (ninety-two) counterbalanced by the death of Kitty Fisher at the youthful age of twenty-six.

The fact that disease did not define their careers is perhaps the most surprising thing. It has been estimated that one in five Londoners had syphilis by their mid-thirties during the last quarter of the eighteenth century – and that was right across the population. How much greater would the incidence have been where the women were engaged, full time, in the sex trade? To make matters worse, the circle of lovers shared among the courtesans who made it to the top of the pile was incredibly small – the same lovers featured over and over again in the various life stories. The Prince of Wales, Lord Cholmondeley, the Duke of Dorset, the Whig politicians loosely grouped under the heading of 'Foxites' are names which crop up over and over again.

So, how come the featured courtesans did not have syphilis, gonorrhoea or chlamydia? The answer is that they almost certainly were infected, but were fortunate enough to have symptoms that were not always evident and which ultimately were not fatal. We know these STIs as separate, individual, bacteria-led diseases: the Georgians lumped them altogether as 'venereal distemper' with no distinction between the treatment for 'the clap' (gonorrhoea) or 'the pox' (syphilis). There was a huge range of salves, lotions, potions and pills sold by doctors and mountebanks which were claimed to cure such diseases, although most treatments involved administering mercury in one form or another. It would be astonishing if the courtesans featured here did not require treatment at one time or another in their careers. Indeed, as we will see in the case of Gertrude Mahon it was strongly hinted that her visit to Montpellier was simply a pretext for treatment, and Mary Robinson was reported to have suffered from 'a fire breaking out'. We can probably discount Gillray's portrait of Elizabeth Armistead as having a face ravaged by the pox – this was simply his way of drawing attention to her scandalous past. There was a no-holds-barred attitude towards gossip about sexual promiscuity, as evidenced by some of the entries in *Harris's List*, where 'venereal distempers' were freely discussed. In all probability all the featured women in this book may have suffered from syphilitic attacks at some stage or other, but were fortunate enough for it not to have been self-evident.

Syphilis, in particular, has a progression which typically involves an initial stage of pain and discomfort followed by a potentially lengthy period of time without symptoms, followed by a secondary stage when symptoms become far more noticeable. Many people would be lucky enough to assume that they had been cured when the initial symptoms disappeared, and never experienced the second stage. Others were not so fortunate. The diarist James Boswell recorded nineteen separate occasions when he was affected by the disease, all of them resulting from paid sexual encounters. He died at the age of forty-five, his death hastened by a combination of venereal disease and the effects of alcoholism.

The fact that STDs ravaged society did nothing to dim the demand for paid sex. At all levels, the offer of sex for sale was completely open. Foreigners complained about being pestered constantly as they walked along the streets. Every publican could offer his customers a list of girls who could be called upon to attend to the needs of a visitor. So called 'jelly houses' acted as pick-up joints while countless 'bagnios' – especially in the area around Covent Garden – were no longer making any pretence of offering hot baths, and instead consisted of as many bedrooms as could conveniently be squeezed into a house, and which could be hired by the hour at any time of the day and night. Sex was going on in the doorways of shops, in the parks and public spaces, in the seedy brothels – and not just in the exclusive seraglios of St James's.

Part II

Toasts of the Town

'A Sketch from Nature' by Thomas Rowlandson.

This section looks at the few, the pinnacle of their profession, who made it to the top. They were acknowledged as the leaders of the demi-monde. Their individual place at the top of the tree may only have lasted a few years – a decade at most – but during their heyday they enjoyed huge adulation and fame. They dominated the gossip columns, they helped flood the print market and they generated the sort of fame we nowadays reserve for reality TV stars. The emergence of these celebrity whores coincided with a true Georgian phenomenon – the growth of consumerism. They echoed the desire for novelty, for style and for ostentation. If ever the phrase 'If you've got it, flaunt it' was true, it was here in London, in the second half of the eighteenth century.

Chapter 6

Fanny Murray

At first sight Fanny Murray is very different to the other celebrity whores whose lives are featured here and she deserves her place because she is such a contrast to the others. She fits into the image of the poor flower girl, catapulted into the limelight; someone who 'was no better than she ought to be'. Not for her a story of being born with a silver spoon in her mouth or escaping from a monotonous education by running away with a dashing swain and then living to regret it. She was no middle-class heroine but someone from the bottom rung of the ladder, who somehow carved a niche as one of the most famous women of the Georgian era. She also differs from some of the other celebrity whores because she retired from harlotry in around 1757, just as the rest of those featured here were being born or being sent off to school.

She was of an earlier generation, one which preceded the explosion in the growth of celebrity linked to the press and to the popularity and influence of artists such as Reynolds and Gainsborough. In her own way she blazed a trail which the others followed and justifies her inclusion because in many ways she was not a typical 'Toast of the Town' as the elite whores were termed. She is also remarkable because she appears to have led a blameless, monogamous married life for over twenty years, having spent the previous fourteen years as one of the most promiscuous and sexually voracious young women ever to have graced the London scene.

Believed to have been born in Bath as Frances Rudman in 1729, Fanny was reported to have become orphaned at an early age. Her father, Thomas Rudman, had been a musician working in that city. He allegedly died in 1741, leaving the twelve-year-old Fanny destitute and living on the streets. This part of the story was based on anecdotes written at the time, but it is possible that these rumours were put out to try and paint Fanny's experience in a better light. The story of the 'poor orphan girl lured into prostitution' sounds better than a 'promiscuous pre-teen who runs off with a randy rake'.

Fanny is believed to have been earning a pittance selling flowers outside the abbey and at the Assembly Rooms when she had the misfortune to come to the attention of Jack Spencer, grandson of the first Duke of Marlborough. He was in his mid-thirties and presumably thought it was a bit of fun to deflower a young street urchin. It is easy to believe that for a few silver shillings Fanny would have naïvely consented (and twelve was regarded as the legal age of consent in such matters). No doubt Spencer promised her protection and financial support, but nothing came of it, and when he deserted her, she fell in with others willing to take advantage of her. After a year of selling her body she found a safe haven at the home of an unlikely hero, the ageing roué Richard 'Beau' Nash.

Beau Nash was the self-appointed Master of Ceremonies at the Assembly Rooms in Bath. For many years he filled the role of arbiter of taste and fashion, laying down rules of behaviour at what was virtually a cattle market for parents wanting to find a suitable marriage partner for their offspring. Beau Nash, often wearing his trademark white fur hat, would call on visitors to the city at their lodgings, ascertain their social status and expectations, meet the young lady or gentleman, and inform the party of the time when they should arrive at the assembly room doors. During the evening he would then effect suitable introductions and would be rewarded for his troubles by being awarded a benefit night twice a year, when all profits would go into his pocket. He was wealthy, he was unmarried and he was in his late sixties. Fanny moved in with him as his mistress when she was fourteen and for a short time he presumably offered her a basic training in how to behave and to succeed in what was very much a man's world. Beau Nash showed her that there could be a comfortable living to be made, that she had something valuable to sell, and that the money she could make was linked to how she behaved, who she mixed with, what she wore, and where she went.

Some idea of Fanny's appearance at this stage in her life is given in a book entitled *Memoirs of the Celebrated Miss Fanny Murray*, published in 1759. There is nothing to suggest that Fanny had anything very much to do with the memoirs – they may have been 'ghosted' for her or they may have been entirely a work of fiction – but they had this to say of her appearance: 'Fanny's person, which already began to testify the marks of womanhood was extremely beautiful; her face a perfect oval with eyes that conversed love, and every other feature in agreeable symmetry. Her dimpled cheeks alone might have captivated, if a smile that gave it existence did not display such other charms as shared the conquest. Her teeth regular, fine and perfectly white, coral lips and chestnut hair, soon attracted the eyes of everyone.'

The *Memoirs* went on to describe her at fourteen – gay, volatile and handsome: 'She dressed equal to any woman in Bath, and perhaps looked as well. It is true she was but of the middle size and though inclined to be plump, she had delicacy enough in her shape to make it agreeable, and beauty enough in her face, to render her at once the grand object of the men's affections, and the women's envy.'

Nash may have clothed her in elegant outfits, he may have taught her 'how to hold a knife and fork' and to make polite conversation, but this was no Eliza Doolittle and she remained ill-educated and uncouth. Despite this, the *Memoirs* state that 'It is not at all surprising then, that she had by this time initiated herself into the company of all the men of quality; or that the demi-reps of fashion should submit to speak to her.' In other words, she was a good social mixer. In time she tired of living with an old man and was lured up to London.

Perhaps this is how most of the whores came to be working in the capital: lured by expectations of wealth, they were drawn to London like a magnet from all parts of the country. But Fanny was perhaps different to many, in the sense that she was no innocent at large. Mind you, she had not, up until then, chosen to be a common whore. Indeed, she had had very little choice at all. Sex kept her fed, clothed and sheltered. If frequenting the lowest dives, the roughest taverns, and the bawdiest brothels meant that she survived, then that appears to have been good enough for her while she was 'learning the trade' as a prostitute.

She fell into the hands of successive procuresses who provided her with borrowed clothing at exorbitant rates, secured by promissory notes which Fanny had small prospect of ever repaying. As Horace Bleackley states in his book *Ladies Fair and Frail*: 'the unhappy girl who failed to pay the exorbitant sum demanded for the loan of these faded garments was hurried without mercy into the Fleet or Marshalsea prisons. Those who fell out of favour with the bucks of the town, and who in consequence found themselves unable to bribe the Watch, were soon dragged before the magistrate and sent to beat hemp in Blackfriars Bridewell. At the best they were used more shamefully than women of the harem; at the worst they were left to rot in the dungeon.'

Fanny proved to be different to many of her contemporaries. She was hopeless at managing money but she worked hard, played hard, and gradually worked herself up to wealthier clients. In time she was able to pay off the tally women and free herself from the tyranny of working for a madam. By then, she had changed her surname from Rudman to Murray and moved into her own garret (shades of Gillray's *The Last Shift* shown in Plate 8) near Covent Garden.

The *Memoirs* paint an interesting picture of Fanny's expenses. They may of course have been entirely fabricated but they suggest that in a single week Fanny might earn just £5 10s 6d, while her outgoings came in at £5 10s, giving her a profit of just sixpence. The expenses are fascinating: her board and lodging ('in a garret, on small beer and sprats') of £1 15s; washing 7 shillings; use of a brocade gown, smocks, stays, shoes, ruffles and petticoats £1 6s 6d. She also had to pay half a guinea (10s 6d) to the constables to stop them arresting her, as well as sundry other expenses relating to her clothing and appearance. It certainly showed how presentation was considered vital if Fanny was to progress beyond the level of giving 'a threepenny stand-up' in a shop entrance. Strutting her stuff alongside the River Fleet, enticing apprentice boys to part with a few shillings in return for what might be called 'a quickie' was never going to make her rich, but it was a means towards an end. The *Memoirs* refer to 'a variety of lovers succeeding each other, the last as welcome as the first'. Fanny almost certainly caught a venereal disease at this stage in her career and the *Memoirs* state 'her goods were damaged, her small stock exhausted in chiurgical fees; her cloaths were pledged upon the same account; her surgeon took his last fee, produced by her last gown.'

Eventually her youthful charms and her wanton enthusiasm captured the attention of the fashionable rakes about town. She would tout for custom in the taverns local to where she lived and at some stage came to the attention of a man called John Harrison, otherwise known as Jack Harris, a businessman and pimp who worked at the Shakespeare's Head Tavern in Covent Garden. For some years Harris had been able to supply prospective customers with details of prostitutes operating in the area, along with their 'specialities', prices and so on. In 1757 Samuel Derrick persuaded Harris to lend his name to a published version of the list and it became a more-or-less annual edition for nearly forty years, under the title of *Harris's List of Covent Garden Ladies*. With a publication figure running into thousands, possibly 8,000, the book was doubtlessly circulated to many more readers on a shared basis. An entry in *Harris's List* was therefore a brilliant form of advertising for any girl lucky enough to be deemed worthy of inclusion. It was a sort of precursor to Tripadvisor: a kind of 'Sexadvisor' showing who was hot and who was not. It took three or four years of living in London before Fanny made the list, appearing as: 'A fine brown girl, rising nineteen next season, perfectly sound in wind and limb. A good side-box piece – will show well in the flesh market – wear well – may be put off for a virgin any time these twelve months. Never common this side of Temple Bar, but for six months. Fit for high keeping with a Jew merchant. NB a good premium from ditto – then the run of the house. And if she keeps out of the Lock [the VD hospital] may make her fortune and ruin half the men in town.'

She was to be found at the First floor at Mrs –'s, milliner at Charing Cross. The entry shows that by then Fanny had acquired sufficient social skills to be considered a good-looking companion to take to the theatre ('a good side-box piece') and was expecting to be showered with the sort of trinkets and rewards which only the wealthy Jewish businessmen could readily afford. Indeed, many prostitutes aimed at the Jewish market. It also showed that for all her experience, Fanny was still able to pass for a virgin (and hence command a far higher price in the market-place).

Entry on the List enabled Fanny to charge customers two guineas a time and this was rapidly increased as word got around about her physical attractions and lascivious appetite. In particular, she started to become famous for what she was wearing – especially on her head. From the age of nineteen she had taken to wearing a straw (or 'chip') hat with an asymmetric brim, worn at a jaunty angle and often tied with a large bow at the nape of the neck. Years later, the *Lady's Magazine* in 1784 was to describe the hat in the following way: 'The late Fanny Murray whose face was very handsome, though somewhat awry, used to wear a hat of her own contrivance, which was so well judged, that it concealed the imperfection of her face, whence it was called Fanny Murray's cock; and became a general fashion: but the misfortune was, that many who wore this hat did not consult her traits, or features, of their faces, did not look near so well, as they had done with any other of a less conspicuous form.'

Wonky face or not, Fanny inspired a rash of imitators, to the extent that a description of a Fanny Murray hat became a shorthand for writers to describe the appearance of ladies of ill-repute, as in the moralistic tale of two siblings, one a prostitute, one virtuous, called *The Sisters* by William Dodd. It came out in 1754 and refers to a group of prominent strumpets wearing 'Fanny Murray'd hats'. One story suggests that Fanny even tried to harness her fame by opening a millinery shop to sell her fashionable hats, but this may simply reflect the fact that the word 'milliner' was often used as synonym for a prostitute, and of course the *Harris's List* entry gives her address as being on the first floor, above a millinery shop. What is certain is that from 1748 onwards, for around a decade, the cocked hat, whether described as the Fanny Murray cock, or the Fanny Murray hat or cap, was immensely popular as a fashion accessory. The *Memoirs* emphasise that whatever Fanny wore was 'the law of fashion' and that her sartorial style was 'the only standard' of female attire.

A painting of Fanny Murray in her youthful prime by Henry Robert Morland was converted into a mezzotint and sold by the thousands. It is shown in the second plate section as plate 5 and reveals a woman in a richly embroidered and beaded gown. It is adorned with a crossed *fichu* – a form of transparent kerchief covering her breasts. Her sleeves are tied with knotted bows and she sports her cocked hat with a close-cap tied under the chin. It is an image of an elegant, confident woman, and the mezzotint was snapped up and pinned on the walls of countless homes by women using it as a fashion plate, as an epitome of good taste.

Equally, it was snapped up in large quantities by men keen to 'have a piece' of Fanny. The circular cut-out miniature of her face, based on the Morland portrait, would be kept between the outer and inner layers of a watch case, hung from a gold chain and worn next to the heart. The British Museum has an example of just such a watch paper, which would have cost threepence – or sixpence for the coloured version. The mezzotint must have also served as an inspiration for many a young shop-girl or domestic servant girl: if you aspire to be seen in a dress dripping with pearls, if you want to be at the cutting edge of fashion, if you want people to look up to you as an icon – become a sex worker.

Not only artists were inspired by Fanny: so were countless poets and writers. One poem, contained in an anthology as late as 1762, referred to the beautiful Fanny with the words:

> What Paint with her Complexion vies
> What Jewels sparkle like her Eyes
> What Hills of Snow so white as Rise
> The Breasts of Fanny Murray

Songs were written in her honour, with one appearing in the *Universal Magazine* in 1755 under the title of 'A song wrote by Mr Boyce on sight of Fanny Murray'. Gin cocktails bore her name, along with ships and numerous racehorses. Hardly a publication of the popular press omitted to include an odd ode, a panegyric poem or a florid description of Fanny's beauty. As one periodical remarked (*The Centinel* of July 1757): 'If Fanny Murray chuses to vary the fashion of her apparel, immediately every Lucretia in town takes notice of the change, and modestly copies the chaste original. If Fanny shews the coral centre of her snowy orbs – Miss, to outstrip her, orders the stays to be cut an inch or two lower; and kindly displays the whole lovely circumference.'

Fanny's 'snowy orbs' were universally admired. The *Memoirs* explain how women copied whatever Fanny wore, even to the extent of going topless when they might have been better advised to stay covered up: 'If she wore a plaid ribbon, plaid ribbons were instantly the fashion. If she cocked her hat before, and wore stays that hid not her snowy orbs the women were all Amazons, and many exposed their want of charms ... because Fanny set the fashion ... In short, Fanny is the only standard for the women's dress, whatever she wears is the law of fashion; her tyranny in mode is complete.'

The eighteenth-century politician Richard Rigby praised 'those fair hemispheres, those orbs of more than snowy whiteness, which seem to pant for release from irksome robes.' Even our modern-day TV reality stars would have been envious of such constant cleavage admiration and attention. Fanny-mania was universal. It was apparently 'a vice not to be acquainted with Fanny; it was a crime not to toast her at every meal, at every sitting.'

As news of her beauty spread, her fees increased. As the *Memoirs* relate, 'a succession of lovers now produced not only a sufficiency to live genteelly, but to amass a considerable sum.' From charging a couple of guineas she moved on to twenty pounds and from there to a hundred guineas. One of her conquests was John Montagu, 4th Earl of Sandwich, who was said to have met her first when she was operating in a brothel run by a Mrs Stanhope. He made her his mistress and because he was regarded as being such a good judge of female beauty Fanny was soon established as the 'reigning Toast of the Town'. William Montagu (brother of John) was apparently so enamoured with Fanny's charms that he had her nude portrait painted and displayed it at his apartments in London, where it was noted by the visiting Philip Yorke, 1st Earl of Hardwicke, and who was at the time Lord Chancellor.

John Montagu loved clubs, in an era when clubs proliferated. In 1746 a new club had started up, under the title of the Order of the Knights of St Francis of Wycombe. Its alternate title was the Order of the Monks or Friars of Medmenham, but in general it has become known quite simply (but inaccurately) as the Hellfire Club. It had been founded by Sir Francis Dashwood, a man who had already formed the Divan Club (open to anyone who had visited the Ottoman Empire) and the Dilettanti Society (for aficionados of the Grand Tour and the wonders of Ancient Rome).

In 1775 Dashwood found a home for his newest society, intending it as a private members club dedicated to drinking wine and fornicating. It was based at Medmenham Abbey to the west of London, on the banks of the River Thames, and because of the religious background to the premises,

'Beauties' showing two fashionable women in 1792 by Thomas Rowlandson.

'Dressing for a Masquerade' by Thomas Rowlandson, showing a group of prostitutes preparing to go to a masked ball.

Plate 1

In 'The audience watching the play' Rowlandson shows that the audience were rather more interested in chatting and socialising than in watching the performance. See chapter 3.

The Prince of Wales drives Mary Robinson to Windsor in a high gig drawn by six goats. Charles Fox leads the procession while Mr Robinson, wearing cuckold's horns, rides his goat backwards. See chapter 11.

Plate 2

Harmless print or revolutionary dynamite? James Gillray shows Charles Fox and his wife, the former Elizabeth Armistead, hosting a National Assembly at their home at St Ann's Hill. It presupposes that the republicans have overthrown the monarchy. What made the print so dangerous was the half-obscured image of the Prince of Wales (extreme right) suggesting that even the prince had republican tendencies. It was enough to make the prince buy up the entire print run and (so he thought) to destroy the copper plate so as to ensure that it could never be used again. See chapter 12.

Vaux Hall by Thomas Rowlandson showing an entirely imaginary audience of celebrated figures promenading at Vauxhall pleasure gardens. In the foreground, Georgiana, Duchess of Devonshire, and her sister Lady Duncannon stand arm in arm while, at right, the Prince of Wales whispers to his mistress Mary 'Perdita' Robinson.

Plate 3

'*A Morning Ramble*', showing fashionable rakes visiting a millinery shop to chat up the young shop assistants, hoping to lead them astray.

The first thing many a successful courtesan aspired to was to drive her own team of horses – and for this she needed to learn how to drive. Here, a driving lesson is in progress.

Plate 4

The rococo rotunda at Ranelagh Gardens, where the nine-year-old Mozart played in 1765.

An Evening's Invitation, with a Wink from the Bagnio. The gentleman has already lost his silk handkerchief and is likely to be parted from his money very soon!

Plate 5

The Whore's Last Shift. Who said that the sex trade was glamorous?

Plate 6

Hats in the final quarter of the eighteenth century, in paintings by Naysmith, Hoppner, Reynolds and Romney.

Plate 7

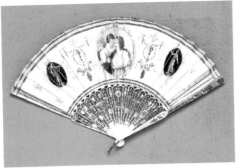

British fans from the late eighteenth century.

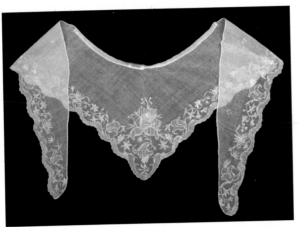

Lace fichu.

The Muff.

Plate 8

(Left) Thomas Rowlandson 'New Shoes' and
(Below) shoes from 1770 and 1800.

Plate 9

Designed by D. RITCHIE Hair Dresser.

Head styles from 1772.

Plate 10

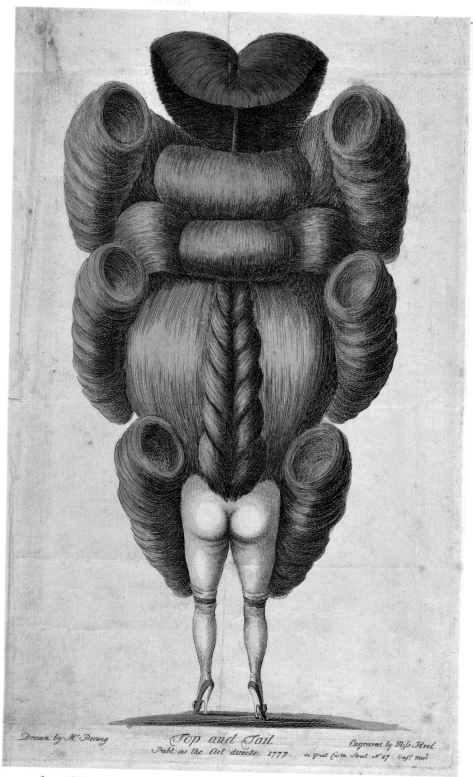

A cartoon from 1777 suggesting that hairstyles had become so vertiginous and all-enveloping that the fashionable lady could dispense with clothing altogether.

Plate 11

Separate views of the Robe à l'Anglaise,
pleated from the shoulder and stitched
closely to the upper part of the body so as to
give emphasis to the bust-line and hips.

Plate 12

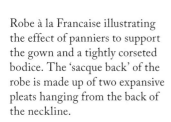

Robe à la Francaise illustrating
the effect of panniers to support
the gown and a tightly corseted
bodice. The 'sacque back' of the
robe is made up of two expansive
pleats hanging from the back of
the neckline.

Plate 13

Fashionable from the 1770s, the Robe à la
Polonaise featured a close-fitting bodice,
with the back of the skirt gathered up into
three separate puffed sections to reveal the
petticoat below.

Plate 14

J-L David's portrait showing the lady wearing a Chemise à la Reine.

Plate 15

Marie Antoinette introducing the scandalous Chemise à la Reine to the world of fashion, in a portrait by Élisabeth Louise Vigée Le Brun (see chapter 11).

Plate 16

members were encouraged to dress as monks, and to select partners from a group of women dressed as nuns. One of the more enthusiastic monks in attendance was the Earl of Sandwich, a close friend of Sir Francis. It is generally accepted that Sandwich brought Fanny along to the gatherings, where she played an enthusiastic part in the orgies and Bacchanalian celebrations. These gatherings became notorious, with suggestions that members studied the occult, worshipped the devil, blasphemed, and generally plotted against the king. One suspects that in fact the members were far too busy getting drunk and fornicating to have either strength or inclination to do anything else.

Astonishingly, Dashwood went on to inherit the title of 15th Baron Le Despencer, served in Parliament, and became Chancellor of the Exchequer, notwithstanding the fact that it was universally agreed that 'of financial knowledge he did not possess the rudiments'. Equally intriguing, the Dashwood family estate, at West Wycombe Park, still houses one of the best-known portraits of Fanny, painted by Adrien Carpentiers in around 1745. It shows her, dripping with pearls, left breast exposed, looking directly at the viewer (see the heading to this chapter).

Fanny's client list expanded to include Henry Gould, who went on to become a judge of the Court of Common Pleas, and Joseph Yorke, British ambassador at The Hague. There were rumours that Prince William Augustus (the Duke of Cumberland, and the youngest son of George II) had a fling with her. She also cavorted with the swindler and confidence trickster Captain Plaistow, as well as with the highway robber James MacLaine. When the heiress Lucy Naomi Strode (née Gough) sought a divorce from her violent husband, Edward Strode, in 1755 she described how her husband initially tricked her into marriage and afterwards had neglected her and spent night after night at the home of Fanny Murray. The divorce petition was reported not just in the proceedings of the House of Lords, but in the newspapers of the day, ensuring that the irrepressible Fanny remained in the public eye.

Meanwhile, she met and captured the heart of Sir Richard Atkins who, in the *Memoirs*, was described as 'a youth just come of age, heir to a good fortune and title.' It went on to state that Fanny was 'the properest woman in the world he could have pitched upon ... She did the honours of his table with that ease and composure that could not be surpassed by a woman of the first fashion.' It was not long before he supplied her with 'a splendid equipage, a numerous retinue, an elegant furnished house and a handsome allowance.' She got a wardrobe of 'gorgeous apparel and a casket of valuable jewels'. She appeared to have hit the jackpot. The *Memoirs* suggest that Sir Richard wanted to whisk Fanny off to Paris, and that she started to learn French. They state, somewhat improbably, that she set off for Calais on her own, on the basis that Sir Richard would follow as soon as his business commitments allowed. The *Memoirs* indicate that she cut quite a swathe in Paris, turning up at the opera, on her own, bedecked in all her finery. She apparently wasn't on her own for long! She was supposed to have visited Versailles, caught the attention of the French monarch, and was eventually joined by Sir Richard. However, in reality there is no confirmation that the French trip ever occurred, and it may simply have been a device to puff up Fanny's beauty and international appeal.

When they returned to Pall Mall 'she lived at ease without immerging into any luxurious dissipations or expensive frolicks,' and when Sir Richard installed her in a house in Richmond he 'suitably furnished it, presented her with a new sedan chair and a number of trinkets.' The *Memoirs* continue by saying that 'she now received the visits of women of character, and ladies of distinction did not scruple speaking her they imitated. She was still the reigning toast; still the standard of female dress; and still the object of every man's desire.'

In practice she was always short of money. The often-told tale is that she asked Sir Richard, yet again, for funds. Horace Walpole takes up the story in a letter written to George Montagu on 20 October 1748: 'I heard t'other night: she was complaining of want of money; Sir R – A— immediately gave her a twenty pound note; she said "Damn your twenty pound, what does it signify?", clapped it between two pieces of bread and butter, and ate it.'

Mind you, the same story of the £20 sandwich was put forward about a number of high-class hookers of the time, including Kitty Fisher. In a way it is not surprising because, in the eyes of the general public, one courtesan merged into another. The same crude ditty about Fanny and her cleavage could be rolled out, with just a change in her name, to praise her successor, Kitty. The same mezzotints were even adapted, by adding the odd feather or two to the hat, or altering the sleeves on the dress, to portray a succession of whores. Anecdotes about one were repeated and applied to another, so that we end up with a sort of composite person, an identikit courtesan. Some might see a parallel in today's celebrity culture – one silicone enhanced beauty can look much the same as the next, face make-up contoured to perfection, wearing much the same skimpy bikini, 'posing up a storm' and 'displaying their ample assets' as the daily newspapers coyly put it.

Nowadays we expect our celebrities to sport the same look of mock-surprise, but today's girls are not the first to master the art of attention-seeking and of manipulating the press for their own advantage. As will be seen in Chapter 8, when Fanny's successor, Kitty Fisher, went riding one day in Hyde Park, she deliberately engineered a fall in front of a group of soldiers, who rushed to rescue the damsel in distress. Exit Kitty in a sedan chair which just happened to be waiting nearby. The press had a field day, with headlines about her being a 'fallen woman' twice over. Cartoonists drew the startling scene – much along the lines of: 'Whoops, silly me. I'm not wearing any underwear today!' The end result: the following days and weeks saw her ride in the park in front of an ever-larger audience hoping for a repeat 'wardrobe malfunction'.

Sadly for Fanny, the money tap was turned off in 1756 on the death of Sir Richard. He was just twenty-eight and the baronetcy came to an end with his death. They were never exactly a golden couple, because Fanny was never entirely faithful to her protector. It was rumoured that she never lost her taste for what might be termed 'a bit of rough' and often indulged her passion with a succession of criminals and low-life. It is also suggested that Fanny and Sir Richard had split up in the year before his death, and that Fanny was looking for ways of supporting herself without resorting to prostitution.

The one thing she never did was save money, and Sir Richard's death was followed swiftly by a descent into abject poverty. She was deserted by her former gallants, and her looks were beginning to fade. The spotlight was passing to the next Toast of the Town – as mentioned above, the young Kitty Fisher. Her creditors wanted to see Fanny thrown into the debtors' prison and in desperation she decided to seek help from the son of the man who had first debauched her. Jack Spencer had died in 1746 but his son John, the first Earl Spencer, was very much in the news. Aged twenty-one, he had just married Georgiana Poyntz at a splendid ball at the Spencer ancestral home at Althorp. Not for John the idea that he wasn't liable for the sins of the father: he recognised that his family had a responsibility to provide assistance. It took the form of an annuity variously described as being of either £160 or £200, linked to Fanny's promise to renounce harlotry. Spencer also did Fanny the enormous favour of introducing her to the popular (but impecunious) Scottish actor David Ross. A much later obituary notice for Ross suggests that:

> About this period [1753] Lord Spencer threw his eyes on him as a proper person to accomplish an act of benevolence and humanity, that will ever reflect the highest credit on his Lordship's heart: the celebrated Fanny Murray had been debauched by his father; to atone for such a fault he considered as an act of justice; he therefore presented her as a wife to Mr Ross with a settlement of £200 per annum. Ross's dispositions demanded such an addition to his fortune; and as the lady retained nothing of her former situation but her charms, the contract was signed, and the marriage celebrated.

Not exactly romantic, was it? But it offered a practical solution to both parties, and, astonishingly, it worked. The couple were well-suited, married on 17 May 1756, and after spending a few years in London, settled in Edinburgh where Ross became manager of the Canongate Theatre. He scraped together enough funds to open the Theatre Royal in Edinburgh's New Town, but it was a financial disaster and by 1770 the couple had moved back to London. Unfortunately for Fanny, her husband was not too inclined towards hard work. His passion in life was food – and drink – and he became increasingly corpulent and immobile. But Fanny appears to have renounced harlotry for the joys of marital bliss and disappeared completely from public view.

She did make a brief reappearance in public in October 1768 when the Danish king, Christian VII, hosted a masquerade ball in London. The king had married Caroline Matilda, sister of Britain's monarch George III. Fanny was specifically invited and appeared in the guise of 'Night'. She was proclaimed as being one of the 'belles of the ball' and features as such in an illustration which appeared in the *Gentleman's Magazine*. It must have been a splendid occasion, with the *Gentleman's Magazine* surmising that 'the value of the jewels worn on this occasion was supposed to amount to no less than two millions.' The report in the *Magazine* continued: 'His Majesty the king of Denmark gave a most superb masked ball at the Haymarket, at which were present the greatest number of nobility and gentry ever assembled together upon any occasion of the like nature. It is computed that not less than 2500 persons of distinction were present. The illuminations were particularly splendid and elegant.'

The rich and famous such as Lord Clive (dressed as an Indian nabob) were in attendance. Singled out for special mention was 'Mrs Ross' being one of the 'characters of more humour but less opulence'. She 'displayed much fancy' in her dress 'of thin black silk, studded with stars, and fastened to her head by a moon very happily executed.'

By then Fanny would have been forty, but having enjoyed the spotlight one final time she stepped back into contented obscurity. She remained with Ross until her death in 1778, aged forty-nine, and as far as can be told, she was happy and faithful throughout her marriage.

Her influence lasted long after she had turned her back on whoring – partly because of the appearance of a notorious book – John Cleland's *Memoirs of a Woman of Pleasure* – which is generally assumed to have been inspired by Fanny Murray and which had been published in 1748. It is better known under the alternative title of *Fanny Hill*, and the central character, an unrepentant whore called Fanny, may well have been based on aspects of Fanny Murray's life and lifestyle. The book was banned, withdrawn from sale, then pirated and circulated in secret until 'Fanny' became synonymous as the ultimate 'tart with a heart', the good time had by all.

Further, unwelcome, fascination with her earlier life came about in 1759 when the book *Memoirs of the Celebrated Miss Fanny Murray* was published. It was one of the very earliest 'whore's memoirs', a genre which was to become popular throughout the next fifty years. It is important to stress that it is a work of fiction and that many of the stories are obvious fabrications. It is unlikely that Fanny played any part in writing the book, and its publication must have caused considerable embarrassment in the Ross household.

One other event, over which she had no control, and which ensured that she retained her notoriety, involved the radical John Wilkes. His constant criticism of the king and the government of Lord Bute had led to a general warrant being issued in April 1763 for the arrest of Wilkes and some forty-eight supporters. Wilkes was able to argue, successfully, that the warrants were unlawfully issued and that as an MP he was immune from arrest on a charge of libel. He was immediately freed, and became a public hero. The government was out to get him and when the new prime minister, the Earl of Sandwich, got hold of an obscene poem, ostensibly written by Wilkes, he sensed the opportunity to nail his opponent. There was bad blood between the earl and Wilkes – both had been members of Sir Francis Dashwood's Hellfire Club when Wilkes had embarrassed the earl with a prank at one of the meetings, involving the release of a baboon dressed up as the devil.

The poem in question was dedicated to the courtesan Fanny Murray and was entitled 'An Essay on Woman'. It was intended as a parody of Alexander Pope's 'An Essay on Man' and was an obscene and blasphemous piece of doggerel which started with the words:

> Awake, my Fanny! Leave all meaner things;
> This morn shall prove what rapture swiving brings!
> Let us (since life can little more supply
> Than just a few good fucks, and then we die)
> Expatiate free o'er that loved scene of man,
> A mighty maze, for mighty pricks to scan.

Later it continues with the words:

> The gasp divine, th'emphatic, thrilling squeeze,
> The throbbing panting breasts and trembling knees,
> The tickling motion, the enlivening flow,
> The ra'turous shiver and dissolving, oh!

Not exactly the sort of poem a happily married couple would want to hear bandied around, especially as ten years had elapsed since Fanny had been involved in the sex trade. Worse was to follow: the Earl of Sandwich wanted to pursue Wilkes for blasphemy, and having inserted some additional lines (about the Holy Trinity being 'cock and balls') in order to make the charge stick, he read out the poem before the assembled House of Lords. Wilkes was convicted of blasphemy and fled the country. Fanny meanwhile was left to face the howls of derision. The fact that the poem was dedicated to her was coincidental – it could have been dedicated to anyone and the poem was not intended to be about her personally. The furore eventually died down and at the age of forty-nine Fanny herself died, in London, on 2 April 1778.

*   *   *

What then is to be made of Fanny? From the moment she was seduced as a twelve-year-old it was obvious that her life would never be entirely respectable. At best she might have been able to look forward to a life 'below stairs' working as a domestic servant. Even if she was not to blame for having lost her virginity to Jack Spencer, Georgian society would never have accepted her – except as an in-your-face, take-me-as-you-find-me harlot. One suspects that she loved sex, loved giving pleasure, loved the way she could use her body to get the things she wanted from life. She walked a tightrope through life, risking descent into abject poverty and the horrors of syphilis and gonorrhoea with every step, but she did so with style and enthusiasm. Yes, she was a whore. Yes, she was a harlot. Yes, she was a mistress. But she was also a warm-hearted, generous, woman who gave money (when she had it) to the Lock Hospital (the venereal disease clinic in Hyde Park). She achieved huge fame, spent a large fortune, lived life to the full, and yet by the time she died she had been almost forgotten. She received no obituary, her cause of death is unrecorded, and her place of burial is unknown. She had a commodity which Georgian society valued highly – beauty – and she milked it for all she could, and in doing so gave a lot of pleasure to a lot of people.

Chapter 7

Nancy Parsons

Nancy Parsons and the Duke of Grafton.

C all her Anne or Annabella, call her Nancy; call her Parsons, call her Horton; call her a professional mistress, call her a gold-digger; call her Anne, Viscountess Maynard. All of them were names and titles applied to someone whose early life is shrouded in mystery, and who gained huge notoriety as the mistress of the prime minister. Later, she became a lover of the Duke of Dorset, then hit the headlines as wife of the second Viscount Maynard, and again, when she was nearly fifty, as a 'cougar' caught up in a ménage a trois with the teenage Francis Russell, 5th Duke of Bedford.

Her place of birth is not known, and suggestions for her date of birth vary between 1735 and 1740. One report states that she was born in around 1735, the daughter of a Bond Street tailor. If that were so, it does not quite fit in with the fact that as an adult she appeared to be well-educated and cultured, quite at home moving in aristocratic circles while operating as the country's *de facto* first lady. Your average daughter of an eighteenth-century tailor, whether operating in Bond Street or not, was unlikely to have been taught anything other than the basic three Rs and arguably would have been ill-at-ease hosting dinner parties at the equivalent of Number 10 Downing Street.

The suspicion must be that she was reasonably well educated. If any of the prints of the time are to be believed, it was not unknown for young schoolgirls to elope from their boarding school with a young swain – presumably only to discover, once lust had subsided, that they were left destitute and with no choice but to resort to sex work to pay the bills.

Whatever her education, she is supposed to have formed an unfortunate connection with a slave ship captain called Horton (or Haughton) and eloped with him to Jamaica. The story goes that the couple split up after a couple of years – or alternatively that he had died – and she returned to London in her late teens, ostensibly 'the widow of Captain Horton'. There is no record of any marriage, and it is quite possible that she adopted a married title in an attempt to appear less disreputable. She had no money on her return and presumably no prospect of returning to her family, so she turned to sex work to make ends meet. She must have had a considerable aptitude and enthusiasm for the work, with one report stating that she was charging clients a guinea a throw, and could earn one hundred guineas in the week. At that stage she was living in London's Soho area, in Brewer Street, above the premises of a perfume-maker.

She soon found that her rates increased rapidly if she moved 'up market'. By 1760 she was 'serving' various aristocrats, including William Petty, the second Earl of Shelburne. He was twenty-three at the time. Later he went on to become Home Secretary and later still, as prime minster, he was the politician who oversaw the peace negotiations with America at the end of the War of Independence. Another client was Richard Rigby, an English politician and Privy Councillor in his forties, who served as Chief Secretary for Ireland and Pay Master of the Forces. She also caught the attention of the wealthy government contractor Arnold Nesbitt, earning her the reproof from Horace Walpole that she was 'one of the commonest creatures in London, one much liked, but out of date.' The barb about her age – by then she was perhaps in her late twenties – is a reminder that in general being a courtesan was a young woman's game, and Nancy had reached her sell-by date.

By 1763 she had become the mistress of Augustus Henry FitzRoy. In 1756 he had first entered Parliament as a young man of twenty-one. In that same year he had married Anne Liddell and she turned out to be quite a handful, not least because of the amount of time and money she spent at the gaming tables. He inherited the title of Duke of Grafton when his grandfather died in the following year, elevating him to the House of Lords. It was a time of political intrigue, with Grafton supporting the Duke of Newcastle, a fierce opponent of Lord Bute because of Bute's mishandling of peace negotiations with France following the conclusion of the Seven Years' War. When Bute was given the push, Grafton was made up to Privy Counsellor. The fact that he was keeping Nancy as a mistress was no surprise – it was almost *de riguer* that young aristocrats should do so. But eyebrows were raised when he installed Nancy, not in some elegant apartment, but in his own London townhouse. His wife, Anne, was pregnant and living at their country home. There she gave birth in July 1764 to what was to be their third child together. The duchess then embarked on a highly public affair with the Earl of Upper Ossory and ended up having his child. Divorce proceedings followed and were finalised in March 1769. The duke was expected to make an honest woman of Nancy, his mistress, and by all accounts she was taken by surprise when instead he hastily married Elizabeth Wrottesley, going on to father another twelve children, nine of whom reached adulthood.

Looking more closely at Nancy's role in these turbulent times in the Grafton household, it is important to remember that polite society tolerated mistresses but did not expect them to be paraded to the detriment of a lawful spouse. Grafton outraged many by publicly inviting Nancy to the races at Ascot and Newmarket. He was a keen racegoer and his jockeys, sporting racing colours of sky blue and with a black cap, were a familiar sight. Such conduct led Horace Walpole to comment that Grafton 'postponed the world for a whore and a horserace'.

In politics, the duke had become ever more important, becoming First Lord of the Treasury and *de facto* prime minister in 1768. Nowadays we do not really bat an eyelid when our premier enters Downing Street, girlfriend in tow, while still married. He can get a divorce, become a father for the sixth (or seventh?) time, get engaged and introduce his fiancée to the queen, and while there may be some odd tut-tutting, no one seriously suggests that a chequered history of personal relationships is a bar to political success. Back in the 1760s it was a problem – it raised the whole question of female influence and of male judgement. If a courtesan could dress like a duchess, hold herself out as a duchess, fill all the roles in public associated with a duchess, then what was the point of being a duchess? The aristocracy had been the ruling class – was it now to be usurped by a 'harlotocracy'?

Such questions may have started in private, but quickly moved into the public domain with the appearance of highly critical but anonymous letters addressed to the duke but released to the press. One of the first was in 1768 and starts by saying: 'Permit me to congratulate you upon a piece of good fortune which few men, of the best established reputation, have been able to attain to,' before going on to say that, 'yours, my Lord, is a perfect character: through every line of public and of private life you are consistent with yourself. After doing everything, in your public station, that a minister might reasonably be ashamed of, you have determined, with a noble spirit of uniformity, to mark your personal history by such strokes as a gentleman … might be permitted to blush for.'

The attack, skilfully disguised as praise, continues: 'I had already conceived a high opinion of your talents and disposition. Whether the property of the subject, or the general rights of the nation were to be invaded; or whether you were tired of one lady, and chose another for the honourable companion of your pleasures … a noble disregard of forms seemed to operate through all your conduct.'

The letter continued:

But you have exceeded my warmest expectations. Highly as I thought of you, your Grace must pardon me when I confess that there was one effort which I did not think you equal to. I did not think you capable of exhibiting the lovely *Thais* [Nancy Parsons] at the opera house, of sitting a whole night by her side, of calling for her carriage yourself and of leading her to it through a crowd of the first men and women in the kingdom. To a mind like yours, my Lord, such an outrage to your wife, such a triumph over decency, such insult to the company, must have afforded the highest gratification.

The letter, which went on to urge the duke to 'obtain a divorce, marry the lady,' was followed by others in a similar indignant vein published under the name of Junius, in the *Public Advertiser*, a London newspaper, during the three-year period from 21 January 1769. The attack savaged Grafton, with one reading: 'It is not that he kept a mistress at home, but that he constantly attended her abroad. It is not private indulgence, but the public insult, of which I complain. The name of Miss Parsons would hardly have been known if the First Lord of the Treasury had not led her in triumph through the opera house, even in the presence of the queen. When we see a man act in this manner we may admit the shameless depravity of his heart, but what are we to think of his understanding?'

Of course, this was incorrect in suggesting that Miss Parsons was an unknown, but being paraded in public on the arm of the first minister certainly did wonders for public visibility and fame. Other more populist publications jumped on the bandwagon, with the *Town & Country Magazine* devoting one of its Tête-à-Tête sections to the happy pair, describing her as 'Annabella – the Female Pilot'. It appears at the head of this chapter.

The entry appeared in March 1769 and paints a fairly favourable picture of Anne/Annabella. She is 'of a good family, but small fortune,' and 'had always moved in polite life.' It also had this to say: 'Annabella is now the happiest of her sex, attached to the most amiable man of the age, whose rank and influence raise her, in point of power, beyond many queens of the earth. Caressed by the highest, courted and adulated by all, her merit and shining abilities receive that applause that is justly due to them. She presides constantly at his sumptuous table, and does the honours with an ease and elegance, that the first nobility in the kingdom are compelled to admire.'

She was renowned for her 'courteous behaviour,' but the article suggested that there was always a risk that she would be perceived as using undue influence on her lover whenever it came to making political appointments. The article concluded that 'cruelty and revenge in a female mind are the sure index of a vicious heart – Annabella knows them not.'

Ironically, by the time the entry appeared in the *Town & Country Magazine* the affair between the two was already over. Caricaturists portrayed Nancy as the gullible woman betrayed in love by a callous man, which somewhat disregards the fact that Nancy had never been 'faithful' to Grafton, and was busy conducting an affair with John Sackville, 3rd Duke of Dorset. Nancy always believed that 'the grass was greener on the other side'. Whether she ever seriously expected the duke to marry her is unclear. In July 1768 the *St James Chronicle* had written an article about Nancy and Grafton, suggesting that the duke's friends were worried about what he would do post-divorce, 'apprehensive, that from his fondness for his mistress, he will unhappily be induced to marry her.'

Nancy must have been embarrassed when what appeared to be the genuine correspondence sent to her by the duke appeared in the press, notably in the *Gentleman's Magazine* and the *Public Advertiser*. These make clear that the duke claimed that he had told Nancy at the outset of their relationship that having an affair with her was 'unseemly, both in my moral and political character and that nothing but the necessity could justify the measure.' In other words, she went into the relationship knowing that he never conceived it to be permanent. He simply needed a companion – whether in bed, running his household, or sharing his life – while he went through the agonies and uncertainties of a divorce. He may have calculated at the outset, quite correctly, that raising the stakes by having a public mistress would help force his wife to agree a divorce.

The duke informed Nancy that 'our former ties are from this day at an end,' and made it clear that he would make a generous allowance available 'with the proviso that your residence be not in these kingdoms – the rest of Europe lies at your choice.' Nancy's response suggested, somewhat naïvely in the light of her affair with the Duke of Dorset, that she was broken-hearted, signing off as 'the unfortunate Ann Parsons'.

There was an explosion of books and articles in print about the marital and amorous activities of Grafton. In 1769 a book entitled *Memoirs of the amours, intrigues, and adventures of Charles Augustus Fitz-Roy, Duke of Grafton, with Miss Parsons, interspersed with a faithful account of Miss Parsons's amours with other persons of distinction* could be bought by an eager public for 1s 6d. They were not memoirs, despite the title, but a complete fabrication designed to gull the public.

Another publication was one described as *A first letter to the Duke of Grafton*, printed for Isaac Fell in London in 1770. It started with the words: 'I shall not therefore, with the multitude, accuse your Grace of having pursued (and that, not in the heyday of your blood) an adulterous lust with all the unguarded folly of boyish effeminacy.' It spoke of the duke 'panting in the withered arms of your mistress at Newmarket,' and continued, 'Nothing less than the conviction of my own senses shall ever prove to me that the English Prime Minister can, in a public theatre, in the presence of his countrymen, in the presence of the representatives of all the crowned heads in Europe, in the presence of his own most moral and most religious Sovereign, sit with doting fondness by the side of an antiquated Figure-dancer, remarkable only for the sickened features of stale beauty, the artificial vivacity of hackneyed prostitution, and the infatuated adoration of a silly keeper.'

Ouch! The 'antiquated figure dancer' would not have liked that one! Speaking of earlier years when divorce was harder to come by, the scurrilous tract continues: 'Adultery, cuckoldom, and divorces were not at that time reduced to the easy and fashionable system at present so favourable to the caprices of the English nobility. Your sense of decency would then have shuddered at the idea of publicly committing your sons to the tuition of Mr Jefferies, and your daughter to the guidance of Mrs Haughton.'

Eventually, Grafton was forced out of office – in part because of the furious attacks on his character by Junius. He remained in politics for many years, became a devout Christian, wrote tracts about the importance of high moral standards, and turned out to be the last divorced prime minister of this country until Sir Anthony Eden nearly two centuries later. It also looks as though he became devoted to Elizabeth, his second wife, and spent forty years with her in faithful harmony.

As for Nancy, her affair with John Frederick Sackville, who became 3rd Duke of Dorset when his uncle died in 1769, was never likely to result in a trip up to the altar. Some felt that it was slightly surprising that it lasted as long as seven or more years. The duke's wandering eye made him a great womaniser and in due course he moved on to younger more vivacious company, in particular Elizabeth Armistead (mentioned in chapter 12). It is debateable whether his greatest passion in life was women or cricket, and both consumed much of his energy and most of his fortune.

While it lasted, the relationship guaranteed that Nancy remained in the public eye, a fame that was magnified time and again as various portraits were painted, all of them copied and circulated as mezzotints.

First came a portrait by Sir Joshua Reynolds, showing Nancy dressed in what was termed 'the Turkish style'. Maybe her status as an 'outsider' influenced the artist's decision to show her, not in formal court dress, but in a slightly exotic loose-fitting gown with a touch of Middle-Eastern allure. The fashion for all-things Turkish had developed in this country after the return to Britain of Lady Mary Wortley Montagu in 1719. She had been married to the British ambassador to Turkey and became a hugely influential figure. Her letters from the Ottoman Empire led to fashions being influenced by styles that were not just Turkish but also Persian, or from the Levant. All were combined as a pastiche of what people were actually wearing in the Middle East, and all were described as being 'Turkish'. The studio records kept by Reynolds show that a 'Mrs Houghton' sat for him three times in 1767 and 'Mrs Horton' sat for him seven times in 1769. It is not known whether the earlier sittings were for a separate portrait – or indeed whether the record refers to Nancy – but there is every likelihood that the 1769 sittings culminated in the portrait shown in the lower image on plate 22.

At much the same time Nancy had her portrait painted by the Scottish artist George Willison. Once more, she appears in Turkish dress, with a long Kashmir shawl wrapped around the silk turban, and fastened with pearl pins. The shawl is crossed behind her neck and draped over the shoulders before being tied at the waist. It was a fashion more akin to that worn by wealthy Indian males, and the painting appears as plate 22 (upper image).

Intriguingly, Nancy also had her portrait painted by Thomas Gainsborough, but sadly it only remains in the form of prints. The original was referred to in Horace Bleakley's book *Ladies Fair and Frail* as being in the possession of the art collector Charles Wertheimer. The book was published in 1909 but press reports refer to a break-in at the Wertheimer home two years earlier, as reported in the *Sphere* magazine of 16 February 1907. The Gainsborough painting was stolen, along with a Reynolds portrait and some elaborate snuff boxes. The haul was described as being worth £70,000, of which £15,000 was attributable to the Gainsborough portrait. None of the items were ever recovered.

There was one further portrait worth mentioning – for the simple reason that it was a complete fabrication, a sort of phoney image taking advantage of the fact that the general public had no real way of knowing what the lady looked like, and could therefore be conned into anything. The deception involved a print made of Anne Elliott, a minor actress and courtesan who died in 1769. It was described as being 'after the portrait artist Tilly Kettle and engraved by James Watson'. It didn't sell, presumably because no one was really interested in Anne Elliott once she had died, so the copper plate used in the engraving was sold, the face tweaked slightly, and then retitled as 'Miss Nancy Parsons'. It demonstrates the way engravings were churned out in bulk – as long as it sold, who cared if it was accurate? To add to the parody, this time it was described as being 'by Housman after Renold' – a spoof on the engraver Richard Houston after Sir Joshua Reynolds. For its time, it was surely much the same as today's influencer on Instagram who uses a photo-shopped image; i.e., it's a blatant attempt to sell, based on a lie.

For Nancy, now well into her thirties and with her looks fading, it must have seemed high time that she got married and obtained some sort of financial security. She managed to catch the attention of the twenty-three-year-old Charles, 2nd Viscount Maynard. They married on 24 September 1776 and visited Italy, leaving behind the comment by the wag Horace Walpole that she was 'the Duke of Grafton's Mrs Horton, the Duke of Dorset's Mrs Horton, everybody's Mrs Horton'.

It has been said that Viscount Maynard was not the sharpest knife in the drawer, and that any lack of intelligence on his part was more than compensated by Nancy's sharp mind. She was perhaps ten to fifteen years his senior. If she thought that being made up to viscountess would be the end of her problems she must have been disappointed, on reaching Naples, to find that polite society refused to accept her on account of her scurrilous past.

Nancy appears to have had a 'seven year itch' and by 1784 had persuaded her husband to accept a nineteen-year-old, Francis Russell, 5th Duke of Bedford, into their household. The trio moved to Nice, and the *ménage à trois* continued until 1787 whereupon Francis returned to London. In due course he went on to become a Whig politician, and to be responsible for much of the development of central Bloomsbury.

That left Nancy and her husband commuting between homes in Nice and Naples, living on their own. They were eventually received by a member of the British royal family, when Prince Augustus (younger son of George III) visited Nice in 1791. The couple led separate lives, with Nancy making frequent solo trips to Italy, where she became a close confidante of the Neapolitan queen. The viscount apparently enjoyed the company of Madame Derville, a dancer who later moved to London and gained a certain notoriety as a courtesan. By 1808 she was one of a number of prostitutes counting the Duke of Wellington as an indebted customer.

One of the last times Nancy was mentioned in the English press was when *The Times* of 15 August 1797 reported that she had no intention of returning to England. She kept out of the public eye, growing old in secluded privacy, and by the early years of the new century had moved to Paris. She apparently lived 'as a religious penitent' and died there in the winter of 1814-15. She was, it was said, much loved by the local community for her good works.

Not many would have placed a bet on Nancy getting to the age of nearly eighty when she started her career as a teenage prostitute. Fairly early on in her career she stopped touting sex for money among the general public, and concentrated on a succession of affairs with wealthy and politically influential people. As a professional courtesan she achieved what few other courtesans aspired to – not just marriage, but a marriage which brought with it a title and a comfortable lifestyle.

Chapter 8

Kitty Fisher

Kitty Fisher takes a fall.

On 12 March 1759 a nineteen-year-old girl, considered attractive by everyone, went for a ride on her horse across Hyde Park. Two years earlier she had started to take riding lessons from Richard Berenger, who went on to hold the post of Gentleman of the Horse to His Majesty King George III, and later wrote books on equestrian skills. In other words, she had been taught properly how to handle a horse. Dressed in a well-fitting black riding outfit, and riding a piebald pony, she looked the picture of elegance as she started to canter along Green Park. As she approached a group of gallant soldiers, resplendent in their army uniforms, the horse was startled and began to bolt. Some of the soldiers realised the danger to the rider and managed to run out in front of the horse, which stopped suddenly, hurling the unfortunate rider headlong onto the turf.

What happened next was the stuff of legends – or at least, of countless songs, ditties, newspaper reports and crude drawings. The rider landed on her backside, legs in the air, clearly displaying the fact that she, like many ladies of the time, had 'gone commando' and was not featuring underwear. A crowd quickly assembled, no doubt intrigued by the sight, but no sooner had they crowded around the poor girl than a sedan chair ('with painted panels and gilded window frames') appeared as if from nowhere and whisked her away. After a stunned silence, someone in the throng announced, 'It's Kitty Fisher; the famous Kitty Fisher!'

Did the incident happen? Probably. Was it a well-engineered publicity stunt? Almost certainly. Did it enhance the fame and reputation of the girl in question, and did she milk that fame and notoriety for all it was worth? Oh yes, without a doubt. Kitty Fisher was already a well-known courtesan, and the press were delighted to be able to report that here was someone who was a 'fallen woman' twice over. The *Universal Magazine* was quick out of the blocks in March 1759 when it published 'On K— F—'s Falling from her Horse.' It rebuked her for her behaviour by pointing out that this was not her first 'fall' and that she should mend her ways.

The incident was gushingly reported in a pamphlet entitled *Horse and Away to St. James's Park* that:

Upon our coming up, we found it to be the celebrated Miss K...y F....r; her military attendant had raised her from the Ground. [...] The nymph was in tears, but rather owing from Apprehensions of her Danger than the sense of Pain; for whether it was owing to any thing her Heroe had said, or from finding the danger over, she, with a prity childishness, stopped the torrent tears, and burst into a fit of Laughing. [...] A superb Chair soon arrived, [...] she flung herself into it, and away she swung through a Crowd of Gentlemen and Ladies, who by this time were coming up. A sort of murmur was heard: but one Gentleman louder than the rest, spoke up, and though what he said was a little interlarded with a flower of rhetorick too common [...] yet the sentiment was honest, and the reprimand such as deserved. "D..n my B...d", says he [...] "if this is not too much. Who the D....l would be modest, when they may live in this state by turning. Why 'tis enough to debauch half the women in London."

It was a common theme – that Kitty was so brazen, so popular, so ostentatious with the trappings of success that any girl would be tempted to become a sex worker just in order to follow in her train.

Even twelve months earlier than the riding 'accident', Kitty had been a sufficient sensation for a certain Thomas Bowlby to write to his friend Philip Gell in Derbyshire: 'You must come to town to see Kitty Fisher, the most pretty, extravagant, wicked little whore that ever flourished; you may have seen her, but she was nothing till this winter.'

Kitty was already used to being the subject of poetic inspiration. For example, Tom Wilkes had composed a piece under the title of 'To Miss Kitty Fisher', and sent it to *The Public Advertiser* for publication back in October 1758. A couple of days after the riding accident she inspired another poem called *On Kitty Fell, a Famous Courtezan's Falling from her Horse* published on 14 March 1759. Oddly, a song called *Kitty Fell* had been published the previous year and it is quite possible that this was about a girl with the surname 'Fell'; no matter, it became a popular ditty applied to the brazen Miss Fisher. The song was reworked as *And luckless Kitty Fell – A song occasioned by the late event* and sung to the same tune as the original *Kitty Fell*. There was even a Kitty Fisher country dance and a book called *Humourous Poetical Dialogue* recognised the value of the publicity brought about by the fall with the words:

> All the world knows
> 'Twas from that very Fall you rose:
> To that, my Dear, you owe your Name,
> 'Twas that wide spread your little Fame.

Before long ships and horses were being named after her: in July 1759 The *Universal Chronicle or Weekly Gazette* reported that: 'Thursday the sweepstakes match of £100 was won by John Ingleby Esqr's grey mare, Kitty Fisher.' Her name was given to a particular bead used as a lace bobbin – still known to this day as 'Kitty Fisher's Eye'. She favoured wearing a particular type of hat, as shown by an article appearing in *The Lounger* twenty years after her death which describes the different types of bonnet in vogue – 'the Quaker, the Shepherdess and the Kitty Fisher'. According to the Whitehall Evening Post or London Intelligencer her famous eyes also led to a striped waistcoat which featured black polka dots being known as Kitty Fisher's Eye.

Meanwhile a caricature of Kitty, legs in the air and displaying her ample charms, appeared under the title of: 'The merry accident, or a print in the morning. A chair, a chair, for the lady'. It appears at the start of this chapter and shows Kitty Fisher sprawled on the ground after falling off her horse; several men quickly gather at the scene of her misfortune as another on horseback leaps a fence exclaiming, 'Oh my Kitty, oh my Kitty, oh my Kitty.'

The ensuing weeks saw a non-stop barrage of comments about her 'accident' and, as the spotlight fell on her, hacks scrabbled to write up her memoirs in order to appeal to the insatiable appetites of the general public. A slim volume under the title of *The Juvenile Adventures of Miss Kitty Fisher* appeared in print, together with an advertisement in *The Public Advertiser* to say that further memoirs were imminent. Outraged, Kitty penned a response, also printed in *The Public Advertiser*, on 27 March 1759: 'Miss Fisher is forced to sue to that Jurisdiction to protect her from the Baseness of little Scribblers and scurvy Malevolence; she has been abused in public places, exposed in Printshops, and to wind up the whole, some Wretches, mean, ignorant, and venal, would impose upon the Public, by daring to pretend to publish her Memoirs.'

Delighted to have goaded her into responding, the press redoubled their efforts to catalogue every move she made, everything she ever said. She was no longer just a star, she was a celebrity in the modern sense of the world. She didn't have to do anything: she was famous simply for being famous.

Kitty appears to have known instinctively what to do with her fame: milk it for all it was worth. And how better to do this than to make sure that her image was splashed across every printshop window in town? How to do that? Go to see that nice young artist Mr Joshua Reynolds, at his old studio in London's Great Newport Street. So it was that within three weeks of falling off her horse Kitty turned up and had her portrait painted. Reynolds shows Kitty with her hands crossed on a ledge and holding a letter which bears a date of 2 June 1759. A strong hint of the sitter's identity is given by the words 'My Dearest Kit' with which the letter commences. She wears an exquisite silk dress with flounced lace sleeves, with a black lace mantilla draped over her shoulders. Around her neck is a four-string pearl necklace and more pearls adorn her hair and ears (pearls were seen as emblems of purity and femininity). She embodies all that was expected of a fashionable and wealthy young lady.

Her gaze is directly at the viewer, but with her head slightly tilted. Before anyone could blink the painting had been converted into mezzotint prints – by Richard Houston, by Richard Purcell, by Edward Fisher and various other artists. John June produced a smaller version of the image specially designed to fit inside a gentleman's watch case. By the middle of July 1759 *The London Chronicle*, *The Public Advertiser* and *The Daily Advertiser* were all carrying advertisements stating: 'Tuesday next will be published, price 2 shillings, a Curious Metzotinto Print of Miss KITTY FISCHER, done from an Original Picture in her own Possession, lately painted from the Life, by Mr. REYNOLDS.'

The words: 'in her possession' are interesting – suggesting that Kitty could afford to commission the painting herself and indicated that she had some control over the production of the various print copies. They sold by the thousand and became omnipresent pin-ups across the country, whether adorning lime-washed walls of country cottages or the plastered interiors of elegant townhouses. It led to the German visitor Giustiana Wynne commenting: 'There are prints of her everywhere, I don't find her beautiful, but the English do and that is what matters.'

The hands-clasped forward-facing pose became a classic, not just for Reynolds but apparently for Allan Ramsay in his 1761 portrait of Lady Susan Fox-Strangways (niece of Lady Caroline Fox). Reynolds used it when painting Lady Selina Hastings (in 1759), Lady Caroline Adair and Margaret Owen (both in 1760), and for Mrs Montgomery and Mrs Irwin the following year. Additionally, he painted two other unidentified sitters in a similar pose, in 1760 and 1762. What this shows is that even though the public could use the 'My Dearest Kit' letter to identify the original sitter as a lady from the demi-monde – never respectable, a beautiful floozy – it was nevertheless an image that others from a higher strata in London Society were happy to emulate.

Who then was this Kitty Fisher? Remarkably for someone who was so famous, so well-reported, so visible as she blazed her trail across the London scene, there is very little hard evidence about her or her life. It is almost impossible to separate the myth from the truth, especially when stories about her are applied willy-nilly to other people. Even her portraits, of which there were many, became interchangeable with images of other women. Kitty Fisher the image was famous: Kitty Fisher the woman was almost unknown.

She appears to have been born in London's Soho area on 1 June 1741 and was baptised nine days later. Her father was German (and the surname was therefore spelled Fischer) and she was given the names Catherine Maria – Kitty for short. In some places her father is described as being a silver-chaser (in other words, someone who decorated silverware by adding a design); in others he was a stay-maker, i.e., making corsets. Whatever his trade, the family were poor and are believed to have spent some time living in Paddington, which at that stage was an insignificant agricultural village, light years away from the City of London even though it was only three miles distant.

When a comic satire appeared in 1759 entitled *Kitty's Stream; or, the Noblemen turned Fisher-men*, under the pseudonym of Rigdum Funnidos, she was described with the words:

> All we know of her
> is this. She was a Milliner.
> Her parentage, so low and mean
> is hardly to be trac'd, I ween.
> Say, has she wit – or has she sense?
> No – nothing but impertinence.

Low-born she may have been, but there is reason to suppose that she received a better education than was generally afforded to young girls at that time. An article in *The Gentleman's Magazine* suggested that she was fluent in French, although, as mentioned later, Casanova suggested that she could speak only English. A milliner she may have been, but that was often an entry ticket to a life of harlotry. The job was not without its moral dangers. An article in *The London Tradesman* stated: 'the vast resort of young Beaus and rakes to millinery shops exposes young Creatures to many Temptations, and insensibly debauches their Morals before they are capable of Vice.'

It went on to warn that:

> Nine out of ten young Creatures that are obligated to serve in these
> shops are ruined and undone: Take a Survey of all common Women
> of the Town, who take their Walks between *Charing-Cross* and *Fleet-Ditch* and, I am persuaded, more than half of them have been bred

milliners, have been debauched in their Houses, and are obliged to throw themselves upon the Town for want of Bread, after they have left them. Whether it is owing to the Milliners, or to the Nature of the business, or to whatever cause is owing, the Facts are clear, and the Misfortunes attending the Apprenticeship so manifest ... it ought to be the last shift a young Creature is driven to.

All the descriptions of Kitty are that she was vivacious, flirtatious and with a sparkling wit. It was therefore no surprise that young gallants laid siege to her and years later there was speculation as to who first succeeded in seducing her. When Edward Thompson wrote his satirical poem *The Meretriciad* in 1763 he pondered on the man's identity:

> Kitty, my Muse will not pretend to say
> Who first deflower'd or brought thee into play;
> So many make pretensions to the fact;
> Since you forgot, they cannot be exact.
> Some say an Ensign, some an am'rous Knight
> A Suburb 'prentice – some a Sergeant Kite
> Many have paid for't, who could well afford,
> A gay Sea Captain and an old Sea Lord;
> Who of all these can we the hero dub?
> It may be one, or all of Arthur's Club

Arthur's Club was a spin-off from White's Chocolate House, occupying premises at 69 St James's Street (now the site of the Carlton Club). The premises of White's Chocolate House had burned down in 1733 and while White's simply moved down the road, its former proprietor, John Arthur, rebuilt the old premises and quickly attracted many of the younger members of White's. What *The Meretriciad* was suggesting was that young Kitty Fisher was passed around the eager membership: she may even have had her naked portrait adorning the club premises. Other commentators suggest that club members agreed to pay a percentage of their gambling winnings as a subscription to pay for Kitty's fees, with one story suggesting that as a result of this 'support' she was able to burn through some 12,000 guineas in less than a year. That is an astronomically high figure. No matter whether it was true, it showed that in the minds of the public here was a lady who really knew how to spend big.

As for the ensign and the knight, there is some conjecture as to whether Kitty's services were enjoyed first by the ensign – Anthony George Martin – or the minor political figure Sir Thomas Medlycott. Some believe that the 'gay Sea Captain' was probably 'a florid young sailor' by the name of Augustus Keppel, who then is rumoured to have given way to Admiral Lord Anson. And when the Tête-à-tête entry in the *Town & Country Magazine* featured Kitty, it was to suggest that she was having affairs with two leading army officers, Field Marshal John, Earl Ligonier and William Stanhope, Second Earl of Harrington. Heady days – sleeping with the top brass of both the army and the navy!

But to start with more down-to-earth matters. Ensign Martin was to go on to become Lieutenant-General Martin and when he died, half a century after his initial liaison, *The Gentleman's Magazine* carried this obituary: 'Lieut.-Gen. Anthony George Martin, who died in May, 1800, at his house in Leicester Square, was, when a young man, considered by the ladies so handsome as to be called by name of "the Military Cupid". He had the reputation of introducing Kitty Fisher into public life. His connection with her was broken off in consequence of his restricted means, he being then only an ensign, but she retained during life her partiality for him, and for his sake was always ready to quit the most wealthy and elevated of her admirers.'

Clearly, as a young man his pockets were not deep enough to support the ambitious Kitty for long. But if Thomas Medlycott swiftly replaced Martin, he too was to prove lacking in means. He did, however, introduce Kitty to all the 'in' places in London: the best box at the theatre, supper in Ranelagh Gardens, masquerades and ridottos at the Opera House, and so on. Whether it was promenading at Islington Spa, or taking tea in Marylebone Gardens, she quickly developed a taste for being seen in all the right places, with all the right people.

What made her attractive to others? Writing in his book *Ladies Fair and Frail* a century and a half later, Horace Bleackley stated that:

all the men admired, and many of the women envied her. From a physical point of view there was reason for the universal admiration, since she was a beautiful girl, though slight, her figure was moulded in graceful curves, and her limbs possessed the roundness and elasticity of perfect health. Her ripe, provoking lips and saucy tilted nose gave her face an expression of roguery, but when she chose the look would soften, and a glance of childish innocence stole into her grey-blue eyes. Dainty to the fingertips, she was always attired with consummate taste, and no woman was more clever in choosing a gown to suit her style of beauty.

Bleackley also commented on Kitty's dress. She would be: 'attired in the first fashion, an easy negligee clinging around her trim figure, and a butterfly cap upon her close curls or else showing her ankles in an audacious short sack and full-dress hoop and wearing a straw hat with upturned brim and waving ribbons. Display was now her ruling passion, adulation the breath of life.'

Other sources such as *The Gentleman's Magazine* of September 1771 suggest that the first person to bring Kitty to the attention of the public was Augustus Keppel. He was the son of the 2nd Earl Albermarle by his wife, Anne Lennox, daughter of the Duke of Richmond – in other words he was well-heeled, well-connected and more than happy to lavish attention on the whore-of-the-moment. Sixteen years her senior, he was at that stage a captain in the navy, going on to become admiral. How did they meet? Quite possibly through an introduction from the artist Joshua Reynolds, who was a friend of both of them. Keppel supported her 'in a state of sumptuous affluence,' but she did not hang about, transferring her favours to a succession of wealthy admirers.

She became famous within a remarkably short period of time and within two months of the legendary fall in Hyde Park the inveterate gossip Horace Walpole wrote to his friend George Montagu about an encounter between Kitty and the nine-year-old Prince Frederick, who was out walking in the company of his elder brother, the Prince of Wales (later to be George III). When Kitty passed by, Prince Frederick told his elder brother the girl's name. 'Who is she?' asked George. 'A Miss,' replied the youngster. 'A Miss,' said the Prince of Wales, 'why, are not all girls, Misses?' 'Oh, but a particular sort of Miss – a Miss that sells oranges.' 'Is there any harm in selling oranges?' 'Oh, but they are not such oranges as you buy – I believe that they are a sort that my brother Edward buys.' (Brother Edward, then a young man of twenty, was the

Duke of York and Albany, and clearly his kid brother had been told all about Nell Gwyn.)

Aside from the Duke of York, her name was linked with Lord Montfort and a couple of earls – of Sandwich and Harrington. She was also alleged to have had an affair with Henry Herbert, 10th Earl of Pembroke and heir to the family estate at Wilton House in Wiltshire – although it is fair to say that he is more often associated with an affair with a different Kitty, his mistress Kitty Hunter. Stories emerged that he paid Kitty Fisher an annuity of £1,000 – a tale that she herself may have happily gone along with as an illustration of her worth. Another protector is likely to have been the wealthy businessman Joseph Salvador, named in the *Oxford Dictionary of National Biography* as her sometime lover. He was a Sephardic Jew, of Portuguese origin, who made a fortune investing in the East India Company, but by the time he met Kitty he had lost a huge amount of money as a result of the earthquake that devastated Lisbon in 1755.

Kitty's popularity soared, with the *Town & Country Magazine* commenting that 'it was impossible to be dull in her company, as she would ridicule her own foibles rather than want a subject for raillery.' Before long 'Fisher-mania' swept across London. Her style in clothing was copied by others, while endless column inches in the press were devoted to her looks, and to describing her latest antics. 'Whether she rolls in her stately carriages, swings in her superb sedan, or ambles on her pye-bald nag, the trappings of luxury which decorate the fair, proclaim the triumphs of her charms, the munificence of her admirers, and the opulence of this prosperous nation,' wrote the *London Chronicle* on 31 July 1759 about 'charming Kitty'. People were proud to think that the country's prosperity meant that even a low-born milliner could strut her stuff with all her finery: 1759 was the year of great victories over the French in North America, in Europe and in India. Conspicuous wealth was the order of the day, in what was called William Pitt's *annus mirabilis* – the decisive year in the Seven Year's War.

Some gasped at her rate of charges – £100 was apparently her going rate. When the ribald *Kitty's Stream* came out in 1759 it included the verse:

> My noble Lord, you know my Price;
> A Hundred, Nothing less, my Lord

> A trifling sum, upon my word!
> A Hundred, you shall ha't my dear
> Here, poor Kitty, take it here.

The same poem went on to suggest that the men of this country would do better to devote their time and wealth in promoting British imperial ambitions and in defeating French interests, but it is hard to imagine that Kitty was too worried about being regarded as unpatriotic. The poem was reissued as 'The Hundred Pound Miss' and this quickly identified her level of charging in the minds of the public.

Some wondered what all the fuss was about, with a popular ballad containing the words:

> What means this strange infatuation,
> That rages at the head o'th' nation?
> Is she alone the finest whore
> Among, at least, an hundred score?
> Are there not fairer on the town
> That walk the streets and take a crown?

Others foretold that the adulation was bad for society, because it meant that people would be led astray as a result of the way they envied her lifestyle. In 1762 a book of verse came out entitled *A sketch of the Present Times and the Time to Come, in an Address to Kitty Fisher*:

> The blushing Maid, at your Appearance, cries,
> Nay, dear Papa, indeed she's very pretty.
> Then whispers to herself, with up-cast eyes
> O ye good Gods, if I was but like KITTY

*   *   *

> Each City Dame, full dress'd, in massy pride
> With feign'd compassion scoffs, indeed 'tis Pity,
> But by warm Fancy check'd, she sighs aside
> O that, for once, I could but change with KITTY

It suggested that all would not end well:

> Love's Fruit should be plucked in its Prime;
> Not left on the Tree until wither'd by Age
> 'Tis a worm-eaten Windfall to Time.

It ends with the assertion that 'thus, Old Maids decay,' and comments that even the best 'Wines kept on the Lees too long' will eventually turn sour and become vinegar.

Not everyone approved of Kitty's style of dress. In October 1759 Lady Caroline Fox wrote to the Countess of Kildare about Lady Northampton: 'She is not a beauty, but so much sense, modesty and air of a woman of fashion both in manner and person make her vastly pleasing. None of the Kitty Fisher style either in dress or manner, which all the young women affect now.' This contrasts with the sycophantic tone of a pamphlet dating from the following year: 'You, Madam, are become the Favourite of the Public and the Darling of the Age.'

She seemed to spend rather a lot of time visiting Reynolds in 1759 – his diary records twenty-one visits, suggesting a developing friendship at the very least. Quite possibly it suggests that the artist turned to her as his muse and lover, and rumours to that effect were current at the time. By the end of 1759 Reynolds had already completed his second portrait of the lovely Kitty, this time in the style of Cleopatra dropping a pearl into her wine glass. Once more, the painting was immediately transferred into printed format. The original is believed to have been commissioned by Sir Charles Bingham, baronet, although it is possible that he was simply the ultimate buyer of the picture. Reynolds may have painted the picture 'off his own bat' in order to showcase his ability to portray beautiful women, or it may have been commissioned by Kitty Fisher herself because she was quite capable of blatant self-promotion. Either way, Kitty as Cleopatra was not exhibited publicly until long after both Reynolds and his muse had died, and the image became famous entirely because of the engraved copies prepared by the likes of Samuel Cousins and Samuel William Reynolds, by James Watson, by Richard Houston, and by Edward Fisher.

The subject of the picture reflects the story that Cleopatra and her lover, Mark Anthony, vied with each other as to who could host the most magnificent banquet. Cleopatra won the wager by dropping her pearl into a goblet containing vinegar and knocking it back in one gulp. It was a story that would have been appreciated by an eighteenth-century audience – the idea of a wager being won by a beautiful and clever woman, triumphing over male strength and political power. In a way the image is a straight 'lift' from one of the paintings Reynolds would have seen when he visited Italy a few years earlier, with the Trevisani painting *of The Banquet of Anthony and Cleopatra*. What Reynolds wanted to convey was that here was a woman who would stop at nothing, and was headstrong, vain and calculating. The pearl signified purity and wholesomeness, and the picture tells us that Kitty was prepared to sacrifice it in a single defining act – the dropping of the pearl into the goblet. It was a metaphor showing female greed and its destructive power.

Reynolds was to go on and paint Kitty over and over again – in 1761, 1762, 1764 and in 1766. And he was not alone in featuring Miss Kitty. A far more down-to-earth image by Paul Sandy in one of his 'Twelve Street Scenes of London' shows a man hawking a ballad about Kitty Fisher, with the visual pun of holding a fishing rod to try and draw in potential buyers. It indicates that by 1760 Kitty was famous 'on the streets' as well as in the Gentleman's Clubs and the high-class seraglios that were crammed into St James's Place. A further famous picture of her was painted by Nathaniel Hone, arch-rival of the prickly Joshua Reynolds, in his 1765 painting showing Kitty with dark eyes looking straight at the audience. Her dark brown hair is dressed high and her loose curls are shown falling shoulder-length. In her left hand she clutches a silken gauze *fichu*, deeply embroidered in gold. Her dress, of a soft oyster-grey colour, is low-cut, but any hint of décolletage is obscured by the *fichu* and by Kitty's hand. Her wrist displays a four-strand pearl bracelet and around her neck there is a simple gold and coral necklace. It is a beautiful image, but what makes it stand out is the small fish bowl in the foreground, at which a cat dangles a paw, trying to ensnare the circling goldfish. It is a rebus, making a pun on the name of the sitter– the cat signifies Kitty and is also the Fisher. Look closely at the rim of the glass bowl and you can see, reflected, six panes of a glass window at which onlookers are staring in. This is Hone's way of showing that Kitty herself lived life inside a goldfish bowl and that she had no privacy, nowhere to hide. Everything was on public display the whole time.

When Hone's portrait came out it was described in the *Public Advertiser* as 'a portrait of a Lady whose charms are well known to the town'. It added to her reputation as a fashion icon – she epitomised elegance and good taste. Giustiana Wynne breathlessly commented: 'She lives in the greatest possible splendour, spends twelve thousand pounds a year and she is the first of her social class to employ liveried servants – she even has liveried chaise porters.'

Everyone must have been aware that the lady parading around in her magnificent coach, drawn by four matching greys, was the fabulous Kitty, because London Society was not used to seeing that sort of ostentatious display, especially from a whore. Little wonder that a report in the *London Chronicle*, 31 July 1759, suggested that if an 'honest countryman' came to London, believing that a person's social status and rank could be shown by their display of outward pageantry, 'he would think that Kitty Fisher was the queen of Great Britain.'

The same Giustiana Wynne recounted a story of rivalry between Kitty and Maria, Countess of Coventry. Maria was also an *arriviste*, a beautiful bombshell who came to London from her home in Ireland, captivating the hearts of many wealthy young men. She settled for marrying Lord Coventry, but his lordship was also enjoying the favours of Kitty and he showered her with gifts. When Kitty met Maria in the park the latter admired Kitty's dress and asked for the name of her dress-maker. This was met by the retort that she had better ask her husband, since the dress was a gift from Lord Coventry. When Lady Coventry rebuked her for her impertinence, Kitty replied that 'she would have to accept this insult because Maria became her "social superior" on marrying Lord Coventry, but she was going to marry a Lord herself just to be able to answer back.'

If correct, it was an interesting insight into gender politics. Kitty knew that ultimately her security, and her acceptance into polite society, was dependent on getting married. Maria had shown the way after being paraded around the marriage market by her doting mother. Kitty hoped for a similar union with titled respectability and there were rumours linking her to the possibility of marriage with Henry Herbert, 10th Earl Pembroke, and to John, 2nd Earl Poulett. The first rumour, spread in a gossipy letter from Elizabeth Montagu to a friend in 1758, cannot have been right because the earl had married in March 1756, when Kitty was an unknown girl of fifteen. She had, said Elizabeth Montagu, been rewarded in lieu of marriage with an annual payment of £1,000, plus an additional £1,000 'for present decorations'. A year later Lady Louisa Conolly, writing to the Countess of Kildare, announced: 'Now for news,

Lord Poulett is to be married to the famous Kitty Fisher, who is really a most beautiful creature of her kind.'

But it was not to be. Kitty appears to have visited Lord Poulett at his magnificent home at Hinton St George in Somerset, but the rumours of impending nuptials were quickly dashed and Kitty returned to an ever-increasing audience of paying customers.

Here was a girl who loved her bling – she adored showing off. She loved pearls, she loved diamonds and she loved flaunting her wealth. This is reflected in the comments made about her by Casanova, who met Kitty when he visited London in 1763. The whole visit was something of a disaster – he had a recurrence of an attack of venereal disease and suffered the indignity of falling head over heels for a young girl who refused to go to bed with him, strung him along and severely dented his reputation as the Ultimate Lover Man. Perhaps to put himself in a better light, he describes meeting Kitty: 'We went to the Walsh woman's, where the celebrated Kitty Fisher came to wait for the Duke of xx, who was to take her to a ball. She had on over a hundred thousand crowns' worth of diamonds. Goudar told me I could seize the opportunity to have her for ten guineas, but I did not want to do so. She was charming, but she spoke only English. Accustomed to loving with all my senses, I could not indulge in love without including my sense of hearing.'

It is interesting that he noticed the diamonds, but her charge was normally ten times the amount quoted. As mentioned earlier, there are other reports suggesting that she could speak French fluently, and it all looks as though it was a case of 'sour grapes' on the part of Casanova. Was she really likely to have chosen to have 'a quickie' while waiting in her finery for the unnamed duke to arrive?

Casanova went on to recount a story about Kitty eating a banknote on a slice of bread: 'La Walsh told us that it was at her house that she swallowed a hundred-pound note on a slice of buttered bread which Sir Richard Atkins, brother of the beautiful Mrs. Pitt, gave her.'

The same story was made at different times about different prostitutes. Sometimes the amount is £20, sometimes £100, sometimes even more. As early as October 1748 Horace Walpole had written a letter to George Montagu, regarding Fanny Murray: 'I liked her spirit in one instance I heard t'other night. She was complaining of want of money; Sir Richard

Atkins immediately gave her a twenty pound note; she said, "Damn your twenty pound, what does that signify!" – clapped it between two pieces of bread and butter, and ate it.'

Clearly there cannot have been a succession of prostitutes so wealthy that they could go around munching banknotes handed out by the unfortunate Sir Richard. The stories are probably all apocryphal but show how the public were happy to believe that the leading harlots of the day were so rich, and their behaviour so extraordinary, that they could afford to waste a sum of money which they would have been happy to have lived off for a whole year in the days before they became sex workers.

Casanova also confided that Kitty had 'prattled like a magpie', thereby echoing the comment made by others that Kitty was a lively chatterbox. There was a story that Edward, Duke of York, made an appointment to meet Kitty at her home in New Norfolk Street, whereupon the two of them gossiped away eighteen to the dozen for the course of an afternoon. On his departure the prince left a draft for fifty guineas – such a low figure that Kitty felt insulted and promptly instructed her servants never to let the man back into her house again. Such stories may or may not have been true, but they show an awareness on the part of the public that Kitty was a greedy little so-and-so – beautiful, charming, talkative but above all, money-grabbing.

Throughout the early sixties Kitty continued to attend the studios of various artists to have her picture painted. Reynolds, operating out of his new and highly prestigious home in what is now Leicester Square, started a number of paintings of Kitty, some of which were probably not finished during Kitty's lifetime. One, showing her in a very relaxed, informal setting, remains unfinished (apart from the head) and depicts Kitty eagerly watching the antics of an exotic parrot. In a similar avian theme, Francis Coates painted her playing with two doves. But there is a problem in attributing many of the 'Kitty' portraits to Kitty Fisher. Artists' notes may or may not be referring to the same sitter. 'Kitty' became a name applied to almost any young lady with a retroussé nose and a pretty face. Not only was 'Kitty' used as a familiar form of the popular name 'Catherine', but because it was also used as a pet name for a cat, and a cat was always associated with uncontrollable female desire, the name 'Kitty' was often bestowed on anyone with a dubious sexual reputation. Then, as now, male hypocrisy was rampant.

A curious thing happened during the course of 1764. Kitty appears to have grown tired of one-night stands and paid encounters and moved in with a man called Mr Chetwynd, posing as his housekeeper, Mrs Brown. They lived together, apparently in harmony, until Mr Chetwynd's health deteriorated to the extent that his doctors advised that he travel to the south of France, where it was believed that the climate might alleviate the symptoms of his illness. In the event, he died in Montpellier and Kitty was left without a protector. Not for long, because she amazed everyone by taking up with a man called John Norris, an impecunious Member of Parliament representing the constituency of Rye. True, he came from 'a good family', but John himself never amounted to much and was something of a wastrel, devoted to gambling. Kitty appears to have regarded him as a challenge – someone she could 'improve'. The family of Mr Norris were not keen on the relationship and the couple therefore travelled to Haddington in Scotland and got married there, at Trinity Church, on 25 October. Returning to England, and realising that the family appeared to have come to terms with their union, they then went through a second form of wedding ceremony on 4 December at London's St George's at Hanover Square.

The next four months appear to have been spent in quiet harmony, with the couple spending most of their time riding together over the Kent countryside, on the Hemsted Park estate at Benenden, lent to them by the Norris family. It was said that she was regarded as Lady Bountiful by the villagers – perhaps a tad surprising given that her generosity can only have been displayed for a very short period – and it was rumoured that she managed to curb her new husband's worst excesses at the card tables. But marital bliss was short-lived – Kitty became seriously ill, possibly suffering from pneumonia or more probably tuberculosis (then known as consumption). There were rumours circulating at the time that she was also suffering from lead poisoning, ingested through her skin by the overuse of cosmetics. There is no evidence of this, because although white lead was common in face powders, both to whiten the skin and then to apply rouge to specific areas, Kitty was not a particularly heavy user of cosmetics, and her portraits never really show her as a 'painted lady'. It was, however, believed to have been the cause of early death in a number of fashionable ladies of the time, including, famously, the Countess of Coventry, with whom Kitty had crossed swords on the topic of dressmakers just a few years earlier.

In the early spring of 1767 the decision was made to travel to Bristol to effect a cure at Hotwells, near where Brunel subsequently designed his suspension bridge. Here, hot springs had been discovered in the Middle Ages, and had been developed as a rival to the more fashionable but overcrowded pleasures of nearby Bath. In the middle of the eighteenth century they enjoyed a certain popularity – not least because John Wesley, the founder of Methodism, was believed to have been cured of a consumptive attack after imbibing the waters. Visiting the hot wells necessitated a three-day journey, which cannot have helped the sickly Kitty. When her carriage stopped at the Three Tuns in Bath, a one-day ride from Bristol, it was realised that she was fading fast. She died there on 10 March 1767. The distraught Mr Norris took her body back to the ancestral home at Benenden, and fulfilling his late wife's instructions, she was buried two weeks later, dressed in her finest ballgown.

If she was indeed born in 1741 that made her just short of twenty-six when she died, but there are other reports that she was born in 1738-9. Either way she was well under thirty when she died. Her death heralded an outpouring of poetic scribblings, including a song in three parts written by Henry Haddington. It appeared with two titles, one, 'Alas, what boast (Upon seeing the celebrated Kitty Fisher in her coffin)' and the other with the alternative title of 'An Elegy on Kitty Fisher Lying in state in Bath.' It contained the words:

Alas, what boast hath blooming youth, since thus Florella lies,
Paleness o'er her damasked cheek and closed her beauteous eyes.
If fade these glories of her face, Ah, why such frailty trust,
When virtue still its sweetness keeps, and blossoms in the dust.

The *Oxford Dictionary of National Biography* refers to an epigram written shortly after Kitty died:

She wedded to live honest – but, when tried,
the experiment she liked not – and so died.

Meanwhile artists such as Reynolds were paid to finish off paintings that were already in the pipeline, or to make new paintings based upon copies prepared in her lifetime. But otherwise Kitty disappeared quickly from public memories. Her life was a shooting star – she arrived on the scene in a blaze of glory and then faded from view, to be replaced by other celebrity courtesans. Her portraits by Reynolds and Hone mean that she is better known today than many of her contemporaries, but nowadays she is perhaps best remembered for a nursery rhyme:

> Lucy Locket lost her pocket,
> Kitty Fisher found it;
> But ne'er a penny was there in't
> Except the binding round it.

There are many explanations for the verse, complicated by the fact that 'locket' was contemporary slang for the vagina, and 'pocket' can also be regarded as a reference to the female sex organ. One explanation suggests that Lucy was a barmaid who also worked as a prostitute, and who lost her provider – her pocket – when her lover transferred his attentions to Kitty. She was therefore 'out of pocket'. An alternative explanation is based on the fact that pockets were sometimes kept detached from the outer garment and it was customary for whores to tie the pocket, in which they kept their cash, around the thigh with a ribbon as a binding. In this case, Kitty's rival had no money in her purse, so all that was in it was the ribbon. Either way, there is a certain irony in the fact that nowadays most people only know of Kitty Fisher through a piece of doggerel which no one understands.

Chapter 9

Frances Abington

Extract from a portrait of Frances Abington by Sir Joshua Reynolds.

There has to be a small element of doubt as to whether Frances Abington deserves to be classed as a whore, but she was certainly a mistress. We can definitely disregard the fact that 'Mrs Abbing-on' made an appearance in Harris's List of 1793. It read:

Mrs. Abbing-on, next door to the Butcher's shop, Store Street. This lady was born of a good family, but being naturally of a forward disposition, she found means to deceive her parents, when a young Hibernian, who seeking out the natural bent of her inclinations, soon found an easy access to the fortress he had long been waiting to storm; but her father dying soon afterwards, my young gentleman was disappointed in his hopes of possessing any fortune at his decease, and therefore soon gave her an opportunity to seek for another keeper, which was one Mr. A-, whose name she now assumes. She lived with him as his wife for some time; he dying, she was again left to shift for herself; but, with prudence and industry, she soon acquired money sufficient to furnish a house.

The entry went on to describe her as, 'genteel, dark hair, black eyes, neat ankles, and about the middle size, is about the age of forty, though seldom owns herself above twenty-five, remarkable for her amorous disposition, and earnest desire to please her customers.' If it had been *the* Frances Abington, it would have described her not as 'about forty' but 'nearly sixty', because she was actually born, as Frances Barton, in 1735.

It would not have been the first time that identity theft intruded into *Harris's List*. Some years earlier a 'Sarah Siddons' had been featured in the List, being described as 'about twenty-three, light hair and eyes, a good skin'. She was said to be 'remarkably good-natured and affable to those who favour her with a visit,' and was always willing to negotiate on her price. But it wasn't *the* Sarah Siddons, famous actress who, at the height of Siddons-mania in 1788, was already thirty-three and the 'Queen of Drury Lane'. Her identity was simply stolen by a prostitute trying to cash in on her namesake's fame, and there can be little doubt that the same deception applied to the entry for 'Mrs. Abing-on'.

That does not mean that the real Frances Abington did not resort to sex work early on in her career. Indeed, it is hard to see how else she could have made ends meet, given that it is thought that she was a street urchin after her mother died in 1749, when Frances was fourteen. Her father was probably a cobbler working in Vinegar Yard, near the Drury Lane theatre. He rarely earned enough to support the family, and Frances – known as Fanny – earned the nickname of 'Nosegay Fan' after resorting to selling flowers on street corners. In the words of an obituary in *The New Monthly Magazine and Universal Register* of 1815, 'her father's earnings were too small to enable him to bestow any education on his children, or even provide them bread; and Frances Barton was obliged when a child to run on errands for a livelihood.'

There are stories that she sang ballads for a few pence, and that she recited ditties in public houses. Almost certainly she became a child prostitute – working in St James's Park and Leicester Fields – but one with a difference: she was determined to advance herself. She appears to have taken on a number of different jobs: as a kitchen maid working for a cook who had close links to the theatre, and as an assistant to a French milliner in Cockspur Street. The term 'milliner' extended to far more than making hats and originally described the range of accessories and fashion items sold by travelling salesmen from Milan. By 1747 *The London Tradesman* could describe a milliner as a retailer who would 'furnish everything to the ladies that can contribute to set off their beauty, increase their vanity or render them ridiculous.' They worked alongside others in the fashion industry: the haberdasher supplied the fabrics, the mantua-maker made up the gowns, the stay-maker made the stays and the milliner brought everything together and actually made things fashionable.

If you wanted to be *a la mode*, you went to the milliner. It was the milliner who supplied the sashes and ribbons, the ruffles and lace panels. It was the milliner who dealt in tippits, gloves and muffs, as well as exotic headwear. So if the young Frances Barton spent time working for a leading milliner it was like embarking on a diploma course in fashion design, and it would have given Frances a background knowledge and an eye for detail which was to stand her in good stead throughout her later life. But, as already mentioned in connection with Kitty Fisher, being a milliner was often the occupation of the lowly prostitute. Indeed, the word 'milliner' had become a pseudonym for 'whore', and every prostitute apprehended by the constable would give her occupation as 'milliner'.

Obviously, this is only circumstantial evidence that Frances was lured into prostitution, but it was an allegation made at the time, and which echoed in later biographies. A contemporary report described her as 'low, poor and vulgar' but stated that she was keen learn new skills and to expand her knowledge, and had accordingly learned to converse in both French and Italian. Another biographer refers to her 'painful and ignoble experiences' and added that her early days were 'miserable, squalid and vicious, but that she strove after a better life.' At one stage in her later career (as an actress) she featured in the Tête-à-Tête column of the *Town & Country Magazine*. The 1777 edition described her affair with the politician William Petty, Earl of Shelburne – a man who went on to become prime minister. The text accompanying their portraits describes Frances's struggles as a friendless orphan, and hints that she was lured into prostitution. It also said that when Lord Shelburne propositioned her she set out a series of demanding terms: 'fifty pounds a week – no visits at her own house – to see what friends she pleased, male and female – no interruption to her dramatic business – a chariot and a set of horses.'

Other scurrilous biographies included the *Secret History of the Green Room*, published in 1795. Describing a time in her career when she had achieved huge success, and had acquired several houses as a result of gifts from male admirers, the salacious report says that Frances:

> now resolved to separate her lovers into two different classes; the first, those whose liberality might enable her to live in splendour; and the second those whom her humour pitched upon. For this purpose, she had various houses in town for her various admirers: her assignation with Mr Jefferson, formerly of Drury Lane, were made at a house near Tottenham Court Road; while my Lord Shelburne, now Marquis of Lansdown, allowed her fifty pounds per week, gave her an elegant house, the corner of Clarges Street Piccadilly, and continued this generosity until he married. Mr Dundas succeeded his Lordship as her humble servant.

In other words, Frances ended up both as a kept mistress and as someone who kept her own lovers, a quite astonishing reversal of the norm, and suggesting someone who was very aware of the power of sex and of the value of money – and indeed of the value of sex and the power of money. If the allegation was true, here was a woman who was determined to eat her own cake and still have enough left to eat quite a lot more, whenever the mood took her.

All this was in the future when in 1755 Frances used her connections in the theatre world to be introduced to Theophilus Cibber, manager of the Haymarket Theatre. She may well have been one of his many lovers, since he was a notorious libertine and had featured in one of the most notorious criminal conversation cases of the century. The crim. con. cases, as they were known, were a precursor of divorce proceedings and in this case involved seedy allegations of threesomes, abduction, theft and cruelty. Theophilus was putting together a company of newcomers to present Susannah Centlivre's *The Busy Body* under the banner of *Bayes's New rais'd company of Comedians*. Frances played the part of Miranda when it opened on 21 August, 1775. Other parts followed in quick succession and her first breeches part, always popular with male audiences keen to admire exposed female legs, was in September that year when she played Sylvia in *The Recruiting Officer*. She was spotted by the comedian Edward Shuter and he offered her a stint in repertory at the old Theatre Royal in Orchard Street, Bath. The following year Shuter offered her a season at the theatre in Richmond, Yorkshire, and while there her commanding performances came to the notice of David Garrick. By the end of 1756 she was appearing at Drury Lane at a salary of thirty shillings a week, a not insignificant sum for a novice. However, it was a frustrating time for Frances, as most of the more prominent female roles went to other actresses, notably Hannah Pritchard and Kitty Clive, and she was left with supporting roles, now and again, rather than continuous employment. The other actresses, especially Kitty Clive, were not happy to see a newcomer in their midst and showed considerable jealousy. For her part, Frances was more than capable of bearing a grudge and of bickering constantly, but she was also acutely aware of the need to develop her skills. She started to learn music and on 21 June 1759 the twenty-two-year-old Frances Barton married her music master, James Abington. He was one of the king's Trumpeters, and he also played at Drury Lane. Following the marriage she dropped her maiden name and used 'Abington' in all theatre bills.

The couple soon fell out with the management at Drury Lane and in November headed off to Ireland and joined John Brown's theatre company, performing at Smock Alley, Dublin. The change of venue marked a huge change in status: she was no longer a singleton of dubious reputation on the bottom rung of the ladder; she was a respectable married woman exhibiting great style and elegance, much sought after by fashionable society. People noticed what she wore, and copied it, never more so than with what became known universally as 'the Abington cap'. It was said that not a single milliner's shop in the whole of Dublin failed to have a window display featuring this universally acclaimed fashion accessory, and suddenly she was looked up to as a fashion arbiter. As one Victorian biographer put it, she 'fairly took the town by storm, and her taste in dress was regarded by the ladies of fashion as so good and correct that it became quite the rage to wear articles bearing her name.' It must all have been an amazing transition for a woman from such a squalid background.

There were two rival theatres in the city and Frances alternated between the Smock Alley and Crow Street premises. For five years her career in

Ireland prospered, but her success on the stage, and her popularity off it, did nothing to help the strains that had developed within her marriage. She was far more successful than her new husband. It cannot have helped when, in 1761, Mr Abington was required to return to England in order to take part in the musical celebrations linked to the coronation of George III. His jealousy was exacerbated because Frances was regularly propositioned by other men and the couple drifted apart, leading to a formal separation under which Frances agreed to pay her husband to stay away from her and not to claim on her earnings.

This freedom enabled Frances to start an affair with a Mr Needham. He was the Member of Parliament for Newry, and was 'a gentleman of family, fortune and learning'. She was devoted to him and when business called him to England she decided to accompany him. When he fell ill, she travelled with him to Bath in the hope of finding a cure but he sadly died there, leaving Frances broken-hearted, but with a very substantial legacy. As the anonymous *Life of Mrs Abington* put it, Mr Needham's heirs 'afterwards discharged, in a very honourable manner, the provision he had made for her, and she was also favoured by the family with a notice that is rarely the consequence of an attachment of such a nature.' Whether or not the inheritance was actually sufficient to buy her several houses in London is unclear, but she returned to the London stage at the request of David Garrick, this time on a salary of £5 a week. She still faced opposition from Hannah Pritchard and Kitty Clive, who managed to 'bag' most of the best female leads, leaving Frances with *The Way to Keep Him*, a comedy in five acts by the Irish playwright Arthur Murphy. He was so delighted with her performance in his play that when he rewrote it some years later he dedicated it to her, writing 'You are entitled to it, Madam, for your talents have made the play your own.'

She also appeared in *High Life Below Stairs*, to huge acclaim, giving her an opportunity to sport 'the Abington cap'. This mob-cap quickly became fashionable in London, just as it had in Dublin, and no self-respecting woman would be seen without it. Frances was mostly playing light, comedy roles, but over time she also took the parts of many of the Shakespearian heroines – as Beatrice in *Much Ado about Nothing*, as Portia in *The Merchant of Venice*, as Desdemona in *Othello* and as Ophelia in *Hamlet*.

In 1771 Frances disappeared from the London stage for several months while she visited Paris – always a cornucopia of delights for a lady of fashion. No record remains of her time there, but she returned to a busy autumn season, followed by a benefit performance the following March – always a profitable occasion for a popular actress like Frances. When she appeared as Miss Notable in Cibber's *The Lady's Last Stake* in April 1772, the artist James Northcote wrote to his brother saying,

'I never saw a part done so excellent in all my life, for in her acting she has all the simplicity of nature and not the least tincture of the theatrical.' When Hugh Kelly wrote *The School for Wives* in 1774 he was so delighted with her playing the part of Mrs Walsingham that he remarked, 'With respect to Mrs Abington, enough can never be said ... she is called the first priestess of the comic muse in this country.'

Her wages were increased despite the fact that she was constantly feuding with theatre manager David Garrick. He became increasingly more irritable at what we would now call her 'diva demands': refusing certain parts; not saying when she was prepared to perform; and insisting on epilogues and prologues being added, changed, or omitted. For six months after her benefit she refused to perform, and instead occupied her time sending vitriolic or sarcastic letters to Garrick. She complained that he would send her a new part to read just hours before she was due to perform it on stage. She also frequently announced that she was unwell and complained that Garrick was bad-mothing her to others. His response? 'The writing of peevish letters will do no business.' Poor Garrick: he had a theatre to run and had to contend with a woman who would send a letter saying, 'I am very much indisposed and desire to be excused when I tell you that I cannot act tomorrow night.' She then went on to say that she was perfectly willing to 'decline receiving any more pay at your office.' This is not what Garrick was used to. As he later wrote: 'I have never yet saw Mrs Abington theatrically happy for a week together.' He warned her that 'such a continual working of a fancied interest, such a refinement of importance, and such imaginary good and evil,' would only result in her missing out on public applause. She skipped rehearsals, and he responded by putting his side of the story in leaks to the London papers. She vacillated endlessly about what date she would agree for her next benefit, effectively messing up the schedule for the other actors and actresses.

Correspondence was sent via lawyers and it seemed likely that Frances would actually retire. One moment there were rumours that she was moving to Paris and was fitting up rooms in a hotel there 'in a superior style'. The next minute she was expected to retire to Wales for the rest of her days.

Garrick may have found her an extremely awkward person to deal with but was able to recognise 'good box office' when he saw it, and was persuaded to increase her pay to £12 per week in 1775. Knowing that people came to the theatre solely in order to see what Frances was wearing, she got paid a clothing allowance of £60 per year, later increased to £200.

Her lifestyle became increasingly opulent: she set up her own carriage, at a time when this was not common among actresses. Her appearance was always commented on in the press, as in, 'Mrs Abington having long been considered in the *beau-monde* as a leading example in dress, her gown on Saturday night was of a white lustering made close to her shape, sleeves to the wrist, and a long train.'

In 1776 she inspired a new range of petticoats, based on a Persian design which Haslewood, in *Secrets of the Green Room*, described as being 'no sooner seen than it was imitated in the politest circles.' Another press article opined: 'Mrs Abington is the harbinger of the reigning fashion for the season – a very beautiful style of petticoat of Persian origin is among the last importations of this admired actress.'

Actresses in the theatre in the eighteenth century felt no restriction requiring them to stick rigidly to 'period' in their performances. Playing a medieval queen or a Roman merchant's wife did not mean rummaging through the theatre wardrobe looking for wimples, or togas. Frances was therefore able to parade around stage like a fashion model displaying the very latest in haute couture. She was described as the 'peculiar delight of the fashionable world,' while Georg Christophe Lichtenberg remarked, 'she seldom appears on stage, when the mode in genteel society does not follow her lead.'

Women did not just come to the theatre to see her costumes, they issued invitations to her to attend them at their private houses and to give advice as to what they should wear. It was an extraordinary turnaround for a girl from the gutter, and the German visitor von Archenholz noted that she had, 'invented herself an occupation quite particular. As she possesses the most exquisite taste she spends a good part of the day in running about London to give advice on the dresses and new fashions. She is consulted like a Physician and fee'd in the handsomest manner ... In this way she is said to make annually nearly fifteen hundred pounds. It is quite sufficient in London to say "Mrs Abington has worn this" to stop the mouths of all Fathers and Husbands'.

Later, she popularised a hairstyle which gave women extra height. Known as 'the ziggurat' with long flowing feathers it proved more popular than her other fashion innovation, no doubt copied from Paris, which involved dusting the hair with red powder. The Press were unimpressed, remarking that although she was the pattern of fashion, 'Mrs Abington has fallen into the absurdity of wearing red powder: her influence on the *ton* is too well known – let her at once deviate from this unnatural French custom.'

However, just as the towering ziggurat was catching on, Frances demonstrated that it was no longer *a la mode*, with the *Gazeteer* of 14 October 1778 announcing, 'the ponderous towering head dress which for some time has been a great weight upon female shoulders, is now lessening almost to its natural size. Mrs Abington has been one of the first to begin this happy reformation in dress, as she made her first appearance in the *School for Scandal*, with her hair remarkably low, which exhibited such evident marks of propriety that all the high heads in the house looked more like caricatures upon dress than real fashion.'

Not everyone was enamoured with the way Frances converted every part she played into an opportunity to look like a shop mannequin. *The Morning Post* felt that she could have 'no pretensions to the *imperious* or *pathetic* in *tragedy*, the *impassioned* in comedy, nor any part where *sentiment* is in the least degree requisite to the character.' In particular the paper objected to the way that her love of fashion meant that she turned 'the elegant woman into the *tinselled queen*'.

What is clear is that with Frances there was little distinction between the way she played her life on stage and the way she played it outside the theatre: she could play the coquette beautifully and she displayed great fashion sense whether on or off the stage. Her life became one of artifice, whether performing in the theatre or mingling with her adoring public. One could say that having been used to extreme poverty in her youth, she now felt far more comfortable playing the lady than ever she did playing the whore.

A further boost to her finances occurred when Frances's lover, William Petty, 2nd Earl Shelburne, decided to take a wife. Frances had been his mistress for some years, following the death of his first wife in 1771. As was considered 'proper for a gentleman' when he married Louisa FitzPatrick in 1779, he paid Frances a lump sum, rumoured to be £500, signifying the end of their relationship. At the age of forty-five, Frances found herself financially secure – she could afford to pick and choose.

There is a certain irony in the fact that just a few months after she appeared in the gossip columns of the *Town & Country Magazine* as Thalia, the Muse of Comedy, Fanny was to star as the queen of gossip in *The School for Scandal*. Written by Sheridan with her in mind for the part of Lady Teazle, the play opened in May 1777. In the opening scene Lady Sneerwell, a wealthy widow, and her servant congratulate each other on placing false gossip and actually name the magazine: Sheridan has Lady Sneerwell make the comment that 'I have more than once traced her causing a Tête-à-Tête in the *Town & Country Magazine* – when the parties perhaps had never seen each other's faces before in the course of their lives.' Curiously, the very same magazine commented enthusiastically about the play describing it as being performed 'with uncommon applause'. The reviewer commented on Sheridan's 'genius and wit' in satirising 'hypocrisy and scandal'. As for Frances, she excelled in the role of Lady Teazle, giving, as it did, another opportunity to wear the very latest in fashions and to exploit her comedic talents. Horace Walpole liked the play – and the portrayal of Mrs Teazle – writing to his friend Robert Jephson on 13 July 1777, 'To my great astonishment there were more parts performed admirably in *The School for Scandal* than I almost ever saw in any play. Mrs Abington was equal to the first of her profession.'

After Garrick retired, Sheridan took over running the Drury Lane Theatre. Frances's salary was still £12 per week but her clothing allowance was doubled and she was given a lump sum of £200 in lieu of a benefit. However, after eighteen years at the same theatre she decided to switch her allegiance and move to Covent Garden, making her first appearance there on 29 November 1782. The move was met with ecstatic applause and it was noted that 'her dress was simple, but perfectly characteristic; the train and petticoat were of white and silver stuff; the body and sash of a dark carmelite satin, with short white sleeves.'

By now Frances was no longer in the first flush of youth, but her popularity was still great and her appearance could command a salary of £30 a night. She had obviously put on a considerable amount of weight and when she appeared as the morose servant Scrub in a benefit performance of Farquar's *The Beaux Strategem* it was reckoned to be a disaster. The part was normally played by a man. The *Public Advertiser* of 11 February may have felt that the character of Scrub 'was well-conceived, and executed with a sprightliness and degree of humour that kept the house in a continual roar of laughter,' but *The Morning Post* of the same day described her manners and deportment as being 'inattentive and torpid rather than active and interesting.' Her 'squeaky' voice did her no favours, even when she tried to disguise it as a man, and the audience felt that the part was beneath her talents and status. Some claimed that she took the part as a result of a wager. The press lambasted her: 'Almost universally she was considered to have fairly disgraced herself and we constantly come across notices and criticisms in which she is roundly taken to task.' The fact is that the public liked to see her in female finery, and they particularly liked seeing her playing the part of rich, titled ladies. They did not go to the theatre to see her as a scruffy servant, and certainly not one which involved her appearing: '*en culottes*, so preposterously padded that they exceeded nature. Her gestures to look comical could not get the least hold of the audience.'

From then on Frances started to wind down her stage performances. She visited Ireland in 1786 and agreed to appear on stage for fifteen nights, at a fee of £500. By 1790 it was generally assumed that she had completely retired from acting, but she made a brief appearance on stage on 14 June 1797 at a charity show intended to raise money for the widows and orphans of men killed and injured in the Battle of St Vincent, a decisive British naval victory at the start of the Anglo-Spanish war. The managers of the Covent Garden Theatre were desperately missing someone of Frances's calibre and persuaded her to come out of retirement. For this they were prepared to fork out £40 for each performance. She appeared as Beatrice in *Much Ado about Nothing* on 6 October 1797 but it led to *The Monthly Visitor* describing her as 'too big and heavy to give any effect to the more gay and sprightly scenes'. Her final appearance was on 12 April 1799, as Lady Racket in Arthur Murphy's farce *Three Weeks after Marriage,* a rehash of his *Marriage a la Mode,* which had first been performed in 1776.

A fellow actor who saw her final performance that night was John Bernard. He wrote: 'The perpetual evidence of youth was in character with her person and her powers; the slimness of her figure, the fulness of her voice, the freshness of her spirits, the sparkle of the eye, and the elasticity of her limbs savoured alike of a juvenility that puzzled the mind … of her it was justly said that "she had been on stage thirty years; she was one and twenty when she came, and one and twenty when she went."' It was perhaps a little too sycophantic – after all, she was by then in her early sixties and everyone knew that she was overweight and nothing like as agile as she once was. But it reflected the general view that Frances was an institution, a true celebrity. No one wanted to believe that she was way past her prime.

In 1806 the husband from whom she had lived apart for thirty years finally died. Throughout those years she had been paying him an annual sum to stay away from her, a payment in lieu of all other claims he might have on her wealth. The capital previously employed in paying that annuity reverted to Frances but although she might be assumed to have been comfortably well off, there were stories that she had invested her money unwisely, and had lost heavily at the gaming tables. She moved from her long-time residence in Piccadilly to Belgravia's Eaton Square and when she died in 1815 it was in a small apartment in Pall Mall. She left various bequests in her will, including donations of £50 to each of the Theatrical Funds at Covent Garden and Drury Lane.

There is no doubt that Frances had celebrity status, very similar to today's stars of the silver screen. But she did not get there on her own. Nowadays we have paparazzi to keep our celebrities in the public eye; back then, that role was taken by the portrait painter. The fact that Joshua Reynolds established his own celebrity status by painting celebrities has already been mentioned, and he clearly had a very soft spot for this particular actress, painting her on at least six occasions. His appointment book is full of her recorded visits. Whether he was in love with her is not known, but he may well have looked to her to take over from the role previously taken by the likes of Kitty Fisher and Nelly O'Brien. He certainly enjoyed the company of the ton's top courtesans.

One of his earliest paintings of Frances was in the late 1760s, when she was in her late twenties. It shows her in the character of Thalia – the Comic Muse – in theatrical costume. She leans against a classical pillar in such a way that the line of her thighs clearly shows through the draping of the garment. The dress is cut low at the front and her head, tilted provocatively, shows her eyes looking directly at the viewer. The painting was immediately copied and the resulting print, etched by James Watson, appeared in 1769. A second portrait was submitted to the Royal Academy for exhibition two years later. Again, it was reproduced as a mezzotint almost immediately, this time by Elizabeth Judkins. Most unusually, Frances is not shown in stage costume but in what appears to be a voluminous and very fashionable cloak. Her gloves are stylish and this time she has turned her head away to one side and therefore not as provocative or immodest in her gaze. She is, however, showing the 'distinguished taste for elegance of dress' noted by her contemporaries.

A third portrait, finished in 1771 and therefore when Frances was in her mid-thirties, is altogether different and is perhaps one of the best-known portraits ever painted by Reynolds. Entitled *Mrs. Abington as Miss Prue in 'Love for Love' by William Congreve* it shows Frances in the role of the rural ingenue Miss Prue, looking directly at the viewer over the back of the chair. She is sporting a wide, black bracelet on both wrists – surely a reference to her role as a style-setter, since that sort of wristband had last been fashionable 150 years earlier. Her thumb brushes her lip in a provocative way – no lady would be shown in such a suggestive manner, perhaps alluding to Frances's reputation as a former prostitute and latterly as a mistress. The portrait is shown as plate 26 and the original is now held as part of the Paul Mellon Collection in the Yale Center for British Art. Intriguingly, the painting was never submitted to the Royal Academy for exhibition and indeed never appeared in public during the artist's lifetime. No engraving of it appeared until 1822, suggesting that this was either a private commission, or perhaps was painted by Reynolds for his personal enjoyment. It has become an iconic image and must have had a similar effect to the modern equivalent, the 1963 photograph of the naked Christine Keeler sitting back-to-front on a chair, facing directly into the camera. Frances was not of course naked, but her provocative pose, her combination of youthful innocence and sexual awareness, would have conveyed much the same message to an eighteenth-century audience.

In 1784 Reynolds exhibited a portrait at the Summer Exhibition of the Royal Academy showing Frances in the role of Roxalana in Isaac

Bickerstaffe's play *The Sultan*. She is in theatrical garb, emerging from behind the stage curtain, and is looking to her left. Within a few years John Keyse Sherwin had copied the image as a mezzotint, released in 1791 when Frances's stage career was nearing its end.

He painted Frances as a fashion icon and even retouched the paintings in order to keep them up to date. For instance, the hairstyle sported by Frances in her portrait as the Comic Muse, painted in 1768, was altered five years later to bring it in line with prevailing tastes. Reynolds paired it with his portrait of Sarah Siddons, as the Tragic Muse, and today both can be appreciated at Waddesdon Manor, a National Trust property near Aylesbury.

Richard Cosway painted Frances, and several others showed her as Thalia, the goddess of comedy. She was painted by the artist James Roberts, one of a series of sixty watercolours on vellum published by John Bell over a twelve-year period from 1776 under the title of *Bell's British Theatre*. Samuel de Wilde, a painter of Dutch descent specialising in actors and actresses, painted her as Charlotte in *The Hypocrite*. John Hoppner, a disciple of Reynolds and a brilliant colourist, painted her in oils in a portrait now on display at the Smithsonian American Art Museum. Her portrait was engraved by T. Cook and published in *The Universal Magazine* in 1783. Charles Reuben Ryley painted her in costume, as did Thomas Hickey, who painted her in 1774 as Lady Bob Lardoon in *The Maid of The Oaks*. De Fesch showed her as Mrs Ford in *The Merry Wives of Windsor*, and Isaac Taylor painted her as Widow Belmour in *Way to Keep Him* in a print published in 1792. It followed a painting by Johann Zoffany under the same title, painted some years earlier and now in the Waddesdon Manor Collection. Daniel Dodd painted the actress in character for the epilogue to Alexander Dow's play *The Tragedy of Zingis*. Edward Francis Burney, nephew of the musicologist Charles Burney, painted her in costume, as did James Sayers, who showed her as 'Scrub' in *The Beaux Strategem* in a 1785 etching. Ozias Humphry painted her in 1789 with water colours and pencil.

In short, one gets the impression that Frances must have spent a considerable amount of her time visiting artists' studios, having her portrait sketched, painted, engraved and recorded in pastels. The portraits were shown in exhibitions, but much more importantly, were copied as engravings, printed by their thousands, and sold to an eager public. In every way, these artists were the eighteenth-century equivalent of the paparazzi, satisfying a huge demand for gossip and fashion news about the famous, the infamous, the glamorous and the rich. The wide publicity was in part down to the efforts of publishers such as John Boydell, mentioned earlier. His firm almost single-handedly kick-started the print market, previously dominated by the French. As an example of his influence, by 1785 the British print industry was exporting British prints to the value of £200,000 a year, at a time when imports had fallen to just £100. Boydell got the Royal Academy Gold Medal for his efforts and ended up as Lord Mayor of London. What the public got was cheap, fine quality prints by the thousand. Engravings by the likes of Bartolozzi, by Walker, by Thornthwaite, flooded the market. Nowadays, we have the internet and today's 'stars' aspire to 'crash the web' with semi-pornographic images. Two-hundred-and-fifty years ago the stars were women such as Frances. They kept their clothes on, but still caused a sensation.

Chapter 10

Gertrude Mahon

Gertrude Mahon, known as 'The Bird of Paradise'.

orn in April 1752, Gertrude Tilson did not have your archetypal family background for a woman who went on to be a leading courtesan. She was no itinerant daughter of a poor family, brought to London, seduced and abandoned to a life of grubby encounters in shop doorways. Instead, she had connections with the Irish aristocracy, had a reasonable education, chose to elope with a ne'er-do-well Irish fiddle player, and then pursued her love of sex by going to bed with rather a large number of wealthy admirers. Arguably, her clientele was less likely to be from the upper echelons – you might say that she preferred quantity to quality – but she led a flamboyant lifestyle which included wearing some fairly outrageous and brightly coloured costumes, often topped off with huge hats. Not for nothing was she known in her later life as the 'Bird of Paradise'. In fairness that soubriquet was also claimed by others – including Mary Robinson – but there is no doubt that Gertrude deserved the title, partly because of her ostentatious dress, and partly because she lived for a while at 6 Paradise Street, Marylebone, and the nickname gave the press an easy way of identifying the object of their comment and ridicule.

Gertrude was born to parents who had both been married before: her mother had been the widowed Countess of Kerry when she remarried. Her new husband, James Tilson, was described as being in the consular service and was known as 'a gay and popular Irishman'. He quickly set about spending his wife's money by building a stately pile at Malpas in Cheshire, which he grandly called Bolesworth Castle. It is not the Victorian pile that still stands today – that was put up in the 1820s when the gothic vision of James Tilson was pulled down. It had been an impressive building, set in beautifully landscaped gardens, and one where the rather spoiled young Gertrude was brought up for the first eleven years of her life.

James then received an appointment as consul in Cádiz in Spain. Off he sailed to take up his appointment, but not until he had moved his wife and daughter to London, putting Bolesworth Castle up for sale. James died after a year in office, leaving his daughter a bequest of £3,000. Gertrude must have found domestic life in London very difficult. She no longer had ponies to occupy her, and her mother turned out to have few maternal qualities. At their home in Wigmore Street, off Cavendish Square, the widowed Mrs Tilson was far more interested in her lapdogs and caged birds than in offering guidance and discipline to her teenage daughter. Mother comes across as a somewhat shallow and vapid character, much given to fussing about with her pets and doing her embroidery rather than in noticing what was going on in the world around her.

Gertrude was a headstrong young girl who developed into a raven-haired flirtatious temptress, a wild-child who clearly revelled in the attention that her looks and behaviour engendered. As an adult, she was just 49 inches tall, and whether you call her 'a pocket rocket', or 'small but beautifully formed', she used her good looks, her sparkling eyes and her diminutive form to attract male attention. The diarist Fanny Burney tells the story of how the sixteen-year old Gertude came to the Burney home in Poland Street, Westminster, for a lesson on the pianoforte given by Fanny's cousin Charles Rousseau Burney. At the end of the lesson the forward young girl deliberately dropped her glove containing a message of love for her tutor. When the hint went unanswered, Gertrude promptly relayed the story to Charles's cousin Hetty (Fanny's elder sister). Doing so suggests an extraordinary level of self-confidence in such a young girl (presumably she was so surprised at being rejected that she was sounding out Hetty to see if her cousin fancied anyone else). It transpired that Hetty was an unfortunate confidante for Gertrude, since Hetty and Charles were childhood sweethearts and ended up getting married to each other. Hetty immediately regaled the rest of her family with the story, delighting Fanny with the titbit of gossip. Fanny wrote in her diary: 'Would you believe it … Miss Tilson, a young lady of fashion, fortune, education birth, accomplishments and beauty has fallen in love with my cousin Charles.' Later, she described Gertrude as 'An amorosa so forward in Cupid's cause'.

A year later and the 'Lilliputian beauty' was launched into London society. The *Morning Herald* was subsequently to describe her as 'A mass of raven hair clustered round her pink cheeks, lustrous black eyes lit up her sweet features.' But one suspects that it was not just her looks that captivated male audiences – it was her coquettish behaviour. She never wasted an opportunity to flirt outrageously, whether it was with a music teacher or a peer of the realm. Her charms attracted the attention of a young Irish musician called Gilbreath (sometimes Gilbert) Mahon. Whatever he earned playing the violin, he squandered on drink and at the gaming tables. He was, however, extremely interested in the £3,000 that Gertrude was going to inherit when she came of age. No matter that he was at least twelve years older than Gertrude (she was seventeen), they decided to elope to France to get married, aware that Gertrude's mother would need to give consent if the marriage were to take place in England.

There is a story that after Gertrude packed her bags and slipped off into the night, heading for the Channel packet at Dover, her mother realised what was going on and sent a posse of men to intercept the young lovers. Apparently, the pursuers caught up with the couple, but the enterprising Gilbreath suggested a libation – and promptly drank the posse under the table. Gilbreath and Gertrude slipped away on the next tide and were married in France in 1769. Gertrude soon became pregnant and her mother presumably felt that it was better to accept the situation. She demanded that the couple return to England and get married 'properly' (there were some doubts as to the validity of the French ceremony). A special licence was obtained from the Bishop of London and the marriage took place at Hanover Square in Westminster on 14 December 1770, when the bride was eight months pregnant. The register noted that the bride was a minor and was married 'with the consent of Rt Hon Gertrude, Countess of Kerry, widow, mother of the said minor.' The young couple's son, Robert Tilson Mahon, appeared on the scene five weeks later.

If Gilbreath thought that this meant that he could now look to his mother-in-law for financial support he was mistaken. In practice the countess was appalled at the idea of her daughter marrying someone without either lineage or financial backing. She could bring herself to play endlessly with baby Robert, but that did not mean that there were any circumstances in which she would allow the young couple to share her home. They stayed in lodgings nearby, and although Gertrude persuaded her guardians to release the income from her inheritance, this amounted to a paltry £150 a year. Disappointed that there were to be no easy pickings, Gilbreath retreated to the gaming tables to seek his fortune. In time, his attentions wandered and after three years he deserted his wife and young child for the delights of the company of another heiress, a Miss Russell, whose brother was one of his gambling companions. He ran off with Miss Russell to Ireland and had nothing further to do with either Gertrude or his infant son.

Gertrude moved back in with her mother but barely a year later the countess died, and Gertrude found herself at a crossroads. On the one hand she was a single mother with a young child, on the other she now received the income from her mother's estate, while the capital was transferred into a trust fund for her son. Society expected her to stay at home and observe a period of deep mourning, and that when that initial mourning period was over she would wear restrained clothing in sober colours, especially when out in public. What society did not expect was for Gertrude to go out immediately and paint the town red. But that is what she did and was soon seen at all the fashionable places, drawing attention to herself with her flamboyant and colourful style of dressing.

Gertrude soon developed a close friendship with a number of other prominent ladies of ill-repute, such as Grace Elliott, who was an occasional lover of the Prince of Wales, and Kitty Frederick, who was the mistress of William Douglas, 4th Duke of Queensberry. Another in her circle was Henrietta, Countess Grosvenor, who had been embroiled in a much-publicised case of criminal conversation when her husband caught her *in flagrante* with the brother of George III. Gertrude became part of a rowdy circle which included the libidinous Lord Lyttleton. She also ensnared the rather randy Lord Cholmondeley, known to all as the Athletic Peer. On one infamous occasion his lordship elected to go to the Pantheon with his two favourite whores, one on each arm: one was Dally the Tall (aka Grace Elliott); the other was the Bird of Paradise.

The Morning Post of 27 January 1776 describes the scene:

The Masqued Ball on Wednesday evening last at the Pantheon, tho' in point of company it might fall short of the expectations of the managers, was the best conducted of any masquerade that ever was given at that house. The great room was rendered unusually brilliant from the disposition of the lamps which, being of one colour, gave a delicacy to the general illumination that charmed the eye of every observer – the dome was remarkably striking.

The company, as usual, was of the mixed kind: comprised rather too much of the lower orders, on account of the severity of the weather, which confining many families of distinction at their country seats, prevented their appearance at this Masque. At twelve o'clock there were about 1200 persons collected together, about two thirds of which were in dominos and these in reality were the only spirited part of the assembly, for the characters were in general as silent and stupid as dullness herself could have desired.

At the top of the free and easy were seen the sentimental Mrs Ell...t and the pretty Mrs M.....n, having each an arm of Lord Ch.....ley, who was well known, tho' he did not unmask the whole evening.

It must have made for a striking sight, the willowy Grace Elliott towering head and shoulders above the diminutive Gertrude, and both of them flirting with their aristocratic companion. He, meanwhile, presumably behaved like the cat that got the cream. The public were left in no doubt: he was enjoying bedroom delights with both the long and the short of the striking pair.

Lord Cholmondeley was twenty-seven years old, and at that stage was unmarried. He had a penchant for keeping company with famous whores: besides Grace and Gertrude there was also Kitty Frederick and he crops up in connection with the stories of both Mary Robinson and Elizabeth

Armistead. These associations did nothing to harm his political career and he became a Privy Councillor in 1783. He inherited Houghton Hall from his great uncle Horace Walpole in 1797, but preferred to live in Cholmondeley Castle in Cheshire, just a few miles from where Gertrude had been brought up in Malpas. Indeed, it is quite possible that Gertrude would have known His Lordship from the time she was a young girl, and could well have been the one who introduced him to her friend Grace.

The Pantheon had first opened as assembly rooms in 1772 and had imposed a strict rule banning admission to 'members of the Cyprian corps' by stating that no one was allowed in unless accompanied by a peer of the realm. By turning up with two whores in tow, Lord Cholmondeley established a precedent which was gleefully followed by all the other prostitutes of note, and soon the Pantheon became notorious as a place for pick-ups and sexual liaisons.

After her mother died, Gertrude clearly felt something was missing from her life – men. And she found them wherever she looked: men would pay handsomely for an evening with the diminutive bombshell. As the *European Magazine* was later to put it: 'From that period may be dated the commencement of those errors, the repetition of which has rendered Mrs Mahon so celebrated in the annals of the bon ton and so remarkable in the history of frail beauty ... she now finding herself totally neglected by her spouse, for whom her passion had long since cooled, opened her ears to the flattery and professions of strangers. A few private intrigues brought in a supply of money.'

The same journal went on to explain that Gertrude soon became an insatiable whore ('one of the most celebrated disciples of the Cytherean Goddess') and found herself 'surrounded with pleasures and plentifully supplied with money.' She was, so the magazine explained, 'passed from hand to hand, constant only to one man, till she saw another who she preferred.'

Her activities quickly found attention in the press, with *The Morning Post* reporting on 9 December 1776 that 'the little Bird of Paradise has at length flown to the continent with a military financier.' On Christmas Day that year the same paper reported, 'Yesterday the Bird of Paradise and her amorous Military Associate Capt T.... of the Guards returned from the continent.' The *European Magazine* was more detailed, explaining that the captain had captivated her heart with his fortune ('or rather, his expensive mode of spending it'). They went to Paris together and 'there sported in all the expensive elegancies pleasures and gaieties of that metropolis,' before running out of money.

Captain John Turner was, with Gertrude's eager assistance, busy burning through an inheritance of £50,000. On their return to London they continued to be seen at balls and ridottos, often in the company of dubious hangers-on. Eventually, Gertrude got bored with Turner. As *The Morning Post* put it: 'The *Bird of Paradise* broke through the upper part of her cage two days ago, flew from her military keeper and perched on the shoulder of Sir John L… as he was driving his phaeton and four through Knightsbridge, who carried her home to Park Place. The forsaken captain is disconsolate.'

Her new paramour was the seventeen-year old Sir John Lade, a horse-mad young baronet who quickly bored Gertrude with his uncouth behaviour. He was too dull for her, and after three weeks she returned to Captain Turner. For a time they lived high on the hog, but money was running out and in due course the good captain was thrown into the debtors' prison. Unwilling to wait for his release Gertrude went back on the game – or as the *European Magazine* expressed it: 'the little Bird of Paradise soon growing tired of her cage, took wing from her mate and sought another fool of fashion to supply her pleasures and extravagancies. She was not however ungenerous to her imprisoned lover, but supplied him with money during his confinement.' Subsequently, the couple drifted apart and within two years the captain's fortunes changed when he met and married an heiress, later going on to become a baronet.

For the newspapers, Gertrude was a godsend. Her diminutive frame, her flirtatious behaviour and her colourful clothing made her stand out in any gathering. Above all, she offset her lack of stature by wearing millinery masterpieces which fully justified the moniker of Bird of Paradise. She had good dress sense, and was often dressed in an elegant manner, even if her clothes were rather more gaudy than good taste dictated. On one occasion she was described as being 'at Vauxhall in glittering plumage, her waist not a span round, her stature four feet one inch, with black hair truly Mahomedan, delicately arched eye-brows smooth as mouse skin, and soft pouting lips.'

If there was no actual news to report, the papers could always fall back on avian puns: she was said to be 'moulting' or, if she was thought to be off-colour, that she had 'eaten too much saffron lately administered in the waters of her cage.' When she travelled to Margate or Brighton she was said to 'wet her plumage every day in the water'. Her success in getting wealthy men to part with their money led one paper to report that this particular bird was, though no larger than a canary, able 'to swallow gold and silver with the facility of an ostrich.'

Her notoriety persuaded the manager of the Covent Garden theatre that she would be an asset on stage and would draw in the crowds. In late October 1780 it was rumoured that the petite Gertrude would appear in a performance of *Tom Thumb*. It was not to be and her first stage appearance was on 12 December 1780 as Elvira in Dryden's *The Spanish Fryar*. Sadly, Gertrude was no actor and although her novelty value meant that she performed before a packed house, her nerves, her tiny voice and her inability to project her personality on such a vast stage resulted in the play being taken off after three performances. She was perhaps fortunate that the critics held back from ripping her to pieces, concentrating instead on commenting upon her beauty. 'Her figure is of the smallest but her features are regular and pretty and her person is remarkably well turned,' warbled the *Morning Chronicle*.

A few more plays followed in early 1781, culminating in an appearance in *The Provok'd Husband* as Lady Townly. The *Morning Herald* of 15 February described her acting as 'intolerable'. More to the point, public curiosity had been satisfied: she was no longer pulling in the punters, and her contract was not renewed. So ended her brief appearance on the London stage. It did, however, mean that she was at the height of her career as a glittering courtesan. She was twenty-nine: she could afford to wear the best gowns that London's couturiers could offer; she was living in a prestigious address at 73 Great Portland Street; and she had taken delivery of a handsome new yellow carriage, a phaeton designed in France. Soon she had added to this a new carriage, known as a vis-à-vis, and soon mastered the art of driving the vehicle with considerable skill, being nicknamed 'Lady Hard and Soft'.

For Gertrude there was just one thing missing – a royal conquest. As will be seen in chapter 11, the Prince of Wales had initially embarked on an affair with Mary Robinson but had then moved on to Grace Elliott. No matter that Grace was Gertrude's friend, she was also her rival and Gertrude would have loved to have been able to score such a victory. She set about trying to engineer an introduction to the Prince of Wales, in effect stalking him by finding out when he was due to attend the opera, or a particular ball, and then making sure that she was also present. The prince did apparently agree to visit Gertrude at her home as part of a raucous party, but if he afterwards succumbed to her charms the public never got to hear of it, and any affair would have been short lived.

It seems that Gertrude was not averse to popping round to one or more of the notorious seraglios which flourished in the area of Pall Mall. One such brothel was in King's Place, where the famous madam Charlotte Hayes had set up in business some years earlier. The establishment was subsequently taken over by Sarah Dubery, and she developed the business by attracting mostly foreign diplomats and wealthy peers. On one such visit Gertrude picked up the Portuguese ambassador, Count Louis Pinto de Balsamo, earning him the title of 'Mahon's pintle' (an old slang word for penis).

If reports in the papers were to be believed, Gertrude spent the summer of 1781 at Margate, which was just emerging as a fashionable seaside resort. That year the *Hibernian Magazine* showed a picture of Gertrude with Colonel Wetwould, and that liaison was followed up in the Tête-à-Tête section of the *Town & Country Magazine*, showing the pair facing each other. The text was not especially kind to the colonel, stating that he was 'twaddling about Ranelagh, the Pantheon, and the St James's chocolate houses, without being able to discover he had any particular connexion with the fair sex, till he became enraptured with the Bird of Paradise the first time he saw her upon the stage.'

The colonel was wise enough to be able to see that his charms would not satisfy Gertrude for long, with the article in the *Town and Country* continuing: 'the colonel himself was heard to say the other evening at Bootle's that the Bird of Paradise was so congenial to the feathered tribe, and so much a bird of passage, as well as Paradise, that he expected she would soon be upon the wing again.'

Gertrude had been the mistress of the wealthy Colonel George Boden for some time but even his pockets were not sufficiently deep to keep up with her profligacy, and running a household with eight live-in servants to support, plus two carriages and six horses to maintain was not cheap. The colonel ended up in the debtors' prison and Gertrude ended up having to sell up and move on. This was despite the fact that she had suddenly come into money of her own when she was left the interest on a legacy following the death of her half-sister Elizabeth. The capital (some £3,000) was held in trust for her son, by then aged twelve.

Despite the extra income at her disposal, Gertrude seems to have gone more 'downmarket' in her tastes. She became the constant companion of Ann Greenhill, popularly known as the Greenfinch, who at that time was the mistress of a notorious captain in the army called John Roper. His drunken, roistering, behaviour led to him being known as 'Captain Toper' but if the *Town & Country Magazine* of 1783 is to be believed the Greenfinch also had a fling with Edmund Boyle, the 7th Earl of Cork and Orrery, featuring in the Tête-à-Tête profile in the April edition that year. But Ann also moved in less salubrious circles, and happily dragged Gertrude along to some of her more disreputable haunts. In this, Gertrude appears to have been encouraged by her friendship with Margaret Cuyler, a notorious whore (and occasional actress) operating out of one of London's infamous brothels in King's Place, near Pall Mall. Margaret's mother may have been a lady-in-waiting to the previous queen and may have brought her daughter up in St James's Palace but it didn't stop Margaret from earning the description as 'a great Jack whore, with no pretensions to manner or beauty' from the diarist and writer William Hickey. She cannot have been entirely without charm though, with the *Morning Herald* on 24 May 1783 describing Margaret as the belle of the ball at a masquerade organised in honour of a visiting French aristocrat (the Duchesse de Chartres) who was visiting London in order to sample English fashion: 'The lovely Mrs C...r appeared in the circle with peculiar éclat ... the beautiful simplicity of her dress proved the delicacy of her taste in that important article, and exhibited her gracefully elegant form to the utmost advantage.' That compliment has to be seen in context of the fact that Mrs Cuyler was not averse to making her services available at higher class brothels in the St James's area. It makes it all the more surprising that the Prince of Wales made an appearance at the masquerade, adding royal support to the idea that even common whores could make their mark in the world as arbiters of fashion.

Mrs Cuyler was fairly dreadful as an actress, but that certainly would not have dissuaded her from suggesting to Gertrude that she could make money by resuming her stage career. Perhaps Mrs Cuyler should have paid more attention to her own stage reviews, with one critic describing her as 'a tall lifeless woman ... exceedingly pallid, and whose features were ridiculously small for her size.'

For now, a return to the stage was ruled out by Gertrude. She decided to spend time on the Continent and in 1784 set off for Montpellier. The papers reported that she had gone to the south of France with 'Mr C..l..t' and the *Rambler Magazine* wrote enthusiastically: 'The Bird of Paradise has taken up her residence in Nanci, in company with Mr C....t, with whom she paired off. The male bird was sent for some time since from England, and, by means of a stratagem which mentioned a relation's death, he was prevail'd upon to come home; he made however a very short stay from his companion whom, on his return he found at constant matins and vespers with the sisterhood of the nunnery on the banks of the Meuse!'

The same magazine wrote on another occasion that Gertrude had gone to Montpellier with someone completely different, and had gone to the famous spa town in order to rid herself of a case of the pox: 'The Bird of Paradise has taken up residence in the South of France, with Sir J...n L...e, to wash in the pool of Montpellier, famous in the ailment of her trade!'

When she returned from France she took up residence in an elegant house in Argyle Street, but financial pressures meant that she accepted an offer from the manager of one of the Dublin theatres to appear there for a short season. She needed the money badly and embarked on a particularly rough crossing from Holyhead to Dublin, before appearing to rapturous audiences in the two roles she had performed in London, as Elvira and as Lady Townly. It wasn't that her acting abilities had improved, simply that Dubliners clamoured to see such a renowned beauty, especially one who was from a noble Irish family and whose clothing was quite magnificent. The sight of her headgear alone made the admission price to the theatre worth paying and 'the Mahon hat' was soon all the rage. Gertrude, meanwhile, managed to ensnare one of the foremost legal minds in the country, John FitzGibbon. He had just been appointed Attorney General and went on to become the Earl of Clare.

By the end of the 1780s Gertrude's future must have looked far from settled: she was in her late thirties and her looks were beginning to fade. Fashions had moved on and the vibrant concoctions that she had previously worn in order to stand out in a crowd no longer seemed appropriate. She may also have been ill – indeed it would have been astonishing if she had not caught venereal disease at some stage or other, and this may well have affected her looks and lessened her appeal. Newspapers hinted as much, but in time the press did something even worse – they disregarded her. In 1790 she was said to be staying at Bath, and that she was 'dead to her former eminence' and 'only alive to epicurism'.

Bath in 1790 would have been a very different city to the one where Fanny Murray had grown up some forty years earlier. Now the entertainment scene involved not one but two assembly rooms, with the Upper Rooms having been opened in 1771. Fashionable and elegant houses had been built by father-and-son architects John Wood at The Circus and the Royal Crescent, and a city of just a few thousand residents in 1700 had grown so rapidly that the census of 1801 showed a population of some 40,020.

But it was the visiting hordes of tourists which inflated the figures even further. The whole place had become the Georgian city of Fun with a capital F. Promenading along the fashionable walkways would have been an overcrowded nightmare. Visiting the theatre would involve sending your servant to queue for tickets first thing in the morning when the box office opened. And if you wanted to visit the Upper Assembly Rooms (always more fashionable than the Lower Rooms) you would have to be vetted first by the Master of Ceremonies, told when to arrive (so that the carriages did not all arrive at the same time and cause traffic chaos) and shown where to sit. By 1790 the Bath that Gertrude visited was at the zenith of its crowded popularity, although subsequently its very popularity doomed it to be overtaken by other playgrounds for the rich and the aspirational (such as Brighton).

At the time when she was staying in Bath the original Pump Rooms were proving to be inadequate, and although the facilities were improved in 1790 the decision was made to construct completely new premises, which opened in 1795. Meanwhile Gertrude ran out of money and her home was repossessed, and all her furniture auctioned off. It was not a good year for Gertrude: 1790 was also the year her son Robert died in India, having signed up four years earlier with the army of the East India Company.

A year or so later Gertrude was mentioned as having ventured to Boulogne, presumably to avoid her creditors, and to be staying with a Mr Parry. There were occasional appearances on stage in minor provincial theatres: at Margate as Lady Teazle in *School for Scandal* at the Theatre Royal in 1794, and in Ireland at Kilkenny the following year. She disappeared from view by 1800, and there was a story that she had moved to the Isle of Man and was 'living under the protection of a Hibernian refugee'. There is no record of either the date or place of her death and all that is certain is that she died forgotten, a sex symbol well past her sell-by date.

Her life had the outward appearance of flamboyance, gaiety and pleasure, and she was remarkable for staying at the top of her game for at least ten years. The seventies and eighties were extraordinary times – times when the whore and the harlot were elevated to celebrity status. It seems undeniable that Gertrude was both, and she revelled in her status, enjoyed the fame, but let fortune slip through her fingers.

Chapter 11

Mary Robinson

Mary Robinson in stage costume.

According to her memoirs, Mary Robinson was born on a night wracked by stormy winds, ostensibly on 27 November 1758. She saw those storms as precursors to a life of hardship and sorrow, a Gothic backdrop to the vicissitudes she later faced. She subsequently wrote that 'through life, the tempest has followed my footsteps, and I have in vain looked for a short interval of repose from the perseverance of sorrow.'

We do not even know if the date of birth is accurate, many believing she was born a year earlier. It may well have been that she docked a year from her true age, just to make her look even more of an innocent-at-large when she was faced with entering adulthood. Like much of her autobiography, Mary was not averse to glossing over the truth and being selective about what she included – and, most significantly, left out.

Mary was the daughter of Nicholas and Hester Darby and records suggest that she may well have been born in 1757, or possibly as early as 1756. Some of the confusion arises because she is thought by some to be the 'Polly Darby' entered in the baptismal records of Bristol's St Augustine-the-Less church in 1756. 'Polly' was a variant of 'Molly', which in turn was a nickname for anyone called 'Mary'. She was one of five children born to the Darbys, who lived at the Minster House in the centre of Bristol, just yards from the mouth of the River Frome. Shipping was brought right into the heart of Bristol, for long the second largest port in the country, just yards from the Darby home.

The Darby household was a perfectly respectable one situated near College Green, next to today's cathedral but at that time adjoining the crumbling ruins of the medieval St Augustine's Minster. Nicholas Darby was a naval captain, possibly born in Newfoundland, who had settled in the mercantile centre of Bristol. The family was well connected – Mary claimed that Robert Henley (otherwise known as the 1st Earl Northington, the Lord High Chancellor) was her godfather. Not for Mary a meteoric rise from the slums, emerging as a flower seller before captivating the hearts of the rich and famous. For Mary it was more a case of a solemn and somewhat melancholy childhood, but one filled with music and literature, followed by a series of bumps in the road as she progressed towards adulthood and an early marriage. Here was a child born into an affluent family, but one who seemed to thrive on melancholia. As soon as she could read she passed her time reading inscriptions on the tombs in the local graveyard – that is, if she wasn't inside the church listening to mournful dirges being played on the organ.

In her memoirs, written towards the end of her life and ending just before they got 'interesting' (i.e., when she started her affair with the young Prince of Wales), Mary writes of the good education she received, albeit one spread over a number of learning establishments. In Bristol she attended the school at Number 43 Park Street run by the five More sisters, of whom the most famous was Hannah More, educationalist, pamphleteer and writer. In practice, much of the teaching was done by Hannah's sisters, Mary, Elizabeth, Sarah and Patty. Hannah had attended the school herself when she was twelve years old, although at that stage it was situated in nearby Trinity Street. The school was unusual in that it provided young girls with an opportunity to study a wide syllabus, including languages such as Italian and Spanish. It was so successful that after a few years the school had moved to its Park Street address and the very young Mary would have set off every morning to walk the few hundred yards across the busy thoroughfare of College Green, past the medieval High Cross, which had been moved to the centre of the Green some thirty years earlier, and to climb the steep hill to where the school was situated. By all accounts she displayed an early interest in playing the harpsichord, reciting elegies, and composing doggerel verse. Looking back at her time in Bristol, Mary wrote that her father's house was 'opened by hospitality' and her father's generosity was 'only equalled by the liberality of fortune'. Every day 'augmented her father's success' as a merchant in prosperous Bristol. 'The bed in which I slept was of the richest crimson damask; the dresses which we wore were of the finest cambric.' But this affluent, loving environment was soon to be shattered by the first of those occasions which must have impressed Mary with the unreliability and perfidiousness of men.

Her father decided to invest everything in a scheme to develop the fishing industry off the coast of Labrador. He became consumed with the idea and announced that he was heading for North America in order to finalise plans. His ambition was to establish a whaling station on Labrador, in competition with the existing whaling stations operated by whalers out of New England. Success would very much depend on getting the trust and cooperation of the native American tribes – the 'esquimaux' as Nicholas Darby called them. In fact there were two quite separate tribes operating in the Cape Charles area of Labrador where Darby wished to settle, and the feuding between the Inuit and the Innu resulted in the Darby settlement being overrun, three of his men being killed, the buildings demolished and some £4,600 worth of damage caused to stock and equipment. Darby had been required to trade for twelve months as a cod fishermen before he could apply for a licence to go whaling, and a year's supply of dried cod was destroyed by the angry natives. In all he lost £8,000 in the venture during a two-year period.

As the weeks became months it became apparent that father's domestic arrangements across the Atlantic included a mistress. And because she was prepared to put up with all the privations and difficulties of setting up a business in Labrador, it was the mistress who earned the loyalty and devotion of Nicholas Darby. His family back home suffered accordingly.

Within a short time the business venture turned into a nightmare. The 'island of promise' turned out to be 'a scene of barbarous desolation'; father lost everything and was declared bankrupt. Worse, he had signed a bill of sale over the house in Bristol, and the failure of the Labrador venture meant that the Darby family were evicted from their home and forced to find inferior accommodation.

So it was that in the tenth year of Mary's life an event occurred that was to be repeated throughout her life – a sudden change linked to pain or sadness, or sometimes both. This first change in her circumstance meant that she was removed from all the things she loved in Bristol – the house, the cathedral organ, her invigorating schooling, her childhood friends and so on – and uprooted a hundred miles away. Her father moved the family to Spring Gardens in London while he resided nearby with his mistress. Mary was sent to a seminary in Chelsea, where she was taught by an extraordinary character called Meribah Lorrington. Later on, Mary would describe her as being the most extensively accomplished female that she ever encountered. She wrote that Meribah's father had insisted that she had 'a masculine education' – one in which she learnt Latin, French and Italian, as well as studying astronomy and mathematics and being able to paint on silk. But this accomplished mentor had one major flaw: she was a raging alcoholic. Mary writes of drink as being Meribah's ruling infatuation, but concedes that 'all I have ever learned I acquired from this extraordinary woman. In those hours when she was not intoxicated, she would delight in the task of instructing me.' The two of them would stay up half the night reading to each other, helping Mary to develop a love of literature and an appreciation of the power of the spoken word. At the age of twelve or thirteen Mary started to compose poems and later arranged to have these juvenile jottings published, but not until after she had married.

Sadly, Mrs Lorrington's descent into intoxicated oblivion meant that the school of which she was in charge had to be closed. Mary attributed the drink problem to 'the immitigable regret of a widowed heart,' and 'the only refuge from the pang of prevailing sorrow.' After those fourteen months of sometimes inspirational teaching from Mrs Lorrington, Mary was moved to a seminary run by a Mrs Leigh in Battersea. She was, wrote Mary afterwards, 'a lively, sensible and accomplished woman ... extremely amiable as well as lovely.' But this proved to be a short interlude in Mary's education. Her father was 'remiss in sending pecuniary supplies' (in other words, he failed to cough up the school fees) and the financially embarrassed Mrs Darby decided to open her own boarding school for young ladies at 5 Park Walk, Little Chelsea. Mary wrote in her memoirs that she taught English literature to the infant pupils at her mother's school, selecting and reading suitable passages for her young charges to read and study. Mary wrote: 'Assistants of every kind were engaged, and I was deemed worthy of an occupation that flattered my self-love, and impressed my mind with a sort of domestic consequence.' She added, 'It was also my occupation to superintend their wardrobes, to see them dressed and undressed by the servants or half-boarders.'

One of the things which comes across most vividly in these memoirs is Mary's love of clothing, and an appreciation of the part played by fashion, by ornamentation and dress. Manners may have maketh the man, but fashion made the woman. Memoirs can often gloss over the truth, or put things in a spectacularly better light than they deserve, but there is no hiding the fact that from an early age Mary was acutely aware of fashion, invariably describing what she was wearing on every significant occasion in her life. As a youngster she had a propensity for wearing what she described as Quaker apparel – plain, somewhat dated garments, lacking in flair and colour. Later she moved on to choosing silks trimmed with ermine, with dresses of various lustres finished with fine lace and so on: and that was even before she became a fashion clothes-horse.

Nicholas Darby felt affronted that his wife was running a school without his permission. He felt it reflected badly on him, so he promptly had the school closed after just eight months – a reminder that in the eighteenth century a married woman could not enter into any business commitments independently of her husband.

Mary adored her mother, whom she describes as the most unoffending of existing mortals with a cheerful temperament and an innocent heart.

In many ways it had been an idyllic early childhood. She had two younger brothers, including George, who went on to become a merchant in Italy. The other brother, William, caught measles and died when he was six years old. The loss had a profound effect on Mary's mother, who, it was said, was nearly deprived of her senses and went into a deep depression. She only recovered her mental equilibrium thanks to the support and guidance of the kindly widow of Sir Charles Erskine.

He had been Lord Advocate, a Scottish judge, and a politician who sat in the House of Commons for twenty years, and who died in 1762. It was not the first time Hester Darby had lost a child – there was also a daughter called Elizabeth who caught smallpox and died at the age of thirty months, some two years before Mary was born.

One year later Mary and her mother received a peremptory demand to meet Mr Darby at his lodgings. By then, Mary had not seen her father for three years. The meeting was, she said, a mixture of pain and pleasure – not least because her mother received 'a cold embrace at their meeting – it was the last she ever received from her alienated husband.'

Mary saw in her father a man who was brave, liberal, enlightened and ingenuous – but also someone who was 'the dupe of his passions, the victim of an unfortunate attachment.' A similar verdict could perhaps be passed upon just about all the men Mary later encountered in her life.

From then on, her father occasionally drifted into Mary's life, only to disappear again. He introduced Mary to the family of her late godfather: the new Lord Northington lived in Berkeley Square and 'always showed Mary the most flattering and gratifying civility.' She was then fourteen years old and described her figure as being 'commanding for my age'. Earlier, she saw herself as swarthy, with eyes that were 'singularly large in proportion' to her face. By now she had grown tall and was showing the signs of irresistible beauty – as well as an overwhelming inner sadness – which was to captivate so many men. Her large eyes, her solemn countenance and her great figure marked her out as a future shooting star.

At that stage she was sent to finish her education at Oxford House in Marylebone. Here she could indulge her passion for writing dramatic poetry, a love that remained with her for the rest of her life. But one particular set of circumstances encountered at Oxford House was to change the pattern of her life. The dancing master at the school was a Mr Hussey, and he was ballet-master at Covent Garden Theatre. He introduced Mary to Thomas Hull, deputy manager of the theatre, and she recited various pieces for him by way of an audition.

An introduction to the great Shakespearian actor David Garrick followed. Garrick was about to retire, but announced that he was determined to appear alongside Mary on her theatrical debut. 'After some hesitation my tutor fixed on the part of Cordelia. His own Lear can never be forgotten.' Mary spoke highly of Garrick. The two clearly hit it off, the old thespian and the young tyro, and she wrote, 'Garrick was delighted with everything I did. He would sometimes dance a minuet with me, sometimes request me to sing the favourite ballads of the day; but the circumstance which most pleased him was my tone of voice, which he frequently told me closely resembled that of his favourite Cibber.' She continued: 'Never shall I forget the enchanting hours which I passed in Mr. Garrick's society; he appeared to me as one who possessed more power, both to awe and to attract, than any man I ever met with. His smile was fascinating, but he had at times a restless peevishness of tone which excessively affected his hearers; at least it affected me so that I never shall forget it.'

This has to be seen against the background that the theatre was a far from respectable place for a young and attractive girl. The theatre at Covent Garden was at the centre of London's vice trade. Not only was the building surrounded by brothels and bagnios, but the theatre itself was a place for making arrangements for sexual liaisons. Courtesans hired the best boxes for the entire season, where they could see and be seen, and where ardent young swains could queue up to secure a lady's favours for a future occasion. The plays themselves were often the occasion for much raucous and lewd behaviour: it was common for the management to offer free admission to the public for the third act, meaning that in front of the stage the pit was filled with revellers only too willing to exchange banter and rude comments with the actors and actresses on stage.

Of course, there were women on the stage who were virtuous and indeed were respected for their acting skills. Sarah Siddons and Susannah Cibber were two who, although not exactly immune from public scandal, at least avoided being tarnished as common whores. Nevertheless, for many in the sex trade walking the boards was seen as a fine way to enhance their business, as an advertisement for their beauty, their elegance and their fashion sense. And of course, if they were acting in a breeches part – in other words appearing on stage disguised as a male, dressed in man's clothing – it meant that they were able to display something which men rarely saw in public – a fine pair of female legs, albeit sheathed in a tight pair of trousers.

One of the contemporaries of Mary was Elizabeth Farren. She had captured the attention of Charles James Fox, the politician and notorious womaniser. He very publicly lusted after her and let it be known how much he was looking forward to seeing her in a breeches part, playing Nancy Lovel in the quickly forgotten play *Suicide* by George Colman. Come the performance and, horror of horrors, the lady's posterior was found to be positively sagging. No pert bum, no approval from Mister Fox. He told the world as much, and the poor girl had to console herself with making the most of the altogether more favourable attentions she got from Edward Smith-Stanley, 12th Earl of Derby. He watched besotted from the box by the stage and finally married her in 1797, and the showgirl thereby became the Duchess of Derby.

Mary and her mother would have been well aware that the suggestion of a stage career would have horrified Mr Darby. But it did offer a modicum of money, much needed in the household, and a date was set for Mary's first appearance. However, it was not to be, because her life took an unexpected turn. Mary was fifteen. Two years earlier she had received a marriage proposal from a much older gentleman. Now she found herself pursued by a naval officer who followed her to her home, sending ardent love letters via servants. It later transpired that he was already married – a lesson in male duplicity which Mary would have been well to have noted more carefully.

Nor was this the only distraction to her career on stage. The Darby family were living in Southampton Buildings near the law firm of Vernon and Elderton. Mary later wrote: 'Opposite to the house in which I resided lived John Vernon, Esq. an eminent solicitor. I observed a young inmate of his habitation frequently watching me with more than ordinary attention. He was handsome in person, and his countenance was overcast by a sort of langour, the effect of sickness, which rendered it peculiarly interesting.' Not entirely by chance, Mary found that her dining companion during an outing to Greenwich was the same young man, a Thomas Robinson. She wrote that a mutual friend explained 'the many good qualities of Mr. Robinson: spoke of his future expectations from a rich old uncle; of the probability of advancement in his profession; and, more than all, of his enthusiastic admiration of me.'

As it turned out, all was not as it seemed. There was no rich old uncle – Thomas was the illegitimate child of a Welsh tailor, and besides, there was an older brother, William Robinson, serving in India in the army of the East India Company and who would have expected to claim whatever inheritance there might be. Furthermore, the indenture which

Thomas would have signed at the commencement of his articles would have expressly prohibited any marriage during the training period. In addition, Thomas had resorted to using money lenders to support his lavish lifestyle and anything that he might have expected to receive on attaining his majority had already been pledged as security for a myriad of loans.

Nevertheless, his suit was favoured by Mary's mother, who naïvely thought that this was a way of protecting Mary from alternative, less suitable, marriage proposals, and of keeping her off the stage and therefore avoiding the risk of further antagonising her father. Mary especially felt indebted to Thomas after her brother, George, fell ill with smallpox. He assiduously cared for George, and indeed for Mary when she shortly afterwards contracted the disease. Mary was not in love, and contemporary reports suggested that the real reason Mary agreed to marry was because she needed an outlet for her rampant sexual desires. The *European Magazine* remarked later that 'she stepped into the nuptial bed with a predetermination to indulge herself liberally in all those pleasures which, under the cloak of matrimony, are too often indulged with impunity.'

The two married on 12 April 1774, when Mary claimed that she was still fifteen, but it was a clandestine union. This was at the express request of Mr Robinson, who wished to keep his marital status a secret until he was fully qualified as a solicitor. This was not surprising, given that his articles of clerkship, as with all training contracts at the time, would have contained a prohibition on marriage. However, for Mary it must have been a difficult decision to accept.

*   *   *

Thus ended the second chapter in Mary's life, and yet again it was to be marked by hardship and disappointment. Not for the first time, Mary discovered that men were not to be trusted.

Why this detailed account of her early life? Because this is the official version, the one given by Mary herself in her memoirs. But inevitably it dwells on the innocence of young Mary: here was a girl thrown into marriage, who but a short while previously was playing with toys and dressing her dolls. It is fair to say that there is another version, one which perhaps is totally salacious and false, but which nonetheless gained credence at the time especially among those who chose to think ill of her. In 1784 a book was published purporting to be a truthful account of Mary's life – and it shows a young woman of rampant sexuality, a nymphet who thought nothing of seducing a young stranger in the back of a coach travelling from London to Bristol, bringing him to a climactic conclusion not once but four times, and all that while her cuckolded husband was sitting on top of the roof of the coach, 'riding shotgun', blissfully unaware of the reason why the coach was giving such a bumpy ride.

The same story suggested that her appetite for sex was uncontrollable, especially once she realised that she could use sex to gain the things she most wanted in life – fine clothes, money and, above all, diamonds. It is not a question of whether this version was true – simply that this is what the public wanted to believe. However hard Mary sought to show her later conduct in a favourable light, she would always appear, in the minds of the public, as a harlot who became a whore, and then went on to become a serial mistress who selected her targets purely upon their social status and wealth.

The immediate effect of the marriage was to postpone Mary's stage debut. She travelled back to her beloved Bristol *en route* to see her new husband's family in Wales, but times had changed in her absence. The Minster House was near-derelict and College Green had become such a busy thoroughfare with visitors promenading to the nearby springs at Hotwells that the High Cross, in the centre of College Green, had been dismantled and carted off to form a garden ornament at Stourhead in Somerset. Mary was, however, able to hear again the sonorous tones of the cathedral organ, and admire the gravestones which she had memorised just a short time earlier. With her husband she crossed the River Severn at Aust and arrived at the Robinson family home at Tregunter. She wore 'a dark claret-coloured riding habit with a white beaver hat and feathers,' which must have made for quite an impression in rural Wales, especially as her husband's sister came out to meet the party wearing 'a gaudy coloured chintz gown, a thrice-embroidered cap, with a profusion of ribbons and a countenance somewhat more ruddy than was consistent with even pure health.' The sister was described as 'Gothic in her appearance ... of low stature and clumsy,' and the two never got on.

Returning to London, the newlyweds set up home in a new house at 13 Hatton Garden and 'furnished it with a peculiar elegance'. Mary stated that she checked with Thomas that they could afford such extravagance, which also ran to a handsome open carriage known as a phaeton, and was assured that they could. She continued, 'I now made my debut though scarcely emerged beyond the boundaries of childhood, in the broad hemisphere of fashionable folly.'

She quickly discovered the extent of her new husband's deceit, and learned of his insolvency, not least because of the regular visits from Jewish money-lenders demanding their money back. None of this stopped her entry into polite society. In her memoirs she described the first time that she went to Ranelagh Gardens: 'My habit was so plain and Quaker-like that all eyes were fixed upon me. I wore a gown of brown lustring with close round cuffs, [it was then the fashion to wear long ruffles] my hair was without powder and my head adorned with a plain white cap and a white chip hat, without any adornment whatever.'

It was a visit to the magnificent Pantheon which helped seal her developing reputation as a leader of fashion: 'At this place it was customary to appear much dressed; large hoops and high feathers were universally worn. My habit was composed of pale pink satin, trimmed with broad sable; my dear mother presented me a suit of rich and valuable point lace … and I was at least some hours employed in decorating my person.'

At the concert at the Pantheon the main focal point was where the Marchioness Townshend was holding court, 'attended by the unceasing murmur of admiration' from all present. Mary Robinson contrived to sit down on a sofa opposite the marchioness and clearly caused something of a stir, deliberately or otherwise, but she adored all the attention she received. Mary later wrote that she could hear 'men of fashion' speaking to the marchioness to ask, 'Who is the lady in the pink dress trimmed with sable?' She was soon recognised by the Earl of Northington, who promptly introduced her to two of the most disreputable rakes and libertines in the country, namely Thomas, 2nd Baron Lyttleton, and Captain George Ayscough. Mary Robinson, by then pregnant, was much embarrassed the next day when she received a visit from those three gentlemen – not least because she was alone and had to handle the visit unaided. As she said, 'At an age when girls are generally at school, or indeed scarcely emancipated from the nursery, I was presented in society as a wife – and very nearly as a mother.'

The motives of the three gentlemen were far from pure and over the ensuing weeks they laid siege to the poor girl, while getting Mr Robinson out of the way by the simple expedient of introducing him to the gaming tables. Here he was happy to gamble away money he did not have, leaving his young wife to the mercies of unscrupulous rakes. Well, that was Mary's version of events.

As for Mary, she returned to the Pantheon, this time bedecked in white and silver, and continued to cut a swathe through the fashionable elite. Her husband neglected her, or else offended her by constantly belittling her and referring to her as 'the child'. Lord Lyttleton eventually confided to Mary that her husband was having an affair with a common whore living in Soho's Princes Street. He obviously hoped that the news would sever any bond of allegiance that Mary might have for her husband. It didn't – but she went round to the house of Harriet Wilmot, confronted her and demanded that she desist seeing her husband. Interestingly, her description of the visit includes mentioning that a new, white lustring sacque and petticoat lay on the bed, and that her nemesis was wearing a dress of printed Irish muslin, trimmed with pale lilac ribbons, while Mary herself was dressed in a 'morning *deshabille* of India muslin, with a bonnet of straw and a white lawn cloak bordered with lace.' It sounds like less of a confrontation between arch-rivals than a cosy description of the fashions of the day.

Whether Mary slept with Lord Lyttleton is unclear. It was denied emphatically by Mary, but the gossip-mongers were not so sure. Lyttleton was a dissolute rake described by Mary as 'perhaps the most accomplished libertine that any age or country has produced,' and he pursued her relentlessly. Others commented that when Lord Lyttleton paid a social visit to Mary he found her 'loose, unattired, warm tender, full of wishes ... her wedded husband gone abroad, the maid dismissed from waiting,' and eagerly took advantage of her situation. The randy lord reportedly 'slipped a purse into her hand, gave her a diamond ring – and whisked her off to bed.' The same story went on to describe how in time Lord Lyttleton, 'being fully satiated with his mistress, whose expenses he found unsupportable, suddenly took his leave.' Reports of the day suggested that she switched her attentions to George Brereton, not because he was particularly handsome or good company, but because he was rich ('was from his ugliness nick-named "Old Scratch", but he had money, an attribute which had great weight with Mrs R. and she attached herself to him ... with a degree of ardour ... that none of her other happy admirers have ever experienced').

Another reported lover was Captain Ayscough. He was Lyttleton's cousin, described at the time as being a 'fool of fashion' and 'a parasite of Lyttleton'. Mary also received the attention of George Robert Fitzgerald, commonly known as 'Fighting Fitzgerald'. On one occasion he allegedly tried to abduct Mary after a visit to Vauxhall Gardens, bundling her into his carriage before Mr Robinson made a timely appearance. This somewhat theatrical event was described in some detail by Mary in her memoirs, but the story may well have been a total invention on her part. Fitzgerald was a somewhat eccentric Irish aristocrat, a renowned womaniser and fighter of duels, and ended up on the scaffold for murdering his father's attorney.

Eventually, the demands of Mr Robinson's creditors became so pressing that the couple fled back to the family home in Wales in order to avoid writs being served. There, Mary's daughter, Maria Elizabeth, was born on 18 November 1774. But there was no avoiding the process-server and in due course the family returned to London, where they were thrown into prison. This was partly a matter of choice for Mary. It was perfectly normal for spouses to join their partner in the Fleet prison, but it was also perfectly normal for men to pay to have whores accompany them inside as they waited for family and friends to raise money for their release, and Mr Robinson was quite blatant in neglecting his wife while fornicating with local prostitutes. Mary, portraying herself in her subsequent memoirs as being whiter-than-white, refers to these whores as women whose 'low licentious lives were such as to render them the shame and outcasts of society.'

Financial support from her husband's family was not forthcoming, but Mary raised a small amount of money from the sale of a book of poetry which she had finished writing prior to her captivity. For nine months she shared the incarceration, never once leaving the Fleet. However, when the opportunity of promoting her poetry book arose, she sent a copy to the Duchess of Devonshire, believing that her patronage and support would be invaluable. And so it proved: the duchess was intrigued by the tale of a poor young girl imprisoned yet refusing to leave her husband's side, and issued an invitation for Mary to pay her a visit at Devonshire House. It was to be the first of many visits for the eighteen-year-old Mary. As ever, she described her initial visit in terms of what she wore to meet the duchess ('a plain brown satin gown').

Another six months elapsed before Mr Robinson was able to reorganise his finances and secure the family's release from prison, after taking out fresh loans and incurring additional debt. Mary took to her freedom with a new determination to enjoy life to the full, immersing herself in outings to Vauxhall, and receiving visits from all her old friends and acquaintances. Among the glitterati to call on her 'at home' in the Robinson apartment in Newman Street was the playwright and theatre owner Richard Sheridan. His visit was unexpected and she greeted him with an appearance which she described as 'carelessly *deshabille*'. She never let on whether she succumbed to the playwright's charms (he was a notorious adulterer and friend of the Prince of Wales). The upshot of their meetings was that she was encouraged to resume her ambition to act on the London stage, despite the fact that she was by then pregnant once more, and would later give birth to a baby girl called Sophia.

Garrick had retired from the stage but agreed to come back in order to coach Mary for her debut role as Juliet in Shakespeare's *Romeo and Juliet*. The play opened in December 1776 and was a resounding success for Mary. For the opening night she wore a dress of 'pale pink satin, trimmed with crape, richly spangled with silver,' set off with a headdress of white feathers. For the final scene she changed into a plain white satin gown with a veil of transparent gauze hanging down to her feet – a simple image of purity and innocence. The crowd adored her, and soon different performances gave her the opportunity to sport different styles ('My dress was white and blue, made after the Persian style; and though it was singular on the stage, I wore neither a hoop nor powder.') There followed more than a dozen appearances in different parts, and before long her fame developed and with it the attention, flattery and attempts at seduction from a host of well-heeled admirers.

If Mary is to be believed, all such entreaties were dismissed out of hand. But if we are to accept the 'unauthorised' *Memoirs*, published in 1784, she named her price, and generally got it, establishing herself as one of the major figures on the sex-for-sale scene. Later, she chose to portray herself as a complete innocent-at-large, writing: 'I had been then seen, and known, at all public places from the age of fifteen; yet I knew as little of the world's deceptions, as though I had been educated in the deserts of Siberia.'

Mary's stage career had to be suspended when her pregnancy became advanced, but not before she was given a benefit night as well as 'a handsome salary'. Sadly, the newborn baby died of convulsions at the age of six weeks and Mary retreated to Bristol to recover her spirits.

When she returned to the London stage it was to perform the whole repertoire of parts for leading ladies: from Lady Macbeth to Ophelia in *Hamlet*; from Cordelia in *King Lear* to Imogen in *Cymbeline*; from Juliet in *Romeo and Juliet*, to Perdita in *The Winter's Tale*. Fame brought endless temptations ('It was now that I began to know the perils attendant on a dramatic life. It was at this period that the most alluring temptations were held out to alienate me from the paths of domestic quiet.')

The Duke of Rutland offered her £600 a year to become his mistress, but if Mary is to be believed, she declined, even though her husband was by then supporting not one but two mistresses in a house in Covent Garden, and was eating through her earnings faster than Mary could appear on stage. To her embarrassment, George Brereton (married to his cousin, the daughter of the Master of Ceremonies at the Upper Assembly Rooms in Bath) tried to blackmail Mary into having an affair with him. He used as his bargaining tool a promissory note signed by Mr Robinson and threatened to call in the debt unless Mary submitted to his demands. It was a pattern of behaviour often used by Brereton, an infamous duellist who thought nothing of murdering a husband if he was ever called out for his adultery. Mary assured the readers in her official memoirs that she outwitted the creepy Brereton. Maybe she just had other fish to fry – her home in the vicinity of Drury Lane Theatre was besieged by admirers. Sheridan himself was continually popping round to offer advice and support, and possibly rather more besides. The young Sir John Lade was a constant visitor, and the politician Charles Fox, and the Earl of Derby, laid siege to her in the green room at the theatre. As she also asserted, she was 'addressed with proposals of a libertine nature by a royal duke, a lofty marquis and a city merchant of considerable fortune.'

Whereas Mary claimed to have maintained her fidelity throughout this time, she also stated that she had acquired 'horses, a phaeton and ponies,' and that her fashion in dress was followed with flattering avidity. ('My house was thronged with visitors, and my morning levees were crowded so that I could scarcely find a quiet hour to study'). She was the centre of attention – and she loved it.

It was generally rumoured that by the autumn of 1789 Mary was having an affair with Sir John Lade, then aged twenty-one and only recently having moved on from gambling away a huge inheritance from a young heiress. He was an extraordinary character – a brilliant horseman, a ferociously fast rider and an inveterate gambler, but hardly a man who would provide Mary with more than a brief period of excitement. Others suspected that her somewhat unconvincing description of the playwright Richard Sheridan as a devoted and conscientious friend simply masked the fact that she was also his lover, while others were already pairing her off with the libidinous Charles Fox.

The stage was set for what was the most auspicious performance of her life – appearing in front of the royal family in an adaptation of Shakespeare's *The Winter's Tale*, playing the part of the female heroine, Perdita. The play told the story of two young lovers, Perdita and the handsome prince called Florizel, who face parental opposition but who ultimately marry and live happily ever after. The date of the Royal Performance was 3 December 1779. King George III and his wife, Queen Charlotte, were in the royal box, while the Prince of Wales, then approaching his eighteenth birthday, was in a box immediately alongside the stage. The prince's party of friends included George Capel-Coningsby (otherwise known as Lord Viscount Malden, and who was the same age as Mary). In her memoirs Mary describes in great detail how the prince fell under her spell that night, how he saw himself as Florizel and Mary as Perdita. Her version paints her as being totally innocent of any form of seduction; others point to the fact that she was constantly making suggestive overtures in the direction of the prince's box, leading one member of the audience to complain that she should have been delivering her lines to the prince on stage rather than to the prince in the auditorium.

Mary's memoirs imply that this was the first time that the pair had met, but the prince's own remarks in letters written at the time suggest that the couple may well have met on at least one previous occasion. Indeed, it is highly probable that this may have been at one of the balls at the Pantheon, or on social occasions at Vauxhall or Ranelagh. Be that as it may, the prince fell head over heels in love (or, at least, lust). Mary describes how Lord Malden was sent round to see her the very next day and how he delivered passionate love letters from the prince. What she does not do is describe how Lord Malden also fancied her something rotten, which must have put his lordship in a somewhat difficult position, trying to persuade the object of his desire to become the mistress of someone else.

Mary goes to great lengths to show how she resisted all the princely blandishments and entreaties, how the prince presented her with a miniature portrait set in a diamond surround, and with a small heart cut in paper bearing the words '*Je ne change qu'en mourant*', and on the other side 'Unalterable to my Perdita through life'. More recent analysis suggests that the love token was at that stage presented as a simple painting and that Mary was the one who subsequently had it mounted in a diamond-studded frame. As such, it features in many of the subsequent portraits of Mary, adding to her wish to be remembered thereafter as the woman who was treated so badly by the prince. What is clear is that Mary was all too well aware that an affair with the prince would mean the end of her career on the stage, would ruin her reputation beyond repair, and could seriously impact on her ability to provide a secure home for her infant daughter. Mary therefore refused to rush into bed – or at least, not with the prince.

The assignations between Lord Malden, representing the prince, and Mary went on and on, for perhaps as long as six months. The press could see for themselves that his lordship's carriage was parked outside the Robinson house at all hours. Rumours abounded that Lord Malden was Mary's lover. Hopping into bed with Mary at the same time as seeking to pimp her on behalf of his royal master was a scandalous and eminently newsworthy piece of gossip. Ironically, it may well have been the news of the double-dealing which ultimately led the prince to go cool on his affair with Mary – to the extent that it was over in rather less time than the negotiations to set it up in the first place.

The constant comings and goings to the Robinson home became a source of constant comment and speculation. Weeks went by, and still Mary refused to meet the prince, explaining via Lord Malden the enormous risk she would be taking. The prince responded by getting Lord Malden to deliver two copies of a contract signed personally by him, effective when he came of age at twenty-one, entitling Mary to a payment of £20,000 as a 'signing-on fee' (this equates to nearly £2 million nowadays). Mary reportedly counter-signed the bond, and the stage was set for the next act in this extraordinary piece of theatre.

The prince instructed his equerry, Captain Jack Willett Payne, to withdraw sufficient money from Coutts, the royal bankers, to cover the rent on a house at Cork Street in Soho. Equipped with furnishings bought from Christie's auction house, Mary moved in with her young daughter, with the prince picking up the tab for a maid, a cook and a footman. The prince, when he wasn't gambling or drinking with friends, would call round for dinner and stay the night with his new lover. He also gave Mary a magnificent new phaeton, painted bright yellow and with dark blue leather upholstery. It reportedly cost some 900 guineas. Pulled by four matching horses and accompanied by servants bedecked in blue and silver livery, Mary made an astonishing sight as she flaunted her new status around town. A phaeton such as this was the modern equivalent of a top-of-the-range sports car being driven with its roof down, in order to gain the attention of all the passers-by.

If Mary's own account is to be believed, the couple did not become lovers until June 1780, after she had separated from her husband. The press got wind of the extravagant gifts made to Mary and soon reports appeared in print. Here, in the *Morning Post* of 22 July 1780: 'The writer [i.e., the prince] has paid the highest compliments to the young lady in question, who could make a conquest in the heart of a young and illustrious personage, at the very moment when he is surrounded by all the beauties of the British Court, vying with each other to capture and ensnare him.'

A few months later another report – in the *Morning Herald* on 4 January 1781 – suggested that all was not plain sailing: 'A certain illustrious young personage is said to have promised that Mrs. R's *establishment* should immediately succeed his own; which, however, remaining still unsettled, though the former arrangement is made, has occasioned some severe reproaches on the part of the now suspicious Perdita.'

The same paper had this to say in its edition of 12 July 1781: 'Fortune has again smiled on Perdita; on Sunday she sported an entire new phaeton, drawn by four chestnut-coloured ponies, with a postillion and servant in blue and silver liveries. The lady dashed into town through Hyde Park turnpike at four o'clock, dressed in blue great coat prettily trimmed in silver; a plume of feathers graced her hat, which even Alexander the Great might have prided himself in.'

Pausing at this point, it is worth noting that in Mary's memoirs she lays much of the blame for having become the mistress of the Prince of Wales at the foot of her feckless husband. But there was another side to the story, one which suggests a far more calculating and promiscuous pattern of behaviour. In her version of events, Mary was abandoned by a husband who ran up enormous debts, especially by borrowing money from his Jewish friend John 'Jew' King. King's own version, published in a series of letters under the title of *Letters from Perdita to a certain Israelite*, points to a brazen whore who extorted money from him in order to fund her own extravagant lifestyle. In other words, she had sex with him in return for a line of credit being advanced to her husband, far beyond what he could possibly afford to repay, just so that she could carry on buying the latest fashions.

A similar 'alternative view' can be applied to the conduct of Mary's mother. By all accounts she pushed Mary into marriage with Mr Robinson, but is it not entirely possible that when she saw her daughter's marriage going the same way as her own she persuaded Mary that 'all men were all bad' and that she should get from them whatever she wanted? That interpretation suggests that Mary simply played hard to get in order to force the prince into promising a massive payment before she would agree to sleep with him. Mary's mother could well have been behind such a strategy, and clearly it worked.

Throughout the affair with the prince, Mary was still appearing on the London stage, but as the initial 'honeymoon period' wore off, the prince started to resent the time Mary spent rehearsing and learning her lines. He became increasingly more temperamental and impatient, and Mary went to see Richard Sheridan to advise him that she was intending to retire from the stage to concentrate on her new responsibilities as the mistress to the heir to the throne.

However, the wandering eye of the prince meant that he had turned his attentions to the courtesan Elizabeth Armistead, with the *Morning Herald* of 8 February 1781 reporting: 'Mrs. Arm.....d has certainly been gratified at last in an *amour* with a certain young personage; and now flatters herself that *her* charms will not be so soon unrivetted, as were those of the once exalted and enviable *Perdita.*'

It looks as though Mary and the prince had first separated in December 1780, but they continued with an on-off arrangement for several months until the terms of a financial separation were agreed upon in September 1781. Initially the prince simply tried to walk away from his bond, knowing full well that a contract entered into by a minor was legally unenforceable.

In desperation Mary let it be known that she was holding love letters from the prince, which would be extremely embarrassing to the royal family if they were made public. Was this blackmail? If so, it was borne out of desperation as Mary had run up bills for some £7,000. But while tradesmen and other creditors were happy to lend when they knew she was the prince's favourite, as soon as he turfed her out of her rented property, sold all the furniture and left her at the mercy of her creditors they were unwilling to wait for their money. She faced imprisonment, having totally 'burnt her boats' in the eyes of the public. She approached the prince, as well as appealing for help from both Charles Fox and Lord Malden. In return for his intercession with the king on her behalf, Fox was believed to have been rewarded in the time-honoured way by fallen women – in bed. It was a relationship that was to continue over several years until Fox found the love of his life – Elizabeth Armistead.

Lord Malden now felt able to be seen escorting Mary around town, but he paid the price for his duplicity in having pursued Mary for his own benefit (rather than for the benefit of the prince) and never again shared the close friendship of the heir to the throne. Mary may well have slept with Lord Maldon 'as a safe port in a storm' after her break from the prince. It certainly wasn't money that Mary expected from him, given that his lordship was unable to access funds from his family until late in 1781, which was when his grandmother died and he received an inheritance. At that stage he started paying Mary an annuity of £200 a year – small beer for a woman of her expensive tastes – and installed her in a rented property in Berkeley Square.

Speculation about the existence of highly embarrassing love letters was rife. Towards the end of 1780 a totally fabricated publication called *The Effusions of Love: Being the Amorous Correspondence between the Amiable Florizel and the Enchanting Perdita* appeared in print, followed in the next year by *The Budget of Love, or, Letters between Florizel and Perdita*. Both were works of fiction, but helped fuel a growing and prurient desire for semi-pornographic details about the royal family. Satirical pamphlets such as the *Poetical epistle from Florizel to Perdita: with Perdita's answer* hit the streets in 1781, and caricaturists started to draw scurrilous depictions of the two protagonists. One of the earliest, and most scathing about the shameless seduction of the foolish but 'innocent' prince, appeared in 1780 under the title of *Florizel and Perdita* ('to the tune of *O Polly is a sad slut*'). It depicts Thomas Robinson as a man who pimped his wife to the prince, but saves its scorn for Mary:

> Her cheeks were vermeil'd o'er with Red,
> Her breast enamell'd White.
> And nodding feathers deck'd her Head,
> A piece for Candle Light.
> Sometimes she'd play the Tragic Queen,
> Sometimes the Peasant poor,
> Sometimes she'd step behind the scene,
> And there she'd play the whore.

As far as the press were concerned, Mary had crossed the line between actress and prostitute. She was now fair game to all her detractors, and the truth was rarely regarded as being in any way necessary to the stories being told. The early 1780s saw the appearance of the Tête-à-Tête gossip column in the *Town and Country Magazine*. Mary Robinson was featured not once but twice, but it is not entirely clear whether the 1780 focus was on Lord Malden or Sir John Lade, or even a fictitious 'composite' lover. Mary is shown as 'The Dramatic Enchantress' and her partner as 'The Doating Lover'. A year later she was 'the Fair Ophelia' to the prince's 'Illustrious Heir' in the same magazine, and although many of the facts recounted are thinly disguised in syrupy language and not-so-subtle implications, the stories were sufficient to have identified the parties to anyone with an interest in the bon ton.

Mary's finances remained desperate and she wrote to George III via Charles Fox, summarising extracts from the love letters which she held. It worked – the king wrote a private letter to the Prime Minister Lord North, which starts with words: 'My eldest son got last year into a very improper connection with an actress and woman of indifferent character ... a multitude of letters passed, which she has threatened to publish unless he, in short, bought them from her ... £5,000 is an enormous sum but I wish to get my son out of this shameful scrape.'

The sum of £5,000 was agreed sometime in September along with an 'understanding' that when the prince reached the age of twenty-one he would give further consideration to the question of an annuity. In practice this eventually ended up as an agreement to make an annual payment of £500 (half of which was to continue to be payable to Mary's daughter in the event of Mary's death). The prince was often remiss in making the payment and needed to be reminded of his obligations.

For the royal family it was an extremely good bargain, commuting the bond of £20,000 for a lump sum of exactly a quarter of the amount claimed by Mary. Her precarious financial position obviously gave her no room to negotiate. When the prince finished with Mary it left her in considerable financial hardship, especially as she had quickly become accustomed to the trappings of success. She had debts of £7,000, and she had an expensive phaeton and horses to support. There were some rumours that she supplemented her income at Mrs Windsor's brothel in Kings' Place.

There are also stories that she went back on the stage for a while, but reports are complicated by the fact that there were several actresses by the name of Mary Robinson on the London stage. This could explain why one audience member remarked in a letter to the *Morning Herald* on 31 March 1783: 'The Perdita is so much improved within these last two years, that she scarcely retains a resemblance of her former self; chiefly owing to her appearing more *en bon point* than she formerly did.' Obviously, *this* Mary Robinson may not have grown a bigger bust; it was most likely to have been her namesake, and it is generally assumed that she departed the stage by the end of 1780 rather than by a much later date of 15 May 1783.

Mary followed up the conclusion of negotiations by making the first of her various trips across the Channel to Paris. It was rumoured that her main rival for the attentions of the Prince of Wales was at that stage the courtesan Grace Dalrymple Elliot, with *The Morning Herald* of 21 October 1781 reporting: 'A Correspondent says that *Dally the Tall* gave a superb fete last night at her house near Tyburn Turnpike, in consequence of the Perdita's departure for the continent, whose superior charms have long been the daily subject of Dally's envy and abuse.'

Following the conclusion of the financial arrangements with the Prince of Wales, Mary Robinson left for Paris in October 1781. Any idea that she was licking her wounds in private disappeared as she threw herself into a round of parties. Her notoriety made her a popular figure with French society and she was immediately pursued both by the Duc de Chartres and the Duc de Lauzun. She was honoured at the opera house and fêtes and balls were arranged in her honour. She was given the name of *La Belle Anglaise* and cut a swathe through fashionable soirées.

Then came her moment of triumph. She was invited to Versailles to meet the queen, Marie Antoinette. Such an invitation naturally necessitated a visit to a Parisian salon to choose a suitable outfit to wear. And not just any salon, but that of the leading *modiste* of the day, the royal milliner/costumier Rose Bartin. She came up with a suitably magnificent little number, a 'pale green lustring train and body, with a tiffany petticoat, festooned with bunches of the most delicate lilac … with a plume of white feathers adorning her head.' How Mary must have loved being attended to by Mademoiselle Bartin, who was famous for conducting 'interviews' with clients while enthroned on a dais in the middle of the room, from where she could direct her underlings as they brought forward fabrics for consideration and styles for approval.

News reached England that Mary would return in the New Year and the *Morning Herald* breathlessly announced on 7 December 1781 that she would bring with her fashions which 'were certain to set the world a-madding'. On 9 January 1782 the same paper was able to report: 'Last night the divine Perdita visited the opera, for the first time since her return from Paris. She was dressed in white satin, with purple breast-bows, and looked supremely beautiful. Her headdress was in a stile that may be called the standard of taste; her cap, composed of white and purple feathers entwined with flowers, was fastened on with diamond pins.'

On another occasion the *Morning Herald* raved about Perdita's pale green dress and her hair braided with 'wheat ears' of silver and gold wire. No matter that Mary had been cast aside by her royal lover; she was news, in a big way. In January 1783 her involvement in a procession of carriages *en route* to St James's Palace to celebrate the queen's birthday caused such large throngs of onlookers that she was forced to turn her carriage round and head home. Her transport arrangements were a constant source of interest. In mid-1783 she acquired a new vis-à-vis, just in time to mark the birthday of the king on 4 June. No understated little number this, it was enthusiastically described in the press:

In the centre of the door panel, on a mantle of pink and silver, lined with ermine, her cypher is painted … The sun appears rising on one side; a coronet of flowers is placed over the cypher, and at the foot a lion couchant … The lining is of rich straw-coloured silk, the fringe and lace of which is pink and silver. The wheels and carriage are pale yellow and silver with silver springs. The harness furniture is ornamented with silver buckles, joints, etc. The hammer cloth is so superb, that it alone amounts to *one hundred pounds*; and the vis-à-vis, including every expense, upwards of *nine hundred guineas*!

Another sensation was caused when Mary decided to do up her box at the opera 'in the French style'. Her trip to Paris inspired her to bedeck her box with pink satin upholstery, and mirrors everywhere. Mirrors gave Mary the chance to see what was going on around her, and also gave the audience – and those on the stage – the chance to see more of her. The actress no longer needed to be on the stage to be part of the performance and could play her part as the 'celebrity in residence' just by turning up and occupying her box.

Not only were there countless scurrilous reports of Mary's sexual conquests (she was described as being 'the Harlot of the Day') but there were endless descriptions of the fashions she wore, wherever and whenever she appeared in public. *The Lady's Magazine* ran a regular update on fashion news and under the heading of 'Fashionable Dresses for May 1783', by a 'Lady of Fashion', it informed its readers: 'Riding habits much worn in the morning; the most fashionable are the *Perdita's* pearl colour, with jonquil yellow facings, and the dark brown with a scarlet waistcoat: plain black or white riding hats, with a large panache of feathers. Hoops almost totally abolished, large tiffany double handkerchiefs, close pinned under the chin, the front of the stay crossed with coloured ribband, large *bouquette* universally worn.'

The December edition went on to describe: 'The *Robinson* hat, white crepe, transparent, bound at the edge with black velvet, and a band of black velvet plain round the crown, edged with a broad flounce of crape in small plaits, and fastened in the front with a diamond buckle.'

Elsewhere readers were informed:

The *Robinson hat* for Ranelagh, white chip, very large, trimmed with a wreath of white roses, and a panache of white feathers on the left side, worn with a hood under the chip, muslin gowns and cloaks, trimmed with *Brussels* lace, likewise introduced at Ranelagh by *Mrs Robinson*. The *Perdita*, a cap of straw; intermixed with ribband; and fastened on with large brilliant pins; a rose of ribband on the left side, with a diamond button and hoop. The *Perdita* handkerchief is elegant but will only suit a fine form. It is composed of three rows of white Italian tiffany laid in small plaits in the manner of a Queen Elizabeth ruff. This part of dress depends entirely upon the wearer.

Readers were told: 'White powder, and little rouge universally worn, the hair very large, and the chignon low behind. Black slippers, and roses, very low heels (unless the wearer is diminutive). Black cloaks trimmed with narrow edging; and white dimity or muslin levettes the fashionable morning dress.'

Then there was a cataract muff named after Mary (falling like a cascading waterfall down below the lady's lap) and when Mary wore gold stockings, embroidered with elaborate clocks (i.e., decorated motifs at the heels), these suddenly became all the rage. But there was one item of dress which became permanently associated with Mary, and it was something that changed the face of fashion: the Perdita chemise. Up until then daytime fashion called for hoops and petticoats to be worn. Mary created a sensation by wearing what the *Ladies Magazine* described as: 'a long dress made of fine muslin, and trimmed with lace, the body to fit close to the waist, in the form of a polonaise; the sleeve long and tight to the arm; a broad cape like a great-coat; a sash of fine muslin trimmed at each end with a broad lace; the front of the dress tied from the bosom to the feet with knots of coloured ribband – without any hoop.'

This really was a game-changer. Female fashions had become almost farcical, with exaggerated cork rumps, or side paniers stretched around elaborate hoops. Dresses – especially court dresses – were made of heavy brocades and had fastenings which required an army of dressers to position, to tighten and to adjust. And then Mary came along, with her light muslins, worn close to the body, showing the natural lines of the wearer. They were easy to put on and easy to take off, and the dress quickly became popular and evolved into the simple Empire line of the

Regency period. Of course, Mary Robinson cannot take all the credit – the outfit was generally known as the *chemise a la reine* in honour of Marie Antoinette, who was painted by Louise-Élizabeth Vigée Le Brun in 1783 wearing just such a costume. The painting is shown in plate 16 and a different version of the chemise is shown in plate 15.

The dress was also described as being the hallmark of the Duchess of Devonshire – which is ironic because initially the duchess thought that the dress was too immodest to be seen in public. But the fact that it was a fashion made popular by the French queen helped overcome her hesitation. The dress became associated with both Perdita and the duchess, which simply goes to show that as fashion icons they were regarded as equals. What they wore at the start of the season was bound to be copied by everyone else by the end of that season.

On 15 October 1782, the *Morning Herald* reported: 'An *amateur* of the Cyprian Corps recommends to our fair countrywomen a total abolition of the *large hoop* and *long petticoat*, and to adopt the *PERDITA*, a system of elegant *simplicity* and *neatness*, which has ever so conspicuously marked the dress of that celebrated *leader* of the *wantons* of the age!' The same newspaper had this to say a month later about the impact that the new style of dress was having: 'The *Chemise de la Reine*, in which Mrs Robinson appeared at the Opera, is expected to become a favourite *undress* among the fashionable women.'

Not everyone approved of a garment that was often transparent and which could reveal much of the female form, with the *Morning Chronicle* reporting: 'The queen's Chemise is the most unbecoming dress that was ever projected among the vagaries of fashion, except for those whom nature has distinguished with a slim and elegant form.'

Many ladies of rank, regardless of whether they had a slim or elegant form, were horrified at the idea of being seen in public in a garment associated so directly with a whore. Nevertheless, the fashion soon caught on, and for fifty years this meant that women enjoyed a freedom of movement and a lightness of dress that was to last until Victorian modesty trussed women up tightly and put them back into hoops and whalebones. For women in the second half of the Georgian era, the new fashion echoed the call for freedom which resonated in revolutions and popular movements for change. It was a dress entirely suited to its time, and Mary Robinson was its most famous protagonist. *Liberté, égalité, fraternité* became the battle cry of revolution – and here was a style of dress that symbolised freedom, was appropriate to all classes, and which came to represent an early version of the feminist movement.

So preoccupied had the press become with news of the minutiae of what Mary said, did and wore that one letter to the *Morning Herald* signed 'Lover of Virtue' complained that whole columns of the paper were 'filled with Mrs Robinson's green carriage. It is of little consequence to the public whether [she] drives four ponies or two coach-horses; whether she paints her neck or her cheeks; whether she sports a phaeton or rides in a dung-cart; whether she is accompanied by a peer or a pimp.'

But if restraint was called for, the press and the reading public were having none of it. Indeed, when the Duchess of Devonshire withdrew from the public gaze during her pregnancy and Mary was out of the country, it was reported that the ladies of the ton had no idea what to wear. Mary really had become someone who was looked up to, revered for her good taste, and given the sort of adulation we would recognise from the treatment of Princess Diana some 200 years later.

The affair between Mary and the prince was long since over but the pairing continued to dominate the public imagination. In 1783, two years after the end of the affair, the caricature of Florizel and Perdita shown in plate 23 appeared. There are two versions, both of them showing the lovers as two plate halves of a single whole, but one with Perdita modestly dressed. The other shows her bare-breasted, pointing out what was seen as rather shocking – the fact that the prince was sharing the breast of a whore. The caricature is a blatant piece of political propaganda, suggesting that although the affair was over the susceptibility of the prince to the charms of a brazen courtesan showed that he was unfit to succeed to the throne – he was tainted by the affair for ever. On the left side of the picture King George III laments 'My son, my son,' while on the other side Mary's husband, Thomas, appears as 'King of Cuckolds' (marked by the pair of horns) supporting a platter which balances the heads of Banastre Tarleton, Charles James Fox and Lord Malden. These three 'alternative Heads of State' – all prominent Whigs – are shown as having been led astray by the insatiable desires of a wanton whore. They are unfit to be seen as rulers of men.

The year 1783 saw a slew of ribald publications, from *Vis-à-vis of Berkeley Square* (described at the time as 'a disgusting attempt at impudence to counterfeit ingenuity') to the *Amours of Florizel, or the Adventures of a Royal Red Cap* and the *Effusions of Love* ('Never have we seen anything more despicable than these two productions, in which the most daring impudence vies with the most abject stupidity'). These semi-pornographic works, which all stressed Mary's role as a whore entrapping men by purveying sex and leading the good astray, may never have been best sellers – at one shilling and sixpence each they were not cheap – but they reflect the prevailing appetite for salacious gossip, linked with an anti-adultery mood in the public at large. Above all, they stress that Mary was not simply an adulteress, she was selling sex in the same way as a common whore. At the time, the word 'whore' was used to cover both categories of women. Mary may not have charged men in cash, but she was paid in carriages, in diamonds, in buckles and baubles. She was portrayed as greedy, vain, conceited, and obsessed with fashion. Her husband was that most despicable of men, someone who acted as procurer and lived off his wife's licentious behaviour. In at least one of the stories the reason given for the prince ending the affair was that Mary gave him a dose of the pox, and in another the 'blameless' young man broke off the relationship the moment he learned that Mary was married. Both stories may have been complete fabrication, but they offer an interesting reflection on eighteenth-century hypocrisy.

Throughout the early months when she returned from Paris, Mary was the mistress of Lord Malden. He may have been her protector and placed her in high keeping, but he also was hard work, and Mary wanted a companion who was altogether more dashing and romantic. No matter that Lord Malden provided her with a carriage which the *Rambler* of April 1784 described as being: 'the admiration of all charioteering circles of St James's – the body was a Carmelite and silver, ornamented with a French mantle, her cypher in a wreath of flowers, the seat cloths crimson, richly ornamented with a silver fringe. Her livery was green, faced with yellow, and richly trimmed with broad silver lace; the harness richly chased and elegantly finished, the inside lined with white silk embellished with scarlet trimmings.'

According to one version of events, sometime in January 1782 Malden introduced his friend Colonel Banastre Tarleton to Mary after a visit to the theatre. The colonel was on half-pay, which meant that he was living on a pension of just £173 per annum. He had served in America where he gained a fearsome reputation during the American War of Independence. An early advocate of what we would now call 'total war', Tarleton was known by the colonists as 'Butcher Ban'. To him, attack was not just the best form of defence, it was the *only* form of defence, and the implication is that he was as energetic in pursuing his love life as he was in pursuing his enemies on the battlefield. Horace Walpole apparently remarked that Tarleton boasted that he had butchered more men and lain with more women than anyone else in the army – a remark which prompted Richard Sheridan to suggest that 'lain with' was too weak an expression: 'he should have said ravished. Rapes are the relaxations of murderers.'

In practice it is likely that Tarleton met Mary, quite by chance, while each of them was visiting the Leicester Fields studio of Joshua Reynolds. The painter's records show that both sitters attended his studio at the end of January 1782 on no fewer than three occasions, on nearly consecutive days.

Tarleton was darkly handsome, a lively conversationalist and an assiduous flirt. One story has it that at Brooks Club, Lord Malden described how faithful Mary was, whereupon Tarleton bet him a thousand guineas that he could seduce the girl. Malden accepted, at which point Tarleton whisked Mary off to a small village outside Epsom for an entire fortnight of love making, returning only to demand his winnings from a humiliated and infuriated Lord Malden. The story in the press suggested that Mary woke up to find Tarleton gone from her bed, and was quite unable to pay the publican for the room in which she had been staying for the past two weeks. She turned to the only person she could ask for help, Lord Cholmondeley, who was happy to oblige with funds, but did so in exchange 'for bedroom duties' throughout the following three weeks. Malden never again helped Mary financially, but was still part of the circle in which she moved. One story has it that she was on her way to plead with Lord Malden for financial assistance when her phaeton overturned, trapping her under the carriage for more than an hour, and that she had to be rescued by Tarleton.

The press loved the tales of Mary's sexual appetite, with scurrilous stories appearing in the likes of *The Rambler* suggesting that on one occasion she fell asleep in the garden, allowing ants to penetrate her undergarments. Who should be on hand to assist her in her hour of need other than a lusty eighteen-year-old gardener, who was able to distract her from her discomfort. Another publication entitled *A sketch of the life of the celebrated Mrs R...* appeared in 1782 in the *European Magazine*. It described her with the words, 'No woman that ever moved in the Cytherean circle, or wantoned in the pleasures of *bon ton* has been more eminent for variety of amours or vicissitudes of fortune, than our heroine.'

A more sympathetic comment – possibly penned by Mary herself – appeared in *The Morning Post* on 29 August 1782 in an anonymous piece described as 'A Hasty Sketch of Perdita by a Gentleman over Head and Ears in Love': 'Formed by the hand of nature for almost every opposite pursuit to that in which the whirl of life has engaged her, Perdita but half enjoys her present situation ... her love is the child of nature.'

Mary had moved in with Tarleton, giving the press a field day. The satirist James Gillray produced a print entitled *The Thunderer*, published in August 1782. It shows Mary as a whirligig – a type of spinning toy – above a public house, legs apart and with a speech bubble asking the question, 'Who'd not love a Soldier?' The pub sign has the words: 'THE WHIRLIGIG – Alamode Beef, hot every Night,' and suggests that Tarleton had stolen Mary from under the nose of the prince. A month later *The Morning Post* of 21 September 1782 gleefully reported:

> Yesterday, a messenger arrived in town, with the very interesting and pleasing intelligence of the Tarleton, armed ship, having, after a chace of some months, captured the Perdita frigate, and brought her safe into Egham port. The Perdita is a prodigious fine clean bottomed vessel, and had taken many prizes during her cruize, particularly the Florizel, a most valuable ship belonging to the Crown, but which was immediately released, after taking out the cargo. The Perdita was captured some time ago by the Fox, but was, afterwards, retaken by the Malden, and had a sumptuous suit of new rigging, when she fell in with the Tarleton. Her manoeuvering to escape was admirable; but the Tarleton, fully determined to take her, or perish, would not give up the chace; and at length, coming alongside the Perdita, fully determined to board her, sword in hand, she instantly surrendered at discretion.

Tarleton was living way beyond his means and on 24 July 1783 left Mary a letter saying that he was being forced to flee to France to escape his creditors. What he did not know was that Mary was carrying his child. She managed to raise promises of funding to clear her lover's debts and set off for Dover, intending to join Tarleton in France, but suffered a miscarriage on the way. It is thought that Mary caught rheumatic fever, leaving her in severe pain and confined to bed for many months. She became paralysed in her legs, something from which she never fully recovered. In later years she was unable to walk without crutches, and had to be lifted in and out of her carriage by servants. At the time it meant a long period of convalescence, but when she was able to return to London, Tarleton followed her and persuaded her to travel to France where each would be able to pursue their literary ambitions – the colonel to write up his *The History of the American Campaigns* and Mary her latest venture into poetry, plays and novels. It seems likely that much of Tarleton's campaign history was actually penned by Mary, but the publishers refused point- blank any suggestion that she should be credited as co-author. The *History* was published in 1787 and was well received, but never a financial success.

The press were not quite sure what to make of Mary's decision to move to France, with the *Morning Post and Daily Advertiser* of Saturday, 25 September 1784 asserting: 'It is not true, that the Perdita is gone into a Convent of Nuns in France; she is indeed retired, but not amongst the female part of the religious; certain friars, it is said, have found her a very warm convert!'

The *Rambler's Magazine* of the same month was rather more accurate when it reported: 'Mrs Robinson has been lately obliged to leave England, for the continent, for the recovery of her health. She has almost lost the use of her limbs, and, upon her journey, was lifted in and out of her carriage. Her disorder is a rheumatic gout of so obstinate a nature that her recovery is doubtful.'

The same magazine wasted no opportunity to heap scorn on Mary. In the section marked 'Female politics of the month' for April 1784 it described Perdita's visit to Ranelagh with the words, 'She had once a pretty face; but she now trowels on the red and white to such a degree as to already have sore eyes in consequence. The passage goes on to say that it was:

rather curious to trace the number of proprietors that the Perdita estate has been under. It was originally pillaged from an extensive common by a petty-fogging attorney; then Lord Lyttleton (the last of that name, not his honoured father) ... then all the manure of Drury Lane was poured upon it, and the plough was scarcely ever out of the ground; a little tiny Viscount then took possession of it and by this time *the thing*, through this variety of cultivation, was so dressed and redressed, so ploughed, so sowed, so drained, so mowed that it was judged worthy of royal notice and covered with no less than a princely erection: but a fire breaking out, the place was abandoned and became a soldier's barrack; since which time it has been a very common place.

Nowadays it is hard to imagine that a newspaper would talk about a woman's affairs in such a way, let alone suggest that she had caught a venereal disease ('the fire breaking out'), but the publishers knew that there was no way that Mary could issue libel proceedings. Defamation has always involved the need to prove damage to reputation, and by this time Mary had no reputation left to damage.

Even as late as March 1784 prints were being produced showing Mary and the prince as an item, as in *The goats canter to Windsor or the cuckold's comfort*, shown in plate 2. The prince and Perdita ride in a gig towards Windsor, with Fox acting as postillion. In the foreground the cuckolded Mr Robinson, riding backwards on a goat, leads two other goats being ridden by Lord North and Colonel Tarleton. It is a comment on the folly of all the people depicted: they may think that they are heading for power (Windsor) but all of them are unfit to be participants in government because they are preoccupied with what lies beneath Perdita's skirts.

The four years that Mary spent with Tarleton in Europe appear to have been happy and productive, with some time being spent at the spa town of Aix la Chapelle 'taking the waters,' or more particularly, taking hot mud baths in the town of St Amand les Eaux near the Franco-Belgian border, in an attempt to alleviate Mary's rheumatic pains. Mary and Tarleton returned to Britain in 1788, settling in Clarges Street, Mayfair. In time, Tarleton was made up to a full colonel and in 1790 was elected Member of Parliament for Liverpool, an unpaid position he held for twenty-one years. Mary's relationship with the dashing colonel became increasingly fraught, especially in the light of opposition from the colonel's family.

On the left, the hooped skirt of 1742 gives the female figure a totally different silhouette contrasted with the narrow, high-waisted gown of 1794. Note the high heels of 1742 and the flat heels of 1794.

Trade Card for Samuel Mann, who made hats, gloves, waistcoats, breeches and hosiery.

Plate 17

'Love' – painted by a vicar!

'Modish' and 'Prudent' by Thomas Rowlandson.

Plate 18

Women's fashions in 1752.

Plate 19

Women's fashions in 1797.

Plate 20

Fanny Murray.

Kitty Fisher.

Plate 21

Portraits of Nancy Parsons.

Plate 22

Mary Robinson as 'Melania'.

FLORIZEL AND PERDITA

Mary Robinson as 'Perdita' combined with the Prince of Wales as 'Florizel'. It was considered a shocking image because it shows the bare-breasted actress joined up to the future king. A more modest version, fully clothed, was also available.

Plate 23

Mary Robinson by George Romney (above)
and Richard Cosway (below).

Plate 24

Three of the most famous courtesans of the day: Mary Robinson as 'Perdita', Grace Elliott (known as 'Dally the Tall') and Gertrude Mahon (known as 'The Bird of Paradise').

Thalia

Malagrida

Publish'd as the Act directs by T. WALKER Nº. 79 Dame Street 1777.

Francis Abington as 'Thalia' and Lord Shelbourne as 'Malagrida' in the scandal-mongering Tête-à-tête section of the *Town & Country Magazine*.

Plate 25

Frances Abington as 'Miss Prue' in William Congreve's 'Love for Love', 1771.

Plate 26

Elizabeth Armistead ('Mrs Charles James Fox') by Joshua Reynolds.

Plate 27

A courtesan at her window.

Plate 28

'*The Political Wedding*' showing the marriage between the Duke of Grafton and Elizabeth Wrottesley in 1769, with Nancy Parsons, left, looking away in tears.

'A Genteel Milliner' – 'milliner' was often a euphemism for a prostitute.

Plate 29

Kitty Fisher's image printed as a watch paper, to be inserted between the outer and inner cases of a gentleman's watch.

Gertrude Mahon.

Plate 30

Frances Abington as Lady Modish.

Elizabeth Armistead and Sir Richard Smith in the Tête-à-tête section of the *Town & Country Magazine*.

Plate 31

Mary Robinson in an engraving by William Birch after Sir Joshua Reynolds.

Plate 32

Mary wrote him adoring poetry, while he kept a mistress and continued with his life as a rake and libertine. He was an inveterate gambler and was constantly facing financial ruin.

It is likely that Mary wrote many of his parliamentary speeches, although the differences between the two people, particularly over slavery, must have caused much friction. Mary was an abolitionist, keen to promote the rights of the individual – all individuals – whereas Tarleton represented a slave-trading city in Parliament. His supporters were the wealthy merchants and land-owners who owed their success to plantations built on slavery, and to the profits made from the trade in human beings.

Finally, Tarleton decided to drop Mary without explanation or ceremony. She is alleged to have opened that day's *The Times* and read the announcement that her lover was engaged to be married to the illegitimate daughter of the Duke of Ancaster, a wealthy heiress called Susan Bertie.

Mary was heart-broken and wrote a novel in which virtuous women were ruined by deceiving men who 'were only after one thing'. The resulting book, *The False Friend*, was a critical success. Half a dozen historical novels followed and for Mary it must have been frustrating because sales were never translated into financial success. In one case she ordered a reprint of her book only to find that demand evaporated, leaving her with printing costs that wiped out the profits on the first print run. On another, she lost money when her publisher, John Bell, was declared bankrupt. Mary also wrote a play, entitled *Nobody*, and it was performed on three nights at Drury Lane in November 1794. It bombed – largely because it satirised the wealthy ladies who spent their time at the gaming tables. Many of them played a notorious game called faro and were involved in running crooked card tables which led to the financial ruin of many innocents. These gambling ladies were also the very people who normally supported the theatre. When they got wind of the fact that they were to be mocked in the new play, they simply sent their servants along to heckle, to protest and to shout down the entire performance: *Nobody* disappeared without trace.

Mary persevered with various books of poems and other publications, the most notable of which was *A Letter to the Women of England on the Injustice of Mental Subordination*. Published in 1799, it met with howls of protest from its male readership, which regarded it as outrageous that such views should be expressed by a woman. It was also far too radical for most women, although her views in many ways reflected those put forward by Mary Wollstonecraft. The two women were never great friends: Wollstonecraft suspected a partiality between her husband, William Godwin, and Mary Robinson, and for some months the two did not see each other, until Mary Wollstonecraft died in 1797, whereupon visits from Godwin were resumed. The two women had similar views about female education and women's rights, but it was unfortunate that both were easily dismissed by men as being 'scarlet women' who had led scandalous lives.

* * *

Mary Robinson, however hard she tried, never escaped from the soubriquet 'Perdita' – which was Latin for 'fallen' – and the name seemed to say all that there was needed to know about her. But it was not the only pseudonym she used when writing: others were Anne Frances Randall, Laura Maria, Tabitha Bramble and Mary Darby. Other names used to describe her were the 'English Sappho', 'la Belle Anglaise', 'the Dramatic Enchantress', and even 'the Madonna of the Eighteenth Century', and all were used at one time or another. No matter the name, however, she never stopped being judged as Perdita, the mistress, courtesan and whore.

Towards the end of her life Mary started her memoirs. They are somewhat light on dates, gloss over a huge number of facts and events, and are generally rather anodyne. Her words may have been influenced by the threat of legal proceedings – there was no way that the monarch was going to allow Mary to publish details of her affair with the heir to the throne, and certainly not to give details of any of the love letters which she had already been paid to destroy. You would not guess from the memoirs that here was a life lived in the spotlight by one of the most famous, beautiful and charismatic women of the Georgian era, someone who was right at the epicentre of Georgian political life.

The speed with which her glamorous life disintegrated must have amazed Mary's friends. Within a decade she moved from being one of the most beautiful and famous figures in the kingdom, someone who could quite literally stop traffic, to a crippled, pain-ridden figure who had to be lifted everywhere – in and out of her bed, in and out of her carriage. She appears to have been given laudanum, based on morphine, in increasing quantities. Nevertheless, she concentrated on her literary efforts. She became, in effect, the 'poet in residence' for the *Morning Post* (ironic, because that was the paper that had been most critical of her in earlier years).

Towards the end of her life (she died at the age of either forty-two or forty-three on Boxing Day, 1800) she may have moved on to a post-revolutionary, classless, style of dressing, but she never once forgot the importance of dress in advancing her cause. She did, however, write poems satirising the absurdity of high fashion, whether for men or women, no doubt seeking to distance herself from her former life. She may well have been instrumental in promoting a regular fashion column in *The Morning Post*, which ridiculed former styles and promoted the simple white muslin dress and sash.

By the age of forty Mary had outlived all of her family apart from her devoted daughter. Her father had died in December 1785 in Russia, where he had served in the Russian Navy, and was buried with full military honours. Five years later her elder brother, John, died in Italy, and her beloved mother died in 1793. When she herself died she was buried, as she had requested, in Old Windsor churchyard. Her daughter, Mary Elizabeth, died just eighteen years later and was interred in the same grave.

What then are we to make of Mary Robinson? If we look at her life from a twenty-first-century perspective her story was no different to many others involving 'the prince and the showgirl' (you only have to think of Koo Stark, who was romantically involved with Prince Andrew). In practice, Mary was part of the romantic life of the Prince of Wales for hardly more than six months, but her role as Perdita, the fallen one, stayed with her throughout her life. By modern standards she was not particularly promiscuous – she may have had a score or more lovers in her wayward youth – and when she met Tarleton she appears to have fallen deeply in love with him and was shattered when he ended their affair after sixteen years.

Was she a whore, i.e., selling her body for money? Certainly not in the sense of having sex with strangers in return for cash. Her partners were invariably successful men from her circle of associates. Yes, she received rewards from these men, either in money or in terms of extravagant gifts, but she was nothing like as voracious in her sexual appetites as her detractors suggested. She used men in equal measure to the way men used her. If men got what they wanted – her body – she made sure that in return she got what she wanted, and her choice was always with players in the First Division, never from the second tier. Whether as friends or lovers, she always associated herself with the movers and shakers: in the political world with people such as the Prince of Wales and Charles James Fox; and from the world of the arts with Richard Sheridan, William Wordsworth and Samuel Taylor Coleridge. And when she fell deeply in love she didn't choose any ordinary man, she chose a brilliant military leader. But like all the other men in her life, Tarleton betrayed her friendship and left her on her own. If she sometimes seems to have wallowed in her own misfortune, it is worth remembering that for the vast majority of her adult life she was in considerable pain, suffering partial paralysis from the waist down. It is little wonder that her own memoirs seem to portray her life as some kind of Greek tragedy. She certainly paid a very high price for her youthful indiscretions.

As a poet, playwright and novelist she is largely overlooked. As a forerunner in the feminist movement she is not given the credit she is due. As a fashion queen she may have been as influential as Princess Diana 200 years later, but fashion is transient and her contribution has faded. Only as a courtesan, as the very first lover of the Prince of Wales, is she remembered. Whoever thought that fame was fair?

Chapter 12

Elizabeth Armistead

Elizabeth Armistead after John Smart.

Of all the courtesans of the eighteenth century, Elizabeth Armistead was perhaps *the* most remarkable: remarkable for the extent of her glittering clientele, remarkable for living to the age of ninety-one, and remarkable for finding true love with one of the most charismatic and rakish politicians of the period.

In July 1766 the *Town & Country Magazine* carried an article about Elizabeth, saying that she could 'claim the conquest of two ducal coronets, a marquis, four earls and a viscount.' In fact, here was a woman who seemed to be able to secure a small army of horizontal admirers: the Prince of Wales, the Duke of Ancaster, the Duke of Dorset, as well as the Earl of Derby and Frederick St John, 2nd Viscount Bolingbroke. She enjoyed trysts with Lord George Cavendish and the fabulously wealthy General Sir Richard Smith, while the Earl of Cholmondeley, Lord Robert Spencer and Lord Coleraine were also benefactors.

Yet this was also a woman who fell in love with one of her clients, a man who happened to be one of the most remarkable politicians of the age. She gave up her career to be with him, paid off his gambling debts, supported him, married him, and outlived him by thirty-six years. By the time she died she was considered a pillar of the community, a world away from the notorious harlot with a voracious appetite who had scandalised London half a century earlier.

Who then was Elizabeth Armistead? Remarkably little is known about her early years. She is believed to have been born in Greenwich on 11 July 1750 as Elizabeth Bridget Cane – or at least that was what the *Public Advertiser* and the *Town & Country* magazine advised their readers. Sources give her father's occupation as being that of a market porter, a herb-seller, a Methodist lay-preacher, or even a cobbler. Maybe all were correct – or none of them. There were rumours that she became a servant girl, or a maid waiting on Frances Abington (or maybe it was Mary Robinson) on the London stage, or that she was a hairdresser's model. Again, all or none of these occupations may be correct.

There is nothing to indicate who Mr Armistead was, or whether he ever married Miss Cane, or indeed whether he ever existed. His may simply have been a name selected by Elizabeth to avoid shame being brought to the family. Equally, there may have been a Mr Armistead who perhaps lured her away from a perfectly respectable upbringing with a promise of marriage, had his wicked way with her and abandoned her in circumstances where she could never resume life with her family. Indeed, there is much to suggest that she was a reasonably well-educated young woman. In her later years she was fond of reading translations of Latin poetry aloud to her husband. She introduced him to the delights of living in the country, of gardening and country walks. She taught herself to play the harp and took up sketching. She was an avid reader and a delightful conversationalist. She kept company with the great and the good – from the Duchess of Devonshire to the son of the reigning monarch – and it is hard to imagine that she would have been able to do this unless she was brought up in what would now be termed a middle-class household, and had been given a reasonable education.

In 1776 the Tête-à-Tête section of the *Town & Country* magazine suggested that the sixteen-year-old Elizabeth had first been led astray by a 'friseur' (i.e., hairdresser) who used her as his model and had taught her that 'the dressing of her hair would be a great ornament to her, and that she would certainly make her fortune if she displayed herself to advantage.' The article recounted that she happily repaid the friseur, identified only as Mr R..., by 'yielding to his amorous intreaties'. The same article suggested that the affair did not last the test of time: 'After some months enjoyment the ardour of his passion subsided, and he was desirous to get rid of our heroine; he accordingly equipped her very genteely, and took a lodging for Mrs A..st..d in the polite part of the town, where, he said, she could not fail to succeed.'

A somewhat different version of events appeared in the same magazine three years later, which suggested that the teenage Elizabeth was abandoned by her father when he decided to desert the household and become a travelling preacher. His daughter had no choice but to survive by 'selling her charms' and did so in one of the upmarket brothels which flourished in Kings' Place in St James's. However, the problem with all such journalistic accounts is that they are all-too-often contradictory, and it was an age in which journalists unhesitatingly invented the facts if they did not know them.

Her name had first appeared in July 1771 when Reynolds noted in his appointment diary that he was scheduled to see 'Mrs Armistead at Mrs Mitchell's, Upper John Street, Soho Square.' Elizabeth Mitchell was a notorious madam who was later known for running a high-class brothel in premises previously occupied by the bawd Charlotte Hayes, at 5 Kings' Place. Mrs Mitchell had a reputation for being able to introduce her male customers to girls who were well bred and well spoken. One of her 'girls' was the celebrated beauty Emily Coulthurst. There is no reason to believe that the young Elizabeth Armistead enjoyed an exclusive relationship with one particular bawd – she may have worked for a succession of brothel-owners. This did not necessarily involve 'living in' and more likely meant being called by a runner as and when she was asked for.

The *Town & Country* suggested that she worked for Jane Goadby, who had helped pioneer the higher-class type of bordello intended to mimic and rival the equivalent lavishly appointed emporiums in Paris. Jane Goadby was famous for training her girls in etiquette and grace, in seductive behaviour and refinement. She offered her clients the *crème de la crème* in female companionship, displayed in elegant and richly decorated rooms. The early portraits of Elizabeth Armistead suggest a well-endowed vivacious young woman, her hair beautifully arranged, who would have fitted in rather well in such an environment. What is not in doubt is that she was soon in high demand and by her late teens was earning a significant amount of money.

One of her early clients was Frederick St John, Second Viscount Bolingbroke. We know this because in 1771 the British Whig politician Charles James Fox described visiting a brothel in the company of a visitor from France. Hearing that Bolingbroke was being entertained in one of the rooms, Fox gleefully kicked open the door and was rewarded by the sight of his lordship enjoying the company of Elizabeth Armistead. It was a story given added irony by the fact that ten years later Fox fell head-over-heels in love with the very same woman.

Bolingbroke was a notorious rake, married to Lady Diana Spencer. Both of them had scandalized society with their affairs, and following his divorce from Lady Diana in 1768, Bolingbroke was associated with a succession of lovers. But Elizabeth was able to ensure that her charms gave her an element of security: she became his mistress, and was set up in 'high keeping'. This meant that she was an 'all expenses paid' lover, given a lifestyle of great luxury. It was to prove to be her big break, the step up towards super-stardom which would last for a whole decade. In those times, ten years at the top was quite extraordinary, indicating a staying power that spoke not only of a woman who was very good at her job, but also someone who was loyal, discreet and charming.

Bolingbroke used his connections to get his lover a job as an actress and she appeared at Covent Garden on 7 October 1774 in the role of Indiana in *The Conscious Lovers*. The programme billed her as 'a young lady never before on any stage' and she went on to play a number of roles including that of Perdita in *The Winter's Tale* and Miranda in *The Busy Body*. In time she moved on to perform on a couple of occasions at The Haymarket. In May 1777 she appeared in a play by theatre-manager George Coleman entitled *The English Merchant*. Clearly she was badly affected by stage fright, her performance being described in the *Morning Chronicle* with the words: 'She last night, at first coming-on, appeared to be much-embarrassed and frightened; the candour and applause of the audience, however, greatly dissipated her fears; and it is but truth to say, that she spoke the pathetic speeches with remarkable sensibility.' The stage, however, was never really her metier. Audiences appreciated her beauty and her magnificent figure, and her voice was good, but she was no actress and the write-ups in the press were generally lukewarm. Arguably, it was this experience of appearing on stage which taught Elizabeth about controlling her image, about inhabiting a role, and about being whoever she wanted to be. These were lessons she put to good use far beyond the confines of the theatre, although her affair with Bolingbroke soon fizzled out.

At a slightly later date she was reported to have 'entertained' George, the eldest son of Lord Bolingbroke. Married and with three children, he went on to become the Third Viscount Bolingbroke. He then appalled society by having an incestuous affair with his half-sister, fathering four children by her before deserting her and entering into a bigamous marriage to a member of the Belgian aristocracy. It does rather suggest a louche, amoral and somewhat close-knit circle of friends with whom Elizabeth Armistead associated.

Another lover was Robert Bertie, Fourth Duke of Ancaster. He was said to have set Elizabeth up as his mistress at a house in Portman Square but *Town & Country* suggested that this was not an exclusive arrangement and that she had a contemporaneous affair with a lieutenant in the army – amid rumours that she had a child by the soldier. That rumour was never substantiated. As for the duke, he caught scarlet fever and died in 1779 at the age of twenty-three and Elizabeth was left looking for a new protector.

Sometime in 1776 she had embarked on an affair with General Richard Smith, thereby showing that she was not averse to sleeping with a commoner – as long as he was obscenely rich. He was a wealthy nabob (in other words he had made his fortune while working in India). The son of a London cheesemonger, he had risen to the dizzy heights of Commander in Chief of the East India Company (Bengal). He appears to have bought his lover a house in London's Bond Street, and settled an annuity on her. For the general, she was the ultimate evidence of his success, a bauble he could exhibit.

The couple's luxurious lifestyle came to a sudden halt when Smith was thrown into prison for corruption, linked to his election to Parliament. Apparently, he had paid fifteen guineas a head to every one of the electorate at Hindon in Wiltshire, one of the most corrupt 'rotten boroughs' in the entire country. You have to admire his perseverance: apart from being sent to prison for six months he was fined heavily, but that didn't stop him standing for re-election. He not only won, but successfully contested two other parliamentary seats in the 1780s and 90s before retiring from politics. In his lifetime he managed to gamble away a huge fortune on horse racing, and also at cards. In particular, he lost heavily to none other than Charles James Fox, who seems to have been associated in one way or another with just about all of Mrs Armistead's paramours.

By now Elizabeth was at the peak of her financial pulling-power having acquired several London properties, including one in Mayfair's Clarges Street. Lord Robert Spencer, known as 'Comical Spencer', was another lover. Part of the Whig circle of friends and a regular companion of Fox at the gaming tables, Lord Robert was a Member of the Board of Trade from 1770 to 1781. He was a charming wastrel, a younger son of the Third Duke of Marlborough and he ended up having a lengthy affair with the beautiful socialite Harriet Bouverie, the wife of his friend and fellow-Foxite Edward Bouverie.

John Sackville, Third Duke of Dorset was for a time the lover of 'The Armistead' (the nickname given her by the press, as if she were a ship being regularly boarded by gentlemen). He was a prolific womaniser with countless affairs, to the extent that it was remarkable that he had time or energy for his main passions in life, namely gambling and cricket. He had an affair with Nancy Parsons, mentioned earlier, under the nose of her other lover, the prime minister of the day. There was also a lengthy fling with the principal ballerina at the King's Theatre, Haymarket. Somehow, he managed to find time to fit in Elizabeth Armistead, but apparently rather left her in the lurch when he abandoned her and went off and had an affair with the Countess of Derby, as well as another one with Lady Elizabeth Foster, mistress of the Fifth Duke of Devonshire. In the end he accepted an appointment to move to Berlin to take up a position as British ambassador to Prussia in 1784, and although he gave up his appointment before it had really started, it took him out of the amorous equation, so far as Elizabeth was concerned.

Elizabeth then shared her favours with Edward Smith-Stanley, Twelfth Earl of Derby. He was a prominent politician who ended up as Chancellor of the Duchy of Lancaster on two occasions, and who was stuck in an unhappy marriage to Lady Derby. As just mentioned, the countess was having a very public affair with the afore-mentioned John

Sackville, Third Duke of Dorset, and possibly to get back at them both, the earl made a very public display of affection for Elizabeth Armistead (a sort of 'You pinch my wife: I'll pinch your mistress'). In March 1779 the earl and Elizabeth Armistead were included in the Tête-à-tête series of profiles and caricatures in the *Town and Country Magazine*. In the article it was claimed that the earl had given her a generous allowance, paid for her to keep two very handsome saddle horses, and shared a house with her in Hampstead. As the magazine reported: 'They seem perfectly well pleased with each other, and his lordship has had so complete a surfeit of matrimony, that this probably may be a lasting alliance.'

The earl lavished money and gifts on her but soon Elizabeth moved on to pastures new. In time the earl's wife died, at the age of forty-four, and within a couple of months the newly widowed Lord Derby married the actress Elizabeth Farren. Just to complete the circle, Ms Farren was the actress who was admired and lusted after by Charles James Fox – or at least until he saw that she had a 'drooping posterior' when he saw her wearing trousers in a 'breeches part'. As mentioned in Chapter 11, a saggy bottom was not to be countenanced, and Fox made it clear, in a most ungallant way, that the admiration and lust had quite disappeared. We can assume from this that Mrs Armistead had a perfectly pert posterior, since Charles was apparently not averse to having her as his companion between the bed sheets, long before they actually fell in love.

For a while Elizabeth divided her favours between the Earl of Derby and Lord George Cavendish, the First Earl of Burlington. The latter was a Member of Parliament for many years, had extensive horse-racing interests, and ended up building Burlington Arcade. The Earl of Derby decided that he wanted her to himself and assumed full responsibility for maintaining her as his mistress. She accompanied him to Winchester when he was moved there as part of the force expecting to repel an imminent French invasion. Later, he set her up in a fine house in the quiet suburb of Hampstead Heath. She subsequently was reunited with Lord George, who then made a second, more substantial settlement on her. Presumably theirs was not an exclusive arrangement: on one occasion Lord George is said to have called on Elizabeth one evening unannounced, only to find the Prince of Wales hiding naked in a cupboard. It must have been an embarrassing encounter for all parties.

The prince had started an affair with Elizabeth when he tired of Mary Robinson. The *Town & Country Magazine* of March 1781 stated that the couple met after Elizabeth had more or less stalked the prince – to the playhouse, to the opera, to his hunting matches. The article continued: 'In a word she became so remarkable that [the Prince] made enquiry about her, and was informed by a trusty page, that she was among the number of come-at-ables.'

Having announced that she was 'a fine woman', and one with whom he would 'like a *tête-à-tête*' the prince sent his page to fix an appointment to meet Elizabeth 'at a certain inn in the neighbourhood of Bushy Park'. The same article went on to suggest that after the initial excitement of a new conquest, the prince found the charms of Mrs Armistead 'rather too antiquated' and made it apparent that he 'languished after youth and variety' and wanted newer, younger companions. Probably finding that the prince could not afford to look after her in the manner to which she had been accustomed, Elizabeth was happy to use her connections 'amongst the catalogue of demi reps ... who, if they could not pass for vestals, might at least, be considered new faces.' She accordingly retained the friendship of the prince, but happily vacated his bed in favour of 'Mrs M.lls, Mrs B.t.n, and Mrs B.y.n.' When the prince tired of those younger companions, he moved on to 'the C.x's ,the C.ith.gts, the Tyl.rs and the C.tle.ns'.

Elizabeth was still seen out and about in the company of the prince, which no doubt helped her retain a high profile. He valued her as a friend even if he could not afford her as a lover. The background to this was that the prince had recently set up his own household, paid for by his father the king, but his allowance was far too small to enable him to live the life of excess to which he quickly became addicted. For a woman in Elizabeth's position, if a man couldn't pay, the man didn't get.

The press were often somewhat out of date as to who was doing what to whom, and continued to suspect that there was a fierce rivalry between Mary Robinson and Elizabeth Armistead. Elizabeth was usually to be seen in her canary-yellow carriage, often outmanoeuvring her rival for column inches in the scandal sheets of the day. By March 1781 the *Morning Herald* was declaring that 'Notwithstanding all the interested assertions to the contrary, Mrs Armist..d is indisputably the reigning sultana of a certain royal paramour.'

In practice, Mary Robinson was pretty well ostracized by the prince, but he was happy to retain the friendship of Elizabeth and continued to move in the lively circle of Whig friends that they shared, including Charles James Fox and Lord Robert Spencer (brother to the Duke of Marlborough). As mentioned earlier, Elizabeth had had an affair with Lord Robert and this may explain why, at some stage in 1781, she acquired from the Duke of Marlborough's estate the lease of a small house with land at St Ann's, near Chertsey in Surrey. It was a property which she retained for the rest of her life. Meanwhile, she still had the premises at Clarges Street in central London, and these had become a frequent meeting place for the pro-Fox Whigs. It is unclear whether Elizabeth was particularly interested in politics, or whether she simply enjoyed the company of politicians; either way, she was a very public figure, very much associated with opposition to the government of the day. And once more she sat for Sir Joshua Reynolds – in time, he was to paint her portrait on at least four occasions.

Some saw her liaison with the prince as a reflection showing how low the Whig party would stoop in order to influence the heir to the throne. As the *Morning Herald* put it in its edition of 24 January 1781: 'There cannot be a stronger proof of the miserable shifts to which opposition are driven, than the reports they so industriously circulate, of a connection between that *High Priestess of Patriotism*, Mrs A.......d and a certain heir apparent.'

The prince was simply not in the same financial league as the rest of Elizabeth's paramours, and she was keen to be free to move on to other lovers, but in such a way as not to humiliate or embarrass him. Their affair had lasted perhaps six months, until the summer of 1781, and at that point Mrs Armistead left London for France, spending a further two months at Spa and two months in Italy. She did not go alone: she was escorted on the first leg of her European sojourn by her former lover the Earl of Derby, and thereafter by George James Cholmondeley, Fourth Earl of Cholmondeley, and also by John Hanger, second Baron Coleraine. The *Morning Herald* kept its readers fully updated as to her progress across Europe, suggesting that she was at Spa either for the sake of her health, 'which was much impaired by her patriotic exertions during the last Sessions of Parliament' (hint, hint, maybe she had the pox), or in an effort to improve her finances by making herself available to the wealthy visitors ('Spa is well known to contain at this time not only the warmest affections but the longest purses'). When she left for Geneva the same newspaper reported that 'The lords Cholmondeley and Coleraine, though not immediately in her suite, saw her no small part of the way, and mean to winter in the same city as this fascinating countrywoman.'

May 1782 saw her return to London and for a brief time she resumed her affair with the Prince of Wales. The *Morning Herald* could not conceal its delight at being able to inform its readers: 'The Armstead [sic] with very subordinate personal attractions, has contrived to out-jockey the whole stud of first rate impures, by the superiority of her understanding – for she has not only outstripped them in the race amorous for a certain Royal sweepstakes, but has contrived to touch the plate, which none of the others could do.'

Elizabeth was no more exclusive with her favours than the prince was with his. It seemed to herald a promiscuous merry-go-round where partners in a small group of friends changed alliances with bewildering speed. But Elizabeth soon detached herself from the dizzy whirl of what might be called aristocratic swingers and quickly found herself gravitating towards the enigmatic Charles James Fox, who had been made up to Foreign Secretary in the administration of Lord Rockingham. He, by then, had just started an affair with Mary Robinson and no doubt Elizabeth took great delight in poaching him from her rival. This time things were different: she was no longer a harlot being passed around within a network of Fox's Whig friends, she was growing increasingly devoted to Fox and Fox alone. The attraction and devotion was mutual – he fell deeply in love with her, as she did with him, and by the summer of 1783 they emerged as a devoted couple.

What did he see in her? Apart from her obvious physical charms she was witty, a good conversationalist and above all a good listener. What did he she see in him? Fox was an enigmatic character – a politician who became a thorn in the side of William Pitt the Younger, and was someone who was constantly arguing for a reduction in the powers of the monarch. He was accused of having republican sympathies and was opposed to British actions against the American colonists during the American War of Independence. He was regarded by many as being unpatriotic – certainly by King George III – not least because of his vehement demands that the government should unconditionally grant independence to the American rebels. In part it was this very public rift with the king which meant that years later Fox was to be denied a state funeral. With the outbreak of the French Revolution, Fox was sympathetic to the rebels in France – at least until details of the horrors of The Terror emerged, leading to the execution of the French king. At the outset of the revolution he was known to have remarked that it was 'much the greatest and best event that ever happened in the world'. He incurred implacable hatred from merchants and landowners with links to the slave trade, because he campaigned for abolition. He was known as 'the man of the people' – loved because of his very obvious human frailties, his sparkling personality and his powers of oratory.

Fox was a brilliant public speaker, but was also, in a sense, destined to be a nearly-man – someone who never quite fulfilled his potential and who never secured the top spot as prime minister. As a young man he had developed a taste for excessive gambling and for sharing his great enthusiasm for life with his friends. In time this circle of friends included the young Prince of Wales. In particular Fox had spent years leading a dissolute life, drinking and whoring, and had never settled down. His gambling debts were astronomic. He went bankrupt in 1772 and 1774 and during the course of his life is estimated to have lost £200,000 in wagers – equivalent to perhaps £18 million nowadays. And then, in 1783, he hooked up with Mrs Armistead.

By that time Fox was heavily in debt. He had few physical charms, was short and plump, and cartoonists generally showed him with a thick six o'clock shadow. Even his friends referred to him by the nickname 'the eyebrow' on account of his beetle brows. It really was a case of Beauty and The Beast. After Lord Rockingham died, Fox lost his job as Foreign Secretary and soon moved into St Ann's with Elizabeth. It was considered quite a modest house for the times, and although it was described as being dark and poky, it had an undeniably charming location, with its land running to around ninety acres. The majority of the land was let out to a local farmer, leaving nearly thirty acres to be used as gardens, woodlands and for grazing sheep. Fox liked to refer to Elizabeth as 'the Lady of the Hill' (meaning St Ann's Hill) and over time he learned to share her interests in plants, in birdlife and in country pursuits. The couple lived quietly and largely out of the limelight, improving the house and gardens and generally enjoying a life of rural simplicity. Elizabeth particularly liked staying at St Ann's in the spring and summer.

In time Fox started to resent the weeks on end that he had to spend in London on parliamentary business, writing to Elizabeth in May 1785, 'You are ALL to me. You can always make me happy in circumstances apparently unpleasant and miserable ... Indeed my dearest angel, the whole happiness of my life depends on you.' That same year Elizabeth acquired the freehold of St Ann's from the Duke of Marlborough, agreeing to pay £2,000 for it but leaving the entire purchase price outstanding on a mortgage, with interest running at £100 a year. Why the need for the loan? Because Elizabeth had sold just about everything in order to clear Fox's debts. Her two annuities were sold, her house in Clarges Street was disposed of, and all her other properties went towards paying off Fox's creditors.

In the early years of their relationship, Fox had seemed to be making most of the running, while Elizabeth had wanted to retain a measure of independence. At an early stage Elizabeth had threatened to end the relationship, prompting Fox to respond: 'No, my dearest Liz, you must not go indeed you must not, the very thought of living without you so totally sinks my spirits that I am sure the reality would be more than I could bear....I have examined myself and know that I can better abandon friends, country and everything than live without Liz. I could change my name and live with you in the remotest part of Europe in poverty and obscurity. I could bear that very well, but to be parted I can not bear.'

Clearly Elizabeth revelled in her new life away from the bright lights of the city. She became an avid reader and would spend hours sitting with Fox while reading aloud translations of Ancient Greek poetry along with passages from the classics. It presents a picture of domestic bliss far removed from the excesses that both parties had enjoyed to the full just a few years previously. For Fox it meant giving up his gambling chums at Brooks's, abandoning the pleasures of the flesh, abstaining from heavy drinking, and keeping away from Newmarket. For Elizabeth it meant forsaking harlotry and turning her back on the heady life of being perhaps the most famous courtesan of her era.

The couple enjoyed entertaining, although the scandalous nature of their relationship meant that not everyone would accept an invitation. A frequent visitor to St Ann's was Lord Holland, son of Fox's elder brother, who would come over from nearby Eton. It was a lively household, full of fun. On occasions the couple brought Fox's two illegitimate children, Harry Fox and Harriet Willoughby, to live with them, as well as Robert St John, the grandson of Mrs Armistead's first patron. So frequently did Robert come to stay that he was to all intents and purposes adopted by the couple. Fox was a year older than Elizabeth and the couple never had children of their own. Given that Elizabeth was only in her mid-thirties when the couple started living together, it is highly probable that she was unable to have children and may well have busied herself in the role of foster parent as compensation for her own inability to conceive.

Many prominent Whig politicians visited the couple at their country retreat. Fox's work commitments meant regular trips to London, and Elizabeth accompanied her lover on many of these visits, apparently willing to accept the fact that many of the functions which he attended were barred to her. He served as Secretary of State on two occasions – a job that entailed long hours, irregular meals, late nights and an opportunity to drink excessively. Thanks to Elizabeth, Fox stayed largely on the straight and narrow. She would wait patiently for him, help him unwind, assist him with drafting his speeches and generally act as a sounding board for Fox's ideas and plans for the future of the country. They were a couple who constantly read aloud to each other. In his *Recollections*, Samuel Rogers recalled that when Fox 'returns fretted in an evening' Mrs Fox 'takes down a volume of Don Quixote or Gilblas, and reads him into tranquillity.' Occasionally, but only occasionally, Elizabeth would go off on her own to visit friends in other parts of the country, or travel down to Bath to take the waters as a remedy for the rheumatism which was starting to affect her badly.

In 1788 the couple decided to go on a European tour, visiting Switzerland, where they stayed two days at Lausanne with the historian Edward Gibbon. The author of the *Decline and Fall of the Roman Empire* was somewhat dismissive of Elizbeth, referring to her as 'a cypher' – presumably an indication of how willing she was to take a back seat whenever she met anyone not in her immediate circle of friends. But Gibbon approved of the effect she was having on Fox, describing his powers as having been 'blended with the softness and simplicity of a child.' From Lausanne the couple headed into Italy, staying there rather longer than anticipated because Elizabeth fell awkwardly and sprained her ankle.

They were forced to hurry home, however, because of news that George III's insanity was likely to lead to a regency. On reaching Paris, Fox sped home across the Channel, leaving Elizabeth to enjoy the pleasures of the French capital on her own. There she remained for two solitary months, blissfully unaware that Fox's dash across France, covering many miles a day on appalling roads in an open carriage and with barely any sleep at all, had left him seriously ill. Many assumed that he was at death's door and when Elizabeth learned the truth, towards the end of January 1789, she hurried back to England, whisked her beloved off to Bath, and ensured that he took a complete rest until his health had recovered fully. Returning to London, Elizabeth found time to sit once more for Reynolds to paint her portrait, while Fox immersed himself in politics. It was a time when Pitt was in his ascendancy and Fox's fortunes, both political and financial, were at their lowest ebb.

It must have been an insecure time for Elizabeth, given that she was now without an income of her own. Her youth and physical charms, so long the guarantee of financial rewards, were beginning to fade. By 1790 she was forty years old and if her portraits are anything to go by, she had started to put on a considerable amount of weight.

By the time that the revolution in France had resulted in Louis XIV being led to the guillotine, the British government were seeking to introduce a raft of measures aimed at preventing insurrection in the United Kingdom: various Treason Acts were followed by the suspension of habeas corpus, the passing of the Aliens Act and the Correspondence with Enemies Act. All of them were opposed by Fox as attacks on the liberty of man. His enemies managed to show him as being unpatriotic, and a traitor, and all but his most devoted friends in the House of Commons deserted him. And yet, by the mid-summer of 1793 a subscription had been raised among the general public and this provided sufficient funds to clear all of his debts and indeed to provide a small annuity to cover his future expenses. It could not have come at a more opportune time. Fox by then was acutely aware that if anything happened to him Elizabeth would have no claim on any part of his estate. In vain he tried to persuade Elizabeth to allow him to use the money to pay off his mortgage on his London property so that he could settle it in trust for her benefit.

Her insecurities cannot have been helped when the banker Thomas Coutts wrote asking if his daughter Frances might be permitted to have a lock of Fox's hair – clearly a coded indication that the Coutts family were looking to see if they could marry Frances off to the charismatic politician. No matter that Fox was twice the age of the twenty-two-year-old Frances. The alliance would certainly have solved all of his financial problems at a stroke, because there is little doubt that a sizeable dowry would have been involved and Fox could reasonably have expected to look forward to raising a family of his own. It seemed to be an inevitable and sensible union – or so it appeared to Elizabeth. She was deeply upset on hearing about the request but charitably offered to withdraw from the scene to allow Fox to proceed.

Fox was having none of it, though, and in 1795 he wrote to his nephew Lord Holland saying: 'I think my affection for her [Elizabeth] increases every day. She is a comfort to me in every misfortune and makes me enjoy doubly every pleasant circumstance of life. There is to me a charm and delight in her society which time does not in the least wear off, and for real goodness of heart if she ever had an equal she certainly never had a superior.'

He also wrote to Elizabeth reassuring her of his loyalty, with the words: 'I cannot figure to myself any possible idea of happiness without you, and being sure of this is it possible that I can think of any trifling advantage of fortune or connection as weighing a feather in the scale against the whole comfort and happiness of my life? Even if you did not love me I could not endure the thought of belonging to any other woman.' In the same letter he wrote: 'I can never be happy without you and you have promised to be ruled in this instance by my determination. That is fixed and if you love me, I shall be happy, if not, I shall be miserable, but still with my Liz, for never can I give my consent to part with her. Do repeat to me my dearest love that you love me tenderly, dearly and fondly for it is such a comf[ort] to me to hear it and read it; and it is true, my dearest Liz, is it not?'

Realising that their status as keeper and mistress was always going to result in a feeling of insecurity – on both sides – Fox proposed marriage. For a time Elizabeth refused, fearing that the scandal would ruin Fox's political career. It was one thing to live openly with your mistress, another to install her as your wife. Others had often conjectured that marriage was on the cards, with *The Times* reporting as far back as 23 January 1789: 'Mrs. ARMISTEAD's marriage to Mr Fox is now mentioned as a certainty; which for ever destroys the hope of a legitimate successor to our great orator's personal and mental estates; the lady having passed that climacteric of life, which shuts out the possibility of children – What a pity!!!'

In practice, marriage was never a certainty, because Elizabeth refused point blank to be a party to something that could ruin the career prospects of the man she loved. However, she finally gave in to Fox's entreaties and agreed to marry him, but only on condition that the union was to remain a secret. Even so, she remained full of doubt until the very last moment, seeking to cancel the wedding arrangements just five days before the ceremony was to take place. Fox talked her round once more, and on 28 September 1795 the two were married at Wyton in Huntingdonshire, in a private ceremony officiated by Rev John Pery. Elizabeth's maid, Mary Dassonville, and the parson's clerk, Jeremiah Bradshaw, acted as witnesses. The married couple returned to St Ann's and quickly resumed their idyllic rural life.

In the ensuing years the house and gardens were dramatically improved. An early nineteenth-century description is of an irregularly shaped house with trellis work in front, and was described by one writer as a 'very interesting and beautiful place, both on account of the extensive prospect obtained from the house and the taste for picturesque beauty and rare plants displayed by Mrs Fox in laying out of the grounds.' This is confirmed in a sketch from the early 1800s showing a cottage orné with trellis-work and a verandah on the south front.

Elizabeth also extended the landscaped area of the garden, taking in a small farm to the west of house, described as an 'attached farm on which are some neatly thatched buildings'. She supervised extensive planting schemes, with avenues of oak trees and the planting of Cedars of Lebanon, some of which survived until well into the twentieth century. Large formal lawns to the south of the house were framed in the 1790s by a Temple of Friendship, a rectangular building fronted by ionic columns. It contained three semi-circular niches containing busts by the sculptor Nollekens, one of which was of Fox and bearing the inscription, 'Given to Mrs Armistead by Earl Fitzwilliam,' along with the date (5 May 1796). Another Nollekens bust, of one of the sons of Lord Bolingbroke, and a bust of Lord Holland adorned the other two niches.

A visitor describing the property some seven years after Elizabeth died wrote of the formal paths leading through a woodland area connecting to the lawns to the north, the area of kitchen garden to the east, and a further area of pleasure ground at the southern end of the site. It was described as offering 'a fine shady walk, bounded on one side by the pleasure grounds, and on the other by a row of Oak trees ... the walks bounded by large clumps and banks of Rhododendrons and Azaleas, with hollies interspersed.'

There was a coach house built to the north-west of the house, separated from it by a walled garden. Built on two levels the walled garden contained several glass houses – very much in vogue in the second half of the eighteenth century. Other features constructed during Elizabeth's tenure were two summerhouses, along with a tea house and grotto, also very much in fashion at the time. The tea house had a single round-headed window on the first floor, reached by a curved exterior wooden staircase, with a chinoiserie trellised handrail. Here, the happy couple liked to take tea and entertain friends, and admire the view of the landscaped gardens. The grotto, downstairs, was built in the 1790s and was constructed on a rectangular plan. It was decorated extensively with shells and decorative stones, including faux stalagmites, and followed the eighteenth-century mania for creating artificial caverns – either as a nymphaeum, in imitation of a classical temple, or a shell-lined grotto or rustic pavilion. In short, the gardens became the height of fashion and good taste.

Years later, in 1837, representatives from the Royal Horticultural Society visited St Ann's and noted that the estate had 'numerous and diversified' walks, as well as a pleasure ground with several buildings, a 'glass-fronted house' which contained Elizabeth's prized collection of plants, including the 'finest specimens of Camellias, in tubs, ever seen'. The RHS admired the fine *Tuxodium distichum*, or Swamp Cypress, which had been planted on the main lawn and stood 30ft tall. The RHS felt that much credit should go to Mr Tucker who had been head gardener for over thirty years, but it is safe to assume that Elizabeth took a keen interest in his work to enhance the site.

Of the interior of the house little is known, but it can be taken that Elizabeth had good taste and was familiar with all the latest trends in décor and furnishing. There is a reference to her owning a painting by George Stubbs entitled *Phaeton with a pair of cream ponies and a tiger-boy*, now in the Paul Mellon Collection at the Yale Center for British Art. She also owned Stubbs's enamel painting of *The Farmer's Wife and the Raven*, probably purchased, at a cost of one hundred guineas, after Stubbs exhibited the picture at the Royal Academy Summer exhibition in 1782. Both are likely to have been in evidence at St Ann's because they were still there when they were auctioned off some time after Elizabeth had died.

When Samuel Rogers wrote about the interior in his *Recollections* he noted: 'In the hall, books and statues. The library on the first floor – small and unadorned – the books on open shelves. In the eating room a portrait of Lord Holland sitting, carefully painted by Reynolds; and of Lady Holland sitting, by Ramsey. Several good old pictures ... The drawing-room prettily furnished with pink silk in the panels, enclosed with an ebony bead, and a frame of blue silk.'

In the 1820s, two decades after Fox had died, Elizabeth embarked on a major refurbishment of the property, so that by the time auction particulars were prepared in the following century the house was said to contain four reception rooms, sixteen bedrooms, and two bathrooms. While it was considerably smaller than this during Fox's lifetime, it was still large enough for a succession of visitors. Prominent Whigs, despairing of seeing their colleague at his old haunts such as Brooks's, happily made the journey out to St Ann's in order to sample the Fox hospitality.

In 1798 Fox appointed John Bernard Trotter as his secretary. Years later, in his memoirs published in 1811, Trotter sought to make money out of revealing what daily life was like in the Fox household, writing: 'When I first had the happiness of knowing Mr. Fox, he had retired, in a great measure, from public life, and was inclining towards the evening of his days ... His habits were very domestic, and his taste for literature peculiarly strong, as well as peculiarly elegant. His love for a country life, and all its simple and never-fatiguing charms, was great.'

The daily routine involved rising in the summer between 6am and 7am (in winter, by 8am). Breakfast was an opportunity for Fox to read aloud from the day's newspaper, and he would then devote his morning to the study of Greek poetry and classical literature. A 'frugal but plentiful' dinner would be taken at 2.30 or 3pm (later in the winter months) and, if the weather allowed, there would then be a long walk to fill the rest of the afternoon. The evenings were spent studying and reading aloud history books, then a light supper – mostly of fruit or pastry – taken at around 10pm. The couple would then retire to bed by 10.30.

The last five years of the century were spent quietly and with great contentment for the couple. Fox decided to write a history of the monarchy covering the reigns of the monarchs from Charles II to George II, intending to highlight the growth in regal powers and the way parliamentary checks and balances had been eroded. He decided that his researches would be aided by a trip to Paris to look at the records held there. This coincided with the passing of the Treaty of Amiens in 1802, bringing a temporary halt to Anglo-French hostilities and enabling British tourists to sample the delights of travel to the French capital. Fox joined the throng of prominent people heading for Paris and on reaching Calais discovered for the first time that the French revered him for the same reason that he was regarded as unpatriotic by the English: he was an unashamed Francophile; he had supported the revolution; he had campaigned for peace at every opportunity. Formal receptions were held in Calais and Lille and it was evident that Napoleon, recently made First Consul, wanted to honour Fox with an audience in Paris. Fox would have known that the First Consul had made it clear that he could not be seen to be associating with adulterous or unmarried couples. He also knew that Elizabeth would greatly enjoy seeing him gain his moment in the spotlight and so he persuaded her that the time had come to reveal their married status. The news was revealed in the London newspapers immediately, with *The Times* of 13 August 1802 declaring: 'For some days past it has been confidently reported, that the Hon. CHARLES FOX had rewarded the constancy and other merits of MRS ARMSTEAD [sic] with his hand at the altar. [...] The wit and accomplishments of this Lady have long been justly celebrated, and she is as much entitled to every privilege that the event we allude to can confer upon her, as many Ladies who preside over fashion in the present laxity of her manners.'

The audience with the First Consul took place on 12 September 1802, and while the Foxs basked in the public acceptance of their union in France, there were inevitably some who were tut-tutting at the idea of a man marrying such an infamous whore and then parading her in public as if her past notoriety was of no consequence. Nevertheless, Elizabeth's charm and quiet good manners impressed most of the people she met, including other English tourists. The few 'antis' were generally won over and when the couple returned to Britain, after an absence of three months, it was to find that most of the fuss had died down. Most importantly, their family and friends stood by them. Besides, at the end of the day most of the people who mattered to them – the Whig supporters and colleagues and their wives – knew which side their bread was buttered: snub Mrs Fox and you would lose the support of her husband. And who were they to moralise when many of them had spent years making a mockery of their own marriage vows?

Caricaturists such as Gillray had a field day, with a particularly unflattering portrayal of Elizabeth in his print entitled *Introduction of Citizen Volpone & His Suite at Paris* – showing Elizabeth as a woman who was as broad as she was long, and with syphilitic sores on her face. The excessive use of rouge on her cheeks and the obvious gaps in her teeth all point to her former occupation. It was of course a monstrous exaggeration – a demonstration that Gillray wanted to remind the world of The Armistead's origins, and drawing attention to the fact that at fifty-two she was no longer the famed beauty of her youth. More to the point, it implies that Elizabeth attended the levée and was introduced to the First Consul personally – a total fabrication. She was never even in the audience, let alone presented to Napoleon. Gillray included her to show that the print was about prostitutes, with Fox prostituting his own beliefs by kow-towing to a dictator who proclaimed to be a republican but who was in fact as much a despot as any monarch.

A steady flow of visitors came to St Ann's to meet and congratulate the couple on their return. The women of the Whig aristocracy came calling, including the Duchess of Devonshire, prompting Fox to write 'with millions of thanks and every grateful feeling.' Equally, when visiting their rented home in London, the Foxes were invited to meet the great and the good, the cream of society. Elizabeth seemed unfazed if she discovered that her host – or more probably the wife of the host – declined to be introduced to her. She never complained at the snub, never tried to intrude where she was not welcome, and never dropped her good-natured façade.

For a time domestic bliss was resumed and Fox made progress on his book about royal powers. He was destined never to finish it and it was published, in an unfinished state, sometime after his death. Meanwhile the political world moved on: William Pitt died in February 1806 and it became clear that despite the implacable opposition of the king, Fox would be invited to join a coalition government. He was appointed Foreign Secretary in what was called the Ministry of All Talents and he threw himself into this most demanding of jobs. Any semblance of a private life was over and the couple moved into a London house called Stable Yard, loaned to them by the Duke of Bedford. Elizabeth was now 'Mrs Secretary' and she effortlessly adapted to a very public role, entertaining visitors and hosting gatherings, as well as trying to protect her husband from the constant demands on his time, especially from place-seekers and sycophants.

Fox was a workaholic, working late into the night, and just as it seemed that things were beginning to normalise, Elizabeth decided to hold a ball. She knew it would either make or break her personal reputation; she had no way of knowing whether she would be accepted as hostess by the 400-plus guests. The ball was to be held at Bedford House, lent by the Duke of Bedford, and was to take place on 19 May. It was a huge success, but the pressure on Fox was beginning to take its toll: he suffered from a succession of bad colds; his legs started swelling; rheumatism was causing him continual pain. It was apparent to his supporters that his declining health might well force him out of office, but Fox was adamant, saying, 'The Slave Trade and Peace are two such glorious things, I can't give them up … If I can manage them, I will then retire.'

In practice he never got the opportunity to retire. The swellings in his legs got worse and he was diagnosed with dropsy – the accumulation of watery fluid in the tissues. Nowadays it would be seen as a symptom of something more serious – for instance, of an oedema due to congestive heart failure. In fact, Fox was suffering from cirrhosis of the liver. According to prevailing medical practice, an attempt was made to drain the excess fluid. In her diary Elizabeth recorded that on 31 August while staying at Chiswick House some thirteen quarts of water were drawn off – more than three gallons of fluid. His health declined rapidly and Fox knew that he was dying. To his wife he said his last words: 'It don't signify, my dearest Liz.' Later, his nephew Lord Holland confirmed: 'If we had not known it before, his last hours would have convinced us that the ruling passion of his heart was affection and tenderness for her.'

* * *

Fox died on 13 September 1806 and for Elizabeth it was to herald a widowhood that was to last for nearly thirty-six years, mostly spent at her beloved St Ann's. Her diaries, held in the British Library, show a woman who lived out her days determined to keep alive the memory of the man she loved profoundly. The entries are rarely about her or her feelings, they are all about her late husband and what he achieved. She received visits from his friends and colleagues, she walked extensively around the countryside near St Ann's, she founded a small school at Ruxbury Road in the local village, and every year on May Day she delighted in the visit of the schoolchildren to her house, all bearing garlands.

Despite her small income she contributed to various local charities, offered support to a number of her servants and their families, and became a much-loved pillar of the community. In order to raise finance she was forced to sell some of her land. On one occasion she was honoured by a visit from her former lover, the Prince of Wales. He was delighted to be reunited, socially, with his old friend and realising the parlous state of her finances, ordered her to be paid a pension of £500 from the Civil List. It was a payment continued by his brother, the Duke of Clarence, when he became king – and indeed by his niece Victoria when she came to the throne in 1837. That alone is a mark of how far she had come, from the seraglios of St James's to the dignified gentility of a widow who was respected by everyone.

Rheumatism and ill health continued to dog her in her old age. In 1840, at the age of ninety, she made a will and in it left an annuity of £60 to her 'good and trusty servant Martha Tucker.' Slightly smaller legacies were left to her cook, her gardener and her coachman, and the residue of her estate, after repayment of her mortgage, was devised to her executors, both of them great nephews of her late husband. She died, a few days short of her ninety-second birthday, on 8 July 1842. Her funeral took place at what was then All Saints Church (now known as St Peter's) in Chertsey. The Duke of Bedford sent an empty carriage, as a mark of respect, and the chief mourners were Colonel Charles Richard Fox – great nephew of her late husband – and his brother-in-law Lord Lifford.

The tradespeople of Chertsey turned out to honour a much-loved local resident, and as the *Windsor and Eton Express* remarked: 'The ceremony was intended to be private but persons of all classes were anxious to show their respect for one who has been so long and justly beloved, and who by her urbanity, kindness, and excessive benevolence, has acquired the esteem of the inhabitants of the neighbourhood of her own residence, St Ann's Hill.'

Around forty of the local tradesmen, all dressed in full mourning apparel, escorted the cortege as Elizabeth completed her life's journey: one that took her from extreme notoriety to social acceptance, from the sex trade to respectability. It was a remarkable transition, from Elizabeth Armistead to Elizabeth Fox, but then, Elizabeth was a truly remarkable woman.

Epilogue

The third Plate from William Hogarth's 'A Harlot's Progress'.

Fame

There is no doubt that the women featured here were in the top tier of their profession, and enjoyed a fame which entitled them to be called the Toast of the Town. The exception perhaps is Frances Abington, whose fame as an actress meant that she was able to escape her past almost entirely. The others never quite managed to reach the point where their fame was not linked, in some way, to the sexual activities of their youth.

Mary Robinson tried desperately to succeed in various areas – as a poet, as a promoter of women's rights – but never shook off the 'Perdita' link. Elizabeth Armistead, because of her great age and her obvious goodness as a person, managed to gain a measure of acceptance notwithstanding her racy past, but one suspects that this was because the public had years and years to adjust to her position as devoted companion and helpmate of Charles Fox. By the time news of her marriage got out she had long retired from harlotry and public scrutiny.

The others were all famous because of, and in spite of, their sexual promiscuity. Those sexy little minxes Fanny Murray, Kitty Fisher and Gertrude Mahon revelled in the fun that was to be had from being a whore in the public eye. They helped create the demi-monde, a world where the public were prepared to set aside conventional moral judgments and measure them for their success, not just in bed but their success at building a career, becoming a role model to thousands of other young women, and for beating the system. It was a fame built upon manipulating the press wherever possible and recognising that there was no such thing as bad publicity.

Fame could be spread by portraits and prints; it could be used to create an exclusivity as well as creating the image of being available to all. 'If you've got it, flaunt it' may be a credo followed slavishly by today's reality TV stars, but they were not the first to do so. In the eighteenth century if you were a famous whore, you did not hide your face and go about your business in private. You would see nothing to be ashamed of. Hence you hired the same box at the opera for every performance that season and made sure that you had a bigger crowd of ardent admirers paying court to you than any of your rivals.

One suspects that some of the women featured here did not get on with their fellow courtesans. Elizabeth Armistead certainly appears to have taken great delight in stealing lovers (for instance the Prince of Wales and Charles James Fox) from her rival Mary Robinson. Conversely, Mary appears to have socialised happily with her rival Grace Elliott (they both bedded the Prince of Wales) and with Gertrude Mahon (who made a play for the prince but lost interest when it became apparent that he wasn't interested in paying).

As a group, the featured women were as talked about among their contemporaries as today's participants in reality TV shows such as Love Island or Big Brother. Although to modern tastes they may not seem particularly attractive, to an eighteenth-century audience they epitomised beauty and sexual allure.

Fortune

It is impossible to compare financial fortunes – there are no records of probate values. All one can say with certainty is that all of them spent money as fast as they earned it. Fanny Murray, in particular, was facing life in a debtor's prison before begging for support from the son of her first lover. Mary Robinson and Gertrude Mahon appear to have lived in fairly straitened circumstances in their later years, and the fact that the elderly Elizabeth Armistead secured a pension from the Civil List is an indication that the fruits of her earlier labours had all been dissipated in repaying her husband's gambling debts and in running the small country estate at St Ann's. So perhaps that is another thing that the seven women had in common – they didn't try and take it with them, they spent it on themselves.

But what of another aspect of fortune – good luck? The first thing to stress is that they were not typical: for every courtesan who made it to the top of the tree there were not just hundreds but tens of thousands of prostitutes who lived lives that were dogged by debt and disease and who ultimately died young, without ever fulfilling their potential. It would certainly seem to be highly fortunate that none of the women featured here had their careers curtailed by disease, although it may well be the case that every single one of them contracted a sexually transmitted disease such as syphilis at one time or another.

What evidence is there for the suggestion that many of the women lived with recurring bouts of syphilis which never moved beyond the first stage? Well, the lack of fecundity is one pointer. It is perhaps remarkable that seven women, all sexually active at the time when they would normally expect to be at their most fertile, managed to produce just two children. This was against the background that contraception (for instance using a condom) was somewhat unreliable. There may of course have been abortions, or secret confinements during convenient trips abroad, but it is far more likely that the lack of offspring was attributable directly to venereal disease. It has been suggested that at least half of all pregnancies with women affected by acute syphilis would have led to miscarriages or stillbirths.

An exposure to STDs would perhaps explain why many of the 'frail sisterhood' moved on from 'general harlotry' to 'serial monogamy' at a fairly young age. By the age of twenty-eight Fanny Murray had married and settled down; Kitty Fisher was three years younger than this when she married; by her mid-twenties Mary Robinson had begun an affair with Banastre Tarleton which was to last, on and off, for fifteen years of fidelity – at least on her part. For all the women listed here, one-night stands may have been features of their youth, but at some stage in their twenties they either married or took stock of what they were offering, raised their game, and aimed for a much more selective – and expensive – clientele. And without fail they made this change possible by a very public display of their success. They weren't happy just to be kept women, answerable to their male patrons: they insisted on their own homes, their own annuities, and control of their own finances.

One other thing that comes across is that many of the women appear to have had a reasonable education, or at least one that was sufficient to enable them to make the transition from whore to companion, and able to converse on a variety of topics. Sure, Fanny Murray and Kitty Fisher seemed to revel in their lustful, brazen promiscuity with very little hint of 'polish', but the others all come across as having received a good education (Elizabeth Armistead being a case in point) or had acquired sufficient skills from working in the theatre to be able to assume an educated persona (Frances Abington comes to mind).

What these women all had in common was that they had high libidos, and a good understanding of what the men in their circle wanted and expected. Sex merely played a part – the men were prepared to pay for good company, with sexual intercourse being just one part of the evening's entertainment. Men wanted 'trophy girlfriends' to drape on their arms, to accompany them to dinners and to the theatre. Not only could they afford the best, but they wanted to show the world that they could do so. The courtesans understood this, played them at their own game, and took the money.

For many of the featured women, their 'elevation to courtesanship' either featured an escape route from an unhappy marriage (Gertrude Mahon, Mary Robinson) or led directly to an advantageous marriage which they would not otherwise have had a right to expect (Nancy Parsons, Fanny Murray, Kitty Fisher and Elizabeth Armistead being cases in point). The odd one out was Frances Abington, who started off as a prostitute, did not marry particularly well, but made the transition to kept woman and thereafter attained a measure of respectability without having to marry. The fact that she also installed her own lovers in her own homes showed a woman who really had learned how to turn the tables to her advantage.

Fashion

One thing which these ladies shared was dress sense – an awareness of the importance of fashion, and its effect on desirability. In modern parlance, looking a million dollars was a key to being attractive, and without exception these women were fashion conscious. They set trends, they pandered to the press, they self-advertised, they sat for portraits, they promoted prints and they paraded their wares in the most public of places, be it Hyde Park, or the opera house, the masked ball or at Ranelagh Gardens.

From our viewpoint, two-and-a-half centuries on, some of the minutiae about fashion in the Georgian era may seem incomprehensible: we don't wear lace-trimmed caps, so the distinction between an 'Abington cap' or a 'Perdita cap' seems irrelevant, but at the time these things mattered. Take the humble straw hat: rarely worn now but almost universally sported by fashionable women in the second half of the eighteenth century. Do you wear them with flowers, or feathers, or be-ribboned? Do you tie a ribbon under the chin or over one ear – or indeed, do you tie it as a top-knot? In many cases your choice would be influenced by the style-makers you saw in the public eye, and that often meant the courtesans. And just as today, when magazines extol the very latest but often very trivial changes in how make-up is applied, or what length sleeves or skirts should be worn, so in the Georgian era the press commented on really minor differences between the fashions of 'yesterday and today'. To be dressed 'a la mode' was important in a way never seen before and as the British Empire spread its tentacles around the globe more and more influences from distant shores– colourful silks, patterned cottons, floaty muslins – entered public consciousness. The leading courtesans did not of course single-handedly create a consumer society, but they were certainly in the right place at the right time to exploit it and to become the face of consumerism.

Occasionally, there would be a major tsunami of a fashion change – a movement such as the one heralded by Mary Quant in the 1960s with mini-skirts worn by such stellar influencers as 'Twiggy' or 'The Shrimp'. The eighteenth-century equivalent was the enormous leap from hooped skirt to the diaphanous muslin chemise worn by the Duchess of Devonshire, although she only did so after first seeing that Mary Robinson had the courage to be seen wearing it in public. Within ten years it seemed that no lady of fashion would be seen out in public unless she was dressed like a Greek statue swathed in almost see-through muslin. The Empire Line, with its fitted bodice ending just below the bust, giving a high-waisted appearance, and a gathered skirt that was long and loosely fitting and skimmed the body, was a world away from the hoops, petticoats and heavily embroidered fabrics worn previously by fashionable women. The French Revolution may have been the catalyst for change, but it was a change made popular in everyday British life by fashion.

The fashionistas managed to succeed in what was very much a man's world – they were business women. Whereas society banned women from the professions, and expected them to confine their activities to the so-called needle trades, or to domestic service, or market trading, these courtesans were brilliant at selling the one thing they had – themselves. This involved their bodies and their company. They sold not just sex, they sold fun. It is worth remembering that for many of their clients – aristocratic and royal – marriage was not about love, or companionship – it was about securing the dynasty. These men did not enter into marriage thinking that it would provide anything other than legitimate offspring. They always assumed that they would look outside the marriage for the things that courtesans could offer – not just sex, but sex within a relationship based on friendship, shared company, and shared experiences. What men were wanting was non-judgmental companionship – someone who would flirt with them, laugh at their jokes, make them feel good about themselves. They wanted good listeners, they wanted their egos massaged, and yes, at the end of it they wanted sex, not just with a view to procreate but for the sheer pleasure of it. Men could do things with their lovers that they would never dream of doing with their wives.

Novelists tended to concentrate on the problems faced by 'titles in search of money' and 'money in search of a title', but this emphasis on marriage as a dynastic institution simply showed that there was a whole class of men who never expected love to be a major component in marriage – particularly at the beginning. After all, they may only have met their bride-to-be on the way to the altar, with George III setting the trend by marrying Charlotte of Mecklenburg-Strelitz just six hours after she first set foot on English soil at Harwich. The marriage contract had been signed the previous month, but the two had never actually met. In the case of the royal couple, you had to say that the marriage worked: they ended up having fifteen children, of whom thirteen reached adulthood. Contrast that with many of the aristocratic unions, where men considered that they had 'done their duty' by fathering a child with a woman they barely knew, and then went back to their mistresses, courtesans and common whores.

In a world where the poor were cripplingly so, and the rich were obscenely wealthy, men with money and titles wanted to flaunt their success. They wanted to be seen out and about with the most expensive courtesans their money could buy, and the women featured here were the Patek Philippe watch, the Karl Lagerfield sable fur coat and the Bugatti Veyron of their day.

What stands out from the women selected in this book is that they understood this, pandered to it and made rather a lot of money out of their male lovers. Georgian society, far from condemning them for their promiscuous lifestyle, lauded them for their success, awarded them with fame and unstinting adulation, and then went out to the shops to buy whatever their heroines were wearing.

Bibliography

Anon: *A Congratulatory Epistle from a Reformed Rake, to John F......g upon the new scheme for Reforming Prostitutes.* Printed for G.Burnet, London, 1758.

Anon: *A Sketch of the Present Times, and the Time to Come: In an Address to Kitty Fisher,* T. Waller, London, 1762 (available online).

Anon: Memoirs of the Celebrated Miss Fanny Murray. J Scott, London, 1759.

Anon: *The Memoirs of Perdita.* G Lister, London, 1784 (available online).

Anon: *The Effusions of Love: Being the Amorous Correspondence between the Amiable Florizel and the Enchanting Perdita.* London, 1780.

Anon: *The Budget of Love, or, Letters between Florizel and Perdita.* London, 1781.

Anon: *Poetical epistle from Florizel to Perdita: with Perdita's answer. And a preliminary discourse upon the education of princes.* London, 1781.

Anon ('MRH'): *Letters from Perdita to a certain Israelite and his Answers to them.* Printed for J. Fielding; W. Kent; J. Stockdale; and J. Sewell, 1781. Available as Gale ECCO, Print Edition).

Anon (by 'A Society of Gentlemen') *The Critical Review or Annals of Literature.* A Hamilton, London, 1783. (Available in digital format).

Anon: *The life of Mrs Abington (formerly Miss Barton) celebrated comic actress.* London, 1888. Available online.

Bee, John (pseud. Badcock, John): *Slang, a dictionary of the turf, the ring, the chase, the pit, of bon-ton and the varieties of life.* London,1823. Available online.

Bleakley, Horace: *Ladies Fair and Frail: Sketches of the demi-monde during the eighteenth century.* Bodley Head, London and New York, 1909 (and available online).

Bourque, Kevin Jordan: *Blind Items: Anonymity, Notoriety, and the Making of Eighteenth-Century Celebrity.* The University of Texas at Austin, 2012.

Byrne, Paula: *Perdita – the life of Mary Robinson.* Harper Collins, London, 2004.

Clayton, Timothy: *The English Print 1688-1802.* Paul Mellon Centre for Studies in British Art, 1997.

Davenport, Hester: *The Prince's Mistress, Perdita: A Life of Mary Robinson* The History Press Ltd, 2006.

Davis. I M: *The Harlot and the Statesman.* The Kensal Press, Buckinghamshire, 1986

De Vrie, Susanna: *Royal Mistresses of the House of Hanover-Windsor: Secrets, Scandals and Betrayals.* Pirgos Press, Brisbane, 2012.

Egerton, Judy: *George Stubbs, Painter – Catalogue Raisonné.* Yale University Press, 2007.

Gamer, Michael and Robinson Terry: *Mary Robinson and the Dramatic Art of the Comeback*. Studies in Romanticism 48 (2009). Available in electronic format.

Hazelwood, Joseph: *Secret History of the Green Room containing authentic and entertaining memoirs of the actors and actresses in the three Theatres Royal*. J Owen, London, 1795 and available in digital format online.

Highfill, Philip; Burnim, Kalman; and Langhans, Edward: *A Biographical Dictionary of Actors, Actresses, Musicians, Dancers, Managers and other stage personnel in London 1660 – 1800*. Southern Illinois University Press, 1984.

Lambert, B.: *The History and Survey of London and its Environs from the Earliest Period to the Present Time*. Hughes and Jones, London, 1806.

Law, Susan C: *Through the Keyhole: Sex, Scandal and the Secret Life of the Country House*. The History Press, 2015.

Linnane, Fergus: *Madams: Bawds & Brothel-Keepers of London*. The History Press, London, 2011.

McCreer Cindy: *The Satirical Gaze: Prints of Women in Late Eighteenth-century England*. Clarendon Press, Oxford, 2004.

McPherson, Heather: *Art and Celebrity in the Age of Reynolds and Siddons*. Pennsylvania State University Press, 2017.

Macolm, J P: *Manners and Customs of London during the Eighteenth Century*. Longman Hurst, London, 1808.

Mudge, Bradford: 'Enchanting Witchery': Sir Joshua Reynolds's Portrait of Kitty Fisher as Cleopatra. University of Colorado at Denver. Available online.

Nussbaum, Felicity: *Rival Queens: Actresses, Performance, and the Eighteenth Century British Theater*. University of Pennsylvania Press, 2011.

Peakman, Julie: *Lascivious Bodies. A sexual history of the eighteenth century*. Atlantic Books, London, 2004.

Pointon, Marcia: The Lives of Kitty Fisher. Journal for Eighteenth-Century Studies 2008. Available online.

Potter, Tiffany (editor): *Women, Popular Culture, and the Eighteenth Century*. University of Toronto Press, 2012.

Ribeiro, Aileen. *The art of dress: fashion in England and France 1750-1820*. New Haven & London, 1995.

Robinson, Mary: *Memoirs of Mary Robinson, 'Perdita'*, from the edition edited by her daughter with introduction and notes by J. Fitzgerald Molloy. Gibbings & Co, London, 1895. Also available online.

Robinson, Mary: *A letter to the women of England and the Natural Daughter* edited by Sharon M Setzer, Broadview Literary Texts, Ontario, 2003 (and available online)

Rogers, Samuel: *Recollections*. Longmans, London 1859.

Trotter, John Bernard: *Memoirs of the Latter Years of the Right Honourable Charles James Fox*. Richard Phillips, London, 1811.

Wood, Gillen D'Arcy: *The Shock of the Real: Romanticism and Visual Culture,1760-1860*. Palgrave, New York, 2001.

Magazines

The Lady's Magazine: or, Entertaining Companion for the Fair Sex, Volume 14, 1783.

The European Magazine, And London Review, Volume 2, London.

The Rambler's Magazine, 1783-88.

Town and Country Magazine or the Repository of Knowledge, Instruction and Entertainment, Volumes XII and XIII, A Hamilton, London, 1780 (available in electronic format).

British Library, Holland House Collection

Fox, Charles James, Letters to Elizabeth Fox, Additional MS 47570, fols 156-217.

Fox, Elizabeth, 'Mrs Fox's Journal' (1806-1841), Additional MS 51476-51507.

Websites

Chertsey Museum https://chertseymuseum.org/St_Anns_Hill

Démodé Couture (specialising in eighteenth century historical costume projects) http://demodecouture.com/

All Things Georgian https://georgianera.wordpress.com/tag/costume-history/

Credits and Acknowledgements

Images included in the text:

Preface: '*A peep into Brest with a navel review*', 1794. Library of Congress.

Part I: '*Liberality and Desire*', by Thomas Rowlandson, November 1788. Author's collection.

Chapter 1:   *General Evening Post*, 26-29 September 1761. Author's collection.

Chapter 2:   '*Kitty Fischer in the character of Cleopatra*'. Engraved by E. Fisher after Joshua Reynolds, shown courtesy of the Lewis Walpole Library.

Chapter 3:   *An audience watching a play at Drury Lane Theatre*. Undated, by Thomas Rowlandson. Yale Center for British Art.

Chapter 4:   '*The Bum Bailiff outwitted, or, the convenience of Fashion*', by S.W. Fores, 1786. Lewis Walpole Library.

Chapter 5:   '*A Bagnigge Wells scene, or, No Resisting Temptation*', Carington Bowles, 1776. Lewis Walpole Library.

Part II: '*A sketch from Nature*', by W.P. Carey (after Thomas Rowlandson) 1784. The Metropolitan Museum, New York.

Chapter 6:   *Fanny Murray* by Adriaen Carpentier. In the public domain.

Chapter 7:   From the *Town & Country Magazine* Tête-à-Tête series, 1769. Courtesy of Lewis Walpole Library.

Chapter 8:   '*The Merry Accident, showing Kitty Fisher taking a tumble*'. Library of Congress.

Chapter 9:   Extract from *Frances Abington*, by Sir Joshua Reynolds. Berser Collection, Denver Art Museum per Wikimedia Commons.

Chapter 10:   '*Gertrude Mahon as the Bird of Paradise*', by Carington Bowles. Lewis Walpole Library.

Chapter 11:   '*Perdita Robinson as Amanda*' with Mary Robinson in the role of Amanda,1777. In the public domain.

Chapter 12:   Elizabeth Armistead in a preliminary sketch by John Smart. In the public domain, per Wikimedia Commons.

Epilogue: William Hogarth's *A Harlot's Progress*, Plate V. The Metropolitan Museum of Art.

Images in plates Section One

Plate 1, Upper: Thomas Rowlandson, *'Beauties'*. The Metropolitan Museum of Art.

Plate 1, Lower: Thomas Rowlandson, *'Dressing for a Masquerade'*. The Metropolitan Museum of Art.

Plate 2, Upper: *The audience watching a play'* by Thomas Rowlandson, 1785. Yale Center for British Art.

Plate 2, Lower:*'The Goats canter to Windsor, or, the Cuckold's Comfort'* from 1784. Lewis Walpole Library, Yale University.

Plate 3, Upper: *L'Assemblée Nationale, or, Grand Cooperative Meeting at St Ann's Hill'* by James Gillray, 1804. Author's collection.

Plate 3, Lower: *'Vaux-Hall'* by Thomas Rowlandson. Image via Metropolitan Museum of Art. In the public domain.

Plate 4, Upper: *'A Morning Ramble, or, the Milliners Shop'* by Robert Dighton. Lewis Walpole Library, Yale University.

Plate 4, Lower: *A Lesson Westward or, a Morning Visit to Betsy Cole'* by Robert Dighton, Lewis Walpole Library, Yale University.

Plate 5, Upper: *The interior of the Rotunda at Ranelagh Gardens*, 1751, by Nathaniel Parr. Lewis Walpole Library, Yale University.

Plate 5, Lower: *An Evening's Invitation, with a Wink from the Bagnio'*, Carington Bowles, 1773. Lewis Walpole Library.

Plate 6: *'The Whore's Last Shift'* by James Gillray, in the public domain.

Plate 7, Upper Left: Detail from painting of Eleanor Ross by Alexander Naysmith. Yale Center for British Art.

Plate 7, Upper Right: Detail from painting *'Cecilia'* by John Hoppner. Yale Center for British Art.

Plate 7, Lower Left: Detail from painting of Mary Hickey by Joshua Reynolds. Yale Center for British Art.

Plate 7, Lower Right: Detail from print of *'Lady Hamilton as the Sempstress'* by Thomas Cheesman, after George Romney. Yale Center for British Art.

Plate 8, Upper Left: British fan, late eighteenth century. The Metropolitan Museum of Art.

Plate 8, Upper Right: British fan, late eighteenth century. The Metropolitan Museum of Art.

Plate 8, Centre: Fichu, late eighteenth century. The Metropolitan Museum of Art.

Plate 8, Lower: The Muff, 1787. Lewis Walpole Library, Yale University.

Plate 9, Top: *'New Shoes'* by Thomas Rowlandson. Lewis Walpole Library, Yale University.

Plate 9, Centre: Silk shoe, British, 1770s. The Metropolitan Museum of Art.

Plate 9, Bottom: Lace-up shoe, 1800. The Metropolitan Museum of Art.

Plate 10: Headdresses from 1772. Lewis Walpole Library, Yale University.

Plate 11: Top and Tail, 1777. The Metropolitan Museum of Art.

Plate 12, Upper: Front and side view of Robe à l'Anglaise. The Metropolitan Museum of Art.

Plate 12, Lower: Rear view of Robe à l'Anglaise. The Metropolitan Museum of Art.

Plate 13, Upper: Robe à la Francaise (front). The Metropolitan Museum of Art.

Plate 13, Lower: Robe à la Francaise (rear). The Metropolitan Museum of Art.

Plate 14, Upper: Robe à la Polonaise (front). The Metropolitan Museum of Art.

Plate 14, Lower: Robe à la Polonaise (rear). The Metropolitan Museum of Art.

Plate 15: Chemise à la Reine in the portrait of Mr and Mrs Lavoisier, by J-L David. The Metropolitan Museum of Art.

Plate 16: Marie Antoinette (otherwise known as The Muslin Portrait) by Élisabeth Louise Vigée Le Brun. In the public domain (original in the National Gallery of Art, Washington).

Images in plates Section Two
Plate 17, Upper: *A section of the Petticoat, or, The Venus of '42 and '94.* In the public domain, per Wikimedia Commons.

Plate 17, Lower: Trade card for Samuel Mann. Lewis Walpole Library, Yale University.

Plate 18, Upper: *Love'*, by Charles White, 1781. Author's collection.

Plate 18, Lower Left: *'Modish'*, by Thomas Rowlandson. Author's collection.

Plate 18, Lower Right: *'Prudence'*, By Thomas Rowlandson. Author's collection.

Plates 19 and 20: Illustrations of fashions in 1752 and 1797 taken from *Manners and Customs of London during the Eighteenth Century* by J.P. Malcolm, 1808.

Plate 21, Upper: Mezzotint of Fanny Murray based on the portrait by H R Morland. In the public domain.

Plate 21, Lower: Mezzotint of Kitty Fisher by Richard Houston, after Joshua Reynolds. Yale Center for British Art.

Plate 22, Upper: Nancy Parsons in Turkish Dress by George Willison. Yale Center for British Art.

Plate 22, Lower: Nancy Parsons by Joshua Reynolds. The Metropolitan Museum, New York.

Plate 23, Upper: 'Mary Robinson as Melania', engraving by John Conde after Richard Cosway, 1792. Yale Center for British Art.

Plate 23, Lower: 'Florizel and Perdita'. Library of Congress.

Plate 24, Upper: Mary Robinson painted by George Romney engraved by J R Smith, 1781. Yale Center for British Art.

Plate 24, Lower: Mary Robinson as Perdita, by Richard Cosway. Metropolitan Museum, New York.

Plate 25, Upper: Perdita, Dally the Tall and the Bird of Paradise preparing to receive company' – frontispiece from the Ramblers Magazine, 1783. In the public domain.

Plate 25, Lower: Thalia and Malagrida', Town & Country Magazine, 1777. Lewis Walpole Library, Yale University.

Plate 26: Frances Abington as 'Miss Prue' by Joshua Reynolds. Yale Center for British Art.

Plate 27: 'Mrs Charles James Fox' (Elizabeth Armistead) by Joshua Reynolds. In the public domain, via Indianapolis Museum of Art.

Plate 28: Print of a (Venetian) courtesan made by John Faber the Younger, 1739. Yale Center for British Art.

Plate 29, Upper: The Political Wedding engraved for the Oxford Magazine, 1769. Lewis Walpole Library, Yale University.

Plate 29, Lower: A Genteel Milliner. Author's collection.

Plate 30, Upper: Kitty Fisher watch-paper, 1759. Per Wikimedia Commons. In the public domain.

Plate 30, Lower: Gertrude Mahon in the Town & Country Magazine Tête-à-Tête series. In the public domain.

Plate 31, Upper: 'Mrs Abington in the character of Lady Betty Modish'. Print by Isaac Taylor, 1777. Public domain.

Plate 31, Lower: Elizabeth Armistead in the Tête-à-Tête series of the Town & Country Magazine from 1776, courtesy of the Lewis Walpole Library at Yale University.

Plate 32: Mrs Robinson, after Sir Joshua Reynolds, engraving by William Birch, 1792. Yale Center for British Art.